1·80 .

ENGLISH
FOR GENERAL CERTIFICATE
AND SIMILAR EXAMINATIONS

Second Edition

BY

G. F. LAMB M.A.

HARRAP   LONDON

By G. F. LAMB, M.A.

ENGLISH FOR LOWER FORMS—BOOKS I AND II
ENGLISH FOR GENERAL CERTIFICATE
PRACTICAL WORK IN PRÉCIS AND COMPREHENSION
EXERCISES IN COMPOSITION AND COMPREHENSION FOR C.S.E.

By G. F. LAMB, M.A., *and* C. C. FITZHUGH, B.A., A.K.C.

INTRODUCTORY PRÉCIS AND COMPREHENSION
PRÉCIS AND COMPREHENSION FOR GENERAL CERTIFICATE
(Ordinary Level)

First published in Great Britain 1954
by GEORGE G. HARRAP & CO. LTD
182–184 High Holborn, London WC1V 7AX

Reprinted: 1955; 1956; 1957; 1958; 1959;
1960 (*twice*); 1961; 1962; 1963

Second Edition, revised, 1964
Reprinted: 1965; 1968; 1970; 1972; 1973;
1975; 1976 (*twice*); 1977

Second Edition © *G. F. Lamb* 1964

ISBN 0 245 55905 1

Printed in Great Britain by Offset Lithography by
Billing & Sons Ltd., Guildford and London

PREFACE

THIS book attempts to satisfy the needs of the student who is preparing for an examination of the General Certificate (Ordinary Level) standard, or who wishes to bring his technique in English expression to this standard even though he may not be taking an examination. It aims at being a practical guide rather than an academically complete course. The book was designed to be used on its own; but, at the request of many teachers, introductory volumes (*English for Lower Forms*, Books One and Two, and *English for Middle Forms*) have now been produced specifically to lead up to it.

I have endeavoured to base the arrangement of the book upon the method usually followed by teachers at General Certificate standard, and to put *first things first*. It seems to me more practical (even though perhaps less logical theoretically) to begin the book with what is by far the most important part of the English course—namely, Composition—rather than to begin with the Word and slowly work up to the Essay by way of the Sentence and the Paragraph. The student is encouraged to get down straight away to the job of choosing a subject, arranging the material, and writing the essay, which is what he will do very early in the normal General Certificate class; he will not leave essay-writing till the end of the year.

It seems to me that by approaching the subject in this way we avoid giving the student the impression that the essay is a mystery that he can hope to penetrate only after a long and painful journey. Moreover, the idea that an essay is built up, word by word, sentence by sentence, paragraph by paragraph, is a misleading one that produces many bad essays. An essay should first be seen in the writer's mind as a whole, with a single main theme. I believe that it is partly the laborious and artificial 'building-up' process that has brought the examination essay into some disrepute as an unreal exercise in Written English. By far the most important thing is that the student should try to find something worth-while to say, relevant to the chosen subject, that is in some way personal to himself. (Of all bad rules the worst, I think, is that the student should "avoid the first person and all confidences and opinions of a personal nature." I quote from a well-known textbook which I myself used at school.) Let him study such finer points of writing technique as paragraphing, effective openings and endings, and the special features of narrative, description, and so on *after* he has got firmly fixed in his mind the principle that the main thing is to have something to say worth saying and to the point, and to say it in an orderly way. Most examining bodies nowadays usually try to give the student an opportunity of doing something better than futile word-spinning on subjects about which he has really no ideas whatever.

I have not equated the examination essay with the literary essay, for the two mediums of expression are usually quite different. No one can be taught to write a literary essay: any one capable of writing one will teach himself. What the ordinary student mainly needs, I believe, is advice on and practice in straightforward expression of ideas. In the main I have drawn examples of the various aspects of essay-composition from competent writers rather than from brilliant literary essayists, because the ordinary student cannot hope to emulate the latter. This type of student gains little from noting how Bacon or Hazlitt or Lamb opened or ended an entirely different kind of essay. This does not mean, of course, that he should not be brought into contact with the work of the great essayists: I hope that he will read and enjoy it as literature. But it is surely undesirable and futile to try to create little Addisons and Lucases.

In other aspects of English besides Composition I have aimed at giving fairly plentiful examples and exercises rather than long discussions, with the idea that the teacher himself will use this material as a basis for class discussion. Incidental exercises inserted in the body of the text are intended, generally speaking, to be worked orally as a piece of immediate practice on what has just been read and discussed.

Punctuation is given a good deal of space, because the correct use of stops plays so large a part in clear and accurate writing, and bad punctuation so commonly goes with muddled writing. The subject of Direct and Reported Speech is treated before Summarizing, for some knowledge of reported speech is often necessary in précis-writing. It is perhaps covered a little more fully than its inherent importance warrants; but it is my experience, and, I believe, that of other teachers, that unless the difficulties are examined in some detail the student receives so little benefit that it is scarcely worth while to deal with the matter at all.

Although it is to be expected that the student will already have had some pract ce in précis-writing before starting to use this book, I have begun the chapter on Summarizing by giving some examples and exercises on writing brief summaries of single sentences and short paragraphs. These are, as it were, five-finger exercises to loosen the student's mental muscles before he tackles the full-length précis.

Questions on comprehension of a given passage—now a common feature of English Language examinations—are mainly based on the passages set for précis, partly because this is the practice in some examinations, and partly to economize in that precious textbook commodity—space.

Similarly, vocabulary questions on précis and other passages, also a familiar type of question in General Certificate examinations, are included in the chapter dealing with vocabulary. In both comprehension and vocabulary exercises precise references are given as to the passage on which each exercise is based; and cross-references are also given at the foot of each relevant précis passage, so that the teacher or student can easily find the appropriate comprehension and vocabulary questions if he wishes to combine these with an exercise in précis-writing.

The question of formal grammar is not an easy one. It does not play a conspicuous part in the modern English Language examination, and examination candidates and ordinary writers can both get by without any special knowledge of grammatical rules. All the same, our language *has* a grammatical basis, and it seems unwise to ignore this altogether, especially as some knowledge of grammar is an aid to the correction of errors in writing. But it is most important that the student should write first and correct and analyse afterwards; so grammar is put towards the end of the book, and not at the beginning. I am aware that the term 'essentials' in the chapter-heading "Essentials of Grammar" would not be similarly interpreted by all teachers. Some grammarians would assert that too much has been omitted; anti-grammarians might say that too much has been included. I have, in fact, tried to effect a reasonable compromise, with a bias towards the elimination of the unnecessary. Some rather elementary matters have been briefly dealt with here, for in my experience it is unsafe to assume that every General Certificate student has a precise knowledge of, say, Transitive and Intransitive, Active and Passive, or even Subject and Predicate; and if these things have *not* been previously understood, then we are walking on quicksand if we try to go beyond them.

In all aspects of English I have included a good many exercises from modern General Certificate (Ordinary Level) papers in order to illustrate the type and standard of questions set by the leading examining bodies.

I tender my grateful thanks to all teachers and others who have offered advice, especially to Mr C. C. FitzHugh, B.A., A.K.C., Senior English Master at Leyton County High School for Boys, who kindly read the manuscript of Chapters VIII and IX and made some helpful suggestions.

G. F. L.

ACKNOWLEDGMENTS

FOR kind permission to reproduce copyright material I offer my grateful thanks to the following publishers, authors, and examining bodies:

Messrs Edward Arnold and Co. and the author, for an extract from *The Epic of Mount Everest*, by Sir Francis Younghusband; the Clarendon Press (Oxford), for an extract from *Modern English Usage*, by H. W. Fowler; Messrs Evans Brothers, Ltd, and the author, for an extract from *B.B.C. Features*, by Laurence Gilliam; Messrs William Heinemann, Ltd, and the author's executors, for extracts from *The Man of Property* and *A Motley*, by John Galsworthy; Messrs Thomas Nelson and Sons, Ltd, for an extract from *London*, by Mary Fox-Davies; Sir Isaac Pitman and Sons, Ltd, for some passages from my *Commentary and Questionnaire on Galsworthy's "Strife"*; Messrs Putnam and Co., Ltd, and the authors, for extracts from *Isles of the Island*, by S. P. B. Mais, and *Single-handed Passage*, by Edward Allcard; Messrs Martin Secker and Warburg, Ltd, and the author's executors, for an extract from *Shooting an Elephant*, by George Orwell; Messrs George G. Harrap and Co., Ltd, for extracts from *These are My People*, by Alan Marshall, *Heroes of Modern Adventure*, by T. C. Bridges and H. H. Tiltman, *I Bought a Mountain*, by Thomas Firbank, *The Book of Discovery*, by T. C. Bridges, *Farming Adventure*, by J. Wentworth-Day, *English for Practical People*, by J. Barclay and D. H. Knox, and *The Polar Regions in the Twentieth Century*, by A. W. Greely; the Editor of *The Daily Telegraph*, for two letters and an extract from an article; the Editor of *The Economist*, for an extract from an article; the Editor of *The Observer*, for an extract from an article; the Editor of *The Times Educational Supplement*, for various articles; the Manager of *The Times*, for an extract from "*The Times*" *Mount Everest Reconnaissance Expedition Supplement*; The University of Cambridge Local Examinations Syndicate, the Senate of the University of London, the Northern Universities Joint Matriculation Board, the Delegates of the Oxford Local Examinations, the Oxford and Cambridge Schools Examination Board, the Southern Universities' Joint Board, and the Associated Examining Board for the General Certificate of Education; and the Director of the National Book League for an extract from an article of mine which appeared in the League's journal, *Books*.   G. F. L.

NOTE. Questions taken from actual examination papers of the leading examining bodies for the General Certificate of Education, whose names are given in the Acknowledgments above, are indicated as follows: (*Cambridge*), (*London*), (*Northern Universities*), (*Oxford*), (*Oxford and Cambridge*), (*Southern Universities*), and (*Associated Examining Board*).

CONTENTS

CHAPTER   PAGE

I. THE ESSAY   15

The Main Stages   15
Paragraphing   29
Opening the Essay   39
Ending the Essay   46
Summary of Chief Points   48

II. TYPES OF COMPOSITION   50

Narrative   51
Description   56
Explanation   65
Discussion and Argument   71
Letter-writing   74
The Short Story   84
Essay Subjects   85

III. PUNCTUATION   90

The Full Stop   91
Question Mark and Exclamation Mark   94
The Comma   97
The Semi-colon   104
The Colon   107
The Dash   107
Quotation Marks (Inverted Commas)   109
The Apostrophe   113
Summary of Chief Points   115

IV. DIRECT AND REPORTED SPEECH   122

Examples of Direct Speech   122
Examples of Reported Speech   122
Changes in Form   123
Some Further Points   127

CHAPTER   PAGE

    REPORTED SPEECH TO DIRECT SPEECH   135
    SUMMARY OF CHIEF POINTS   138

V. SUMMARIZING (PRÉCIS)   139
    PRÉCIS OF A SENTENCE   139
    PRÉCIS OF A SHORT PASSAGE   141
    MORE ADVANCED PRÉCIS   147
    EXAMPLE OF ADVANCED PRÉCIS   149

VI. COMPREHENSION AND STYLE   171
    COMPREHENSION TESTS   171
    LITERARY STYLE   179

VII. VOCABULARY   182
    THE MEANING OF WORDS   182
    THE CHOICE OF WORDS   195
    SPELLING   203

VIII. ESSENTIALS OF GRAMMAR   211
    PARTS OF SPEECH   211
    PHRASES AND CLAUSES   221
    ANALYSIS OF SENTENCES   223
    SYNTHESIS   234

IX. ERRORS TO AVOID   238
    ERRORS IN THE USE OF WORDS   238
    ERRORS IN STYLE   243
    GRAMMATICAL ERRORS   246

X. FIGURES OF SPEECH   253

    INDEX   259

CHAPTER I

THE ESSAY

ENGLISH Composition, often under the title "The Essay," forms the first question in most English Language examinations.

It is easy to see why this is so. One of the chief aims in studying English is to learn to express one's thoughts effectively; and in a written examination the ability to express ideas can best be shown in a connected composition of some kind. Exercises in punctuation, précis, constructing sentences, choosing suitable words, correcting errors, analysing passages, parsing words—all these may play a useful part in English practice. But they are a means to an end; and that end is the ability to express ideas clearly and coherently in writing.

There is no mystery about writing essays. It is largely a matter of deciding what to say, and then saying it as clearly and interestingly as possible. Practice helps a great deal in this, as it does in most other crafts.

THE MAIN STAGES

There are three main stages in writing an essay for examination purposes:

1. Choosing the subject.
2. Collecting and sorting out ideas.
3. Writing the essay.

Choosing the Subject

This is an important part of the proceedings: a bad choice of subject can prevent you from writing a good essay. Essay subjects are usually set to give scope to candidates of differing interests and talents. Try to find the topic which best fits your own interests. It is most advisable to choose a subject, if there is one, about which you have some personal knowledge. We write best about what we know best. A great deal of bad writing (not only in examinations) arises from hazy knowledge of the subject.

Let us look at an essay paper from a school-leaving examination to indicate the kind of consideration that the student should give to each subject. It may be added that the points to be considered in choosing an essay subject are roughly the same whether the composition is to be written in half an hour, an hour, or an hour and a half.

EXAMPLE

Write an essay on one of the following subjects:

(*a*) A famous river.

(*b*) A national hero (or heroine).

(*c*) My most amusing (or unfortunate) experience.

(*d*) Recreation.

(*e*) What do you think are the three most useful modern inventions?

(*f*) Give an account of a debating (or musical) society to which you belong (or would like to belong).

The choice here is a fair one, and most people should be able to find at least one subject on which they can say something worth reading.

(*a*) *A famous river*. This subject is probably intended to appeal particularly to the student with an interest in geography. If geography is one of your subjects, and in the course of your work you have made some study of (say) the Amazon, the Mississippi, the Nile, or the Thames, you should be equipped to tackle this topic.

Any general reading you may have done which is relevant (for instance, Ballantyne's *Martin Rattler* has reference to the Amazon, Edna Ferber's *Show Boat* deals with the Mississippi, and the story of H.M.S. *Amethyst* is closely connected with the Yangtze) might also incline you towards this subject. Similarly, some personal experiences on the Thames or the Wye might well encourage you to choose this topic, and would certainly be helpful. You should, however, beware of choosing the subject too readily on the strength of having read about, or boated on, a small section of a famous river. This sort of knowledge could and should be used in your essay, but it would need to be backed by at least some knowledge of the course and main features of the river. A punting excursion from Richmond to Kingston, for instance, would not by itself be sufficient to make the river Thames a good choice.

One other caution. The title includes the word 'famous'. Your local river cannot be regarded as suitable for this essay unless it is one which almost everybody has heard of. If there is a serious doubt in your mind on this point it would be better to choose another subject if possible.

(b) *A national hero* (*or heroine*). This subject is no doubt for the particular benefit of the student interested in history, who should have sufficient knowledge of at least one historical figure to be able to write a sensible account of him or her. You would not need to have a very detailed knowledge of the character's life—there would probably not be time to reveal such knowledge even if you had it—but you should be able to explain clearly *why* he has become a national hero, and to give some account of his career at least in broad outline.

Give a little thought to the wording of the title. The character you choose must be a *national* figure—that is to say, he must have achieved fame through what he has done for his nation; and he must be a character generally admired by the nation concerned. Joan of Arc, Boadicea, Nelson, Drake, Florence Nightingale, Garibaldi, Washington, Nurse Cavell, Kitchener, Nansen, Captain Scott, Montgomery—one of these would certainly meet the case.

(Note that there is no indication in the wording of the title that the British nation is meant.) A famous person whose achievement was scientific or humanitarian rather than national might be less suitable. Such great figures as Pasteur, Lister, Marconi, Mme Curie, even Livingstone, are perhaps international rather than national heroes; and if one of these was chosen it would be necessary to stress the prestige he or she had brought to the nation concerned. Again, few statesmen would fit the title. Cromwell, Burke, Gladstone, Disraeli, were undoubtedly great national figures, but they were hardly looked upon as heroes by a whole nation. Whether national feeling was right or wrong does not enter into the matter. On the other hand, Lloyd George and Sir Winston Churchill, though regarded with divided feelings, perhaps, in peace-time, were unquestionably national heroes during the First and Second World Wars respectively, and could suitably be dealt with from the wartime angle.

Attention of this kind given to the wording of the essay title is not time wasted, for an essay which did not really meet the title would certainly be penalized by loss of marks.

(c) *My most amusing (or unfortunate) experience.* Almost any candidate should be able to write on this subject. But you should not rush into it too hastily. You have to make sure that the episode you are thinking of dealing with has sufficient substance for an essay of the allotted time. You do not want to find, after you have started, that all you really have to say could be put in a few lines, and then have to resort to obvious padding. Thus you may once have slapped a perfect stranger on the back in the belief that you were greeting a friend, but it would not be easy to use so slight an incident as the subject of an adequate essay— though an able writer, by skilfully filling in the background, might succeed. On the other hand, your first attempt at cycling, or ice-skating, or sailing could very well make a good theme for an amusing experience; or you might write a good essay on the time when you got lost on a moor in the mist, or when it rained the whole time during a camping week-end.

One caution may be necessary to the writer on an amusing experience. You are not expected to try to write in the manner of P. G. Wodehouse or any other humorous writer. The humour should lie in the experience itself, and not in a facetious style.

(*d*) *Recreation.* This is rather a tricky subject. Most people could probably manage to say *something* about recreation, but few people would find much worth saying. The subject is too general to be treated from the angle of personal experience, and too vague to offer much scope to the candidate with some specialized knowledge. It would be easy here to fall into the danger of giving, in effect, a mere list of recreations, with a brief comment on each. It would also be quite unsatisfactory to write on a single recreation.

The term 'recreation' covers a very wide field. By dictionary definition it could include anything from cricket or football to snakes and ladders, or reading, or going to the cinema. Before deciding to choose a topic so imprecise you need to make sure that you understand the full implications of the term, and that you can bring them together in an essay with a definite theme. The sort of essay most likely to hit the mark is a reflective one, discussing the part which is and which ought to be played in our lives by recreation, and drawing upon specific types of recreation to illustrate the ideas put forward. Probably many essays on this subject would be rather dull.

(*e*) *What do you think are the three most useful modern inventions?* This subject is perhaps included for the particular benefit of the student with a scientific bent.

You are limited to three inventions, no more and no fewer, and this limitation should be strictly observed. In deciding which inventions to deal with you should bear in mind that you would not have time to say very much about each, and that an invention which could be dealt with compactly might have an advantage over one (*e.g.*, wireless communication) which is wide in scope and rather vague, especially if the essay is a half-hour one. You should be able to describe the invention clearly, and to say why you have chosen it.

In addition to the number 'three' there are three other operative words in the title. Let us take them one by one, beginning with the most important. You are required to **write on 'inventions', and you should** consider carefully the **difference between an invention and a discovery.** Newton did not invent the law of gravity; he discovered it. We *discover* what is there already, such as a physical feature (*e.g.*, a river) in unknown country, or a natural phenomenon, such as steam or electricity; we *invent* a device or a machine. Thus James Watt did not invent steam. He discovered (or rediscovered) the power of steam, and invented an improved steam-engine. No one invented electricity (it was in existence long before William Gilbert conducted his experiments in the sixteenth century), though we can correctly speak of the invention of the electric telegraph or of the telephone. Atomic power is a discovery; the atom bomb is an invention.

You are limited to modern inventions; and although the term 'modern' is rather vague, it would be safest to keep as near to the twentieth century as possible. Thus the aeroplane and even the petrol motor-car might well be admissible, but not the printing-press, the telescope, or the steam-engine.

Thirdly, the invention must be 'useful'; and you should be careful to explain in what respect it deserves the epithet.

This subject need not, I think, be taken solely from the scientific standpoint. Even the non-scientist may have sound ideas on what inventions have been of most service to man, and should be able to explain the reasons for his choice even if he cannot give a detailed account of the invention. Humour need not be ruled out. A candidate who could argue half-humorously in favour of (say) the rubber hot-water-bottle, the electric-razor, and the collar-stud might get good marks if his essay were really well-written, and not merely facetious or flippant.

(*f*) *Give an account of a debating* (*or musical*) *society to which you belong* (*or would like to belong*). This may seem a fairly easy subject to write about; and it certainly has the advantage of enabling you to make use of personal experience. But before rushing to choose it make sure that you really have something to say about it. Many dull essays are written on such subjects by candidates who find, after they have started, that they can do little more than give a list of subjects debated. Be on your guard. Lists and catalogues of names always make bad essays. A description of the formation of the society, a brief impression of the kind of debate or concert that usually takes place, neat portraits of some of the outstanding debaters or members, and an esti-mate of the value of the society to yourself and to others— these points might form the basis of an interesting essay.

The second phrase in brackets gives the candidate who does not happen to belong to a debating or musical society the opportunity of using his imagination and ideas in sketching an ideal one.

We have considered each of the essay titles in detail in order to show the kind of thought that should be given to them when you are making your choice. It is unlikely, however, that you will require to give this attention to every title on the paper. There will probably be one or two that definitely do not appeal to you. Cross these out, and concentrate your attention on the others, narrowing down your decision, after due consideration, as soon as possible.

One point remains. What is to be done if none of the essay subjects seems to offer any possibilities?

There are two answers to the question.

The first is that you should look again at the list of subjects. It is a common experience among candidates to feel, after the first quick look at the paper, that there is no topic on which they can write. This is due partly to over-anxiety, partly to the fact that most people's ideas take a little time to come to the surface. If you go through each subject in turn, trying to see the implications in the wording of it (in the way we have just been considering), you will probably find that you have more ideas on at least one or two of the subjects than you first thought.

If in spite of this careful consideration you still find yourself baffled, you must regard yourself as exceptionally unlucky in your paper, or else exceptionally narrow in your range of interests. You might then use the device (sometimes known as the 'tin-opener') of putting the questions "What? Where? When? Why? How?" to the most likely of the subjects.

Let us take "Recreation" as an example, and apply our questions. *What* is recreation? *Where* do we most often indulge in it? *When* do we usually take it? What purpose does it serve? (I.e., *Why* do we have recreation?) *How* can we best obtain it? The answers to these questions may help to get your thoughts to flow. If you jot the answers down you may be able to find an idea which could form the basis of an essay. Try it now as an exercise in stimulating the flow of ideas.

The 'tin-opener' is at times a useful way of getting the mind working, and it is certainly better to use it than to remain staring at a blank sheet of paper. But such expedients are not likely to result in a very convincing essay. They are merely desperate remedies for mental blankness. Your real aim should be to find a subject which interests you and about which you have something to say.

EXERCISES

1. (a) Which of the subjects on p. 16 would you choose? Explain briefly why you would choose it.

(b) Write an essay on the subject you have chosen. (The time spent on your essay may be based on the time allowed for the essay in an examination you may be taking, though at this preliminary stage you may find it better to concentrate on writing an interesting essay than to adhere too strictly to a fixed time.)

2. It is, as we have seen, important to pay careful attention to the wording of the essay subjects. Say briefly what noteworthy differences you would expect to find in essays on each of the following subjects and the kind of material you would include:

(i) (a) A famous mountain.
   (b) Famous mountains.
   (c) Mountains and mountaineers.
   (d) Mountains.
   (e) A mountaineering exploit.
   (f) Mountaineering.
   (g) Mountain-climbing in Britain.
   (h) Accidents on mountains.
   (i) The mountaineer.

(ii) (a) My favourite television programmes.
   (b) Television.
   (c) My favourite television programme.
   (d) The B.B.C.
   (e) Television programmes.
   (f) Watching television.
   (g) My ideal television programme.
   (h) Should the B.B.C. remain a Government-controlled monopoly?

3. Examine the following list of essay subjects. Say briefly what points would need to be considered concerning each subject.

(a) A famous mountain.
(b) Which well-known historical figure would you most like to meet if you had the opportunity, and why?
(c) My favourite television programmes.
(d) The choice of a career.
(e) Pioneers of medicine.
(f) School magazines.

4. Write an essay on *one* of the above subjects.

Collecting and Sorting Out Ideas

Enough has already been said to show the danger of plunging into a subject without a little preliminary consideration. But even after you have chosen your subject some careful thought is necessary before you begin to write. It is foolish to embark upon an essay with only a hazy idea of what you are going to say. You should jot down on rough paper the ideas that you have in mind, partly so that you do not forget them in the hurry of writing the essay, partly so that you can be sure of arranging them in the best way. Your essay should hang together; a series of disconnected thoughts is unsatisfactory not only to an examiner but to any other reader.

Students are often told to plan their essays carefully, and are sometimes supposed to build up quite elaborate plans before they begin writing. There is a danger, however, in carrying planning to excess. For one thing, you will not have time in most examinations to follow a scheme that is too elaborately divided and subdivided, even if you have time to work out such a scheme. If the essay is to be a half-hour one the plan will need to be quite simple. Moreover, some people cannot write to too rigid a scheme; their spontaneity would suffer.

None the less some kind of outline scheme is necessary to ensure unity and logical sequence in the essay. Sometimes the best way of arranging your essay may be so clear in your mind that you need only the briefest of notes to aid your memory. But more usually some preliminary sorting out of ideas on paper is desirable; and the less certain you are of what you are going to say, the more important it is to get your stray thoughts down in black and white so that they can be seen, considered, and arranged.

Let us take an example from the list of essay subjects already examined.

A famous river. We will assume, to begin with, that the

river you know best is the Thames. You have boated on one or two sections of it. You have a rough idea of its course, and of the chief towns and villages through which it flows. You know that it has some commercial importance in London. You have seen the lights twinkling on it at night. You know some of the bridges under which it passes. You know it has played its part in history (perhaps you are a little vague about this). You may have seen pictures of it frozen over in earlier days. You know that a water-bus service is run over the London section, and that fair-sized ships can come up as far as London Bridge. You know of Henley Regatta, and that the Oxford and Cambridge boat race is rowed from Putney to Mortlake.

To fling down these ideas on to paper would result in a very unsatisfactory piece of writing. There must be some general idea underlying your essay, some main impression which you are trying to convey. What that impression is will depend on your own interests and on the kind of knowledge that you happen to possess.

If you have a fair idea of the course of the Thames your underlying idea might well be to trace this course from source to mouth. Your plan in this case might be a division of the river into four sections, with a general summing up:

A

1. Source—Thames Head—rivulet in Cotswolds—placid stream through meadows—Lechlade.
2. Oxford to Windsor—has widened into river—steamers—beauty spots, pleasure-haunts (Cliveden, etc.)—many locks (*e.g.*, Boulter's).
3. Windsor to Putney—Londoner's playground—Runnymede, Hampton Court, Richmond (personal experiences here).
4. London River—commercial shipping—barges—Pool of London—water-bus service—unusual views of London—historic places (Parliament, Tower, Wapping, Greenwich).
5. Charm of river in many moods—sunny day, dull day, night-time.

It might occur to you that the course of a river has some resemblance to the course of a human life, and that a description of the river might be based on this main theme. In this case your plan might run:

B

1. Its birth (Thames Head) and infancy (source to Lechlade).
2. Its adolescence (Lechlade to Teddington—last lock—becomes tidal after this).
3. Its growing manhood (suburban London to mouth—sweeps out to sea as young man goes out into the world).

If your knowledge of the precise course of the river is limited you might deal with the subject under certain topics, in which case your plan could be on these lines:

C

1. Boating—picnics on river, steamer trips, week-end camping punts—some favourite places—Richmond (personal experience), Maidenhead, etc.
2. Sporting contests—Henley Regatta—Oxford and Cambridge boat race—many sailing clubs—Royal Thames Yacht Club.
3. Charming scenery and villages (personal recollection).
4. Interesting bridges—Marlow, Hampton, Lambeth, Waterloo, London, Tower. (Describe two or three of these.)
5. Historic interest—Oxford, Windsor Castle, Runnymede, Hampton Court, London.
6. London River—not without own beauty—views from bridges, Pool of London, scene at night.

One more example, where the interest is mildly historical rather than geographical:

D

1. Thames has been called "liquid history."
2. Free use of river in medieval times—pageantry—King's barge —hundreds of watermen employed—sometimes frozen in winter— fair—roasting of ox.
3. Historic scenes connected with river—Runnymede and Magna Carta, Hampton Court and Wolsey, Oxford and Civil War, Shakespeare and Southwark, Greenwich and Charles II, Old London Bridge, Tower of London.
4. Modern development of river—shipping—docks—pleasure— bus service.

5. Future of river—relief to London traffic system?—return to medieval liveliness?

None of these plans is intended to be regarded as a model for an ideal essay. They are merely indications of the various ways in which ideas on a subject can be gathered together in order to give an essay some sort of coherence. The examinee essay-writer has to shape his ideas and arrange his plan to suit whatever knowledge he possesses, without recourse to reference books. The plan should be devised to make the best use of this often limited knowledge.

You are deliberately not asked to write an essay based on any of the above plans. Your essay-plan should be your own: the planning is an integral part of the essay writing, and should be as personal to you as the essay itself. You cannot expect to write a satisfactory essay to somebody else's plan. The plan is merely *your* way of arranging *your* ideas.

EXERCISES

1. (i) Put down briefly your various ideas on *three* of the following subjects. (ii) What is the *main idea* you would try to convey in writing the essay? (iii) Make a brief plan to show the *arrangement* you would probably follow:

    (*a*) A railway station in a big city.
    (*b*) Cycling for convenience and for pleasure.
    (*c*) What qualities do you think the ideal newspaper should have?
    (*d*) A visit to a cricket (or football, or netball, or hockey) match.
    (*e*) The stars.
    (*f*) Criticize or defend the habit of reading detective stories.

2. (i) Criticize the given plan for the following essay subject, paying careful attention to the wording of the title. (ii) Suggest briefly a better arrangement of ideas.

Science in the Modern World

    (*a*) The atom bomb—wireless communication—science taught in all schools to-day—importance of science in the modern world.
    (*b*) Electricity—refrigerators—electric lighting—other forms of lighting.
    (*c*) Marconi—Galileo and the telescope—discovery of electricity.
    (*d*) Wireless—the B.B.C.—should it be monopoly?

Writing the Essay

This is, of course, the most significant process of all. Important though it is to give sufficient time to choosing your subject and arranging your ideas, if your composition does not get much further than this it will be of little value to anybody, whether you are writing for an examination or for any other purpose. The final result is what you will be judged by.

Let us stress once again that reasonable time spent in finding the most suitable subject and in jotting down your ideas about it is time well spent. It is far better to take ten minutes or so doing this than to rush at once into your essay, scribble vigorously for ten minutes, and then have to nibble your pen-holder while you wonder how on earth to continue.

This clearly emphasized, we may go on to add that the time spent in these preparations must be within reason. Rigid rules cannot be laid down, for Composition is a personal art; but, broadly speaking, you should not take more than about a third of your time in preliminaries. Seven or eight minutes in preparing a half-hour essay, fifteen to twenty minutes in preparing a longer one—these figures may be taken as rough guides to the amount of time you will be able to spare. When this time has gone by you would be well advised to finish off your plan quickly and get started on the writing of the essay.

Some people try to write the whole essay in rough first and then transcribe it, after revision, for the examiner. (Many professional authors write out their work more than once, and nearly all revise very carefully what they have written.) But you will need to be very expeditious to write your essay twice in an examination. Do not risk it unless you have discovered in practice that you can safely do it in the time allotted.

EXERCISE. Write an essay on one of the subjects already prepared in Exercise 1, p. 27.

PARAGRAPHING

If a piece of writing is not divided into paragraphs it is apt to be difficult and tedious to read. Even a short essay or article needs paragraphing. As for a full-length book, imagine a long novel going on for two or three hundred pages without any paragraph breaks! To read it would be like walking along a fifty-kilometre road with a wall on each side and no seats or gates anywhere on the way.

The beginning of a new paragraph is both a resting-place for the eye and a signpost indicating that a new development in the writer's line of thought is being opened.

Unity of Theme

A good writer has a definite theme (or central idea) for each of his paragraphs, and you can follow the train of his thought by noting these themes. Quite often the theme is expressed in a sentence or phrase in the paragraph itself— sometimes the opening sentence. (Such a sentence is known as the *topic sentence*.) At other times the theme is implied in the paragraph, though not directly stated: it should be possible for the reader to write it down in a few words. Both methods of paragraph construction are correct provided that there *is* a theme and that the author keeps to it. He should not, in the same paragraph, stray to some other topic.

Good paragraphing leads the reader naturally from one point to another. Bad paragraphing leaves him mentally confused.

Consider the following paragraphs (*A* and *B*):

A. George Bernard Shaw is a contradictory figure in English drama. He was one of the leaders in the movement that encouraged dramatists to make their plays resemble real life; yet he has also shown a delight in fantastic ideas. Together with John Galsworthy, he helped to found the 'drama of ideas,' writing plays which dealt seriously with social follies and social evils; yet no one has contributed more wit, fun, and humour to the theatre. Even the older generation of theatre-goers look upon him as a veteran; yet his plays are still regarded as 'modern' in the theatre of to-day.

This paragraph, introducing an essay on Shaw, has a clear *unity of theme*—namely, the contradictory or paradoxical nature of Shaw's dramatic achievement. (Is there a topic sentence?) The whole paragraph contributes to this theme by illustrating various aspects of the apparent contradictions. The essay would naturally go on to discuss Shaw's different achievements, in the theatre and perhaps elsewhere, in a little more detail.

> *B.* George Bernard Shaw has written many plays on various themes. He is one of the greatest of modern playwrights. Shaw was a man of causes, and above all an idealist, and so great was his enthusiasm that he always wrote forcefully and with great wit. *Arms and the Man* and *Man and Superman* are two of his best plays. He is one of the founders of the 'drama of ideas.'

There is NO true *unity of theme* here. Although all the sentences are about George Bernard Shaw, they do not present any particular aspect of him either as a man or as a writer.

The first sentence tells us that he wrote many plays on various themes. Had the writer proceeded to develop this topic, pointing out some of the different themes which Shaw has dealt with in his plays (the Salvation Army, the medical profession, marriage, dictatorships, housing, etc.) and stressing their variety, then the paragraph would have had a definite theme. As it is, the writer merely puts together a number of separate, unrelated sentences about Shaw.

We must keep a sense of proportion in the matter of paragraphing. The first thing in writing is to say something interesting in lively and accurate English, and careful paragraphing is not a substitute for this. But it remains true that intelligent paragraphing can play a useful part in enabling you to express effectively what you have to say, and you must bear it in mind as you plan and write your essay.

EXERCISES

1. Which of the following paragraphs have *unity of theme*? Say what the theme is. Show where the other paragraphs fail to achieve unity.

(*a*) Cycling is one of the healthiest of sports. Not only does the bicycle bring its rider into the fresh air of the countryside; it also provides him with vigorous exercise, and gives him a needed change of scene. There is no better way of keeping fit than by regular cycle-trips into the country. The best way to clean a dirty bicycle-chain is to soak it well in paraffin before oiling it. It is essential to oil a bicycle frequently to keep it in good condition.

(*b*) I once asked an old merchant skipper what he considered the greatest danger afloat, and he at once answered "Fog." Then after thinking a moment he added, "And fire." Fire is bad enough on land, but when a house catches fire one can usually get out in time to save one's life, and one can call up the fire brigade to help put out the flames. But a fire at sea is a dreadful business; the only refuge is the boats, and there may be no ship within hundreds of kilometres to give any sort of help. Then, think of fire on a ship loaded with explosives!

(*c*) Lighthouses may be roughly classed under two headings: those built on solid land and those constructed upon wave-washed reefs. Building the former is as simple as building a church, and one can be completed in a few months; but the latter present a thousand and one problems to the builder, and a single structure may take years to complete. Among the difficulties are tides, waves, shifting sands, fierce currents, and gales. The builder's task is one long struggle against the pitiless sea.

(*d*) The most terrible battle that lighthouse-builders have waged with stormy seas was in the building of a lighthouse at Smith's Point in Chesapeake Bay. Lighthouse-keepers lead very lonely lives. There are many stories of heroism of lighthouse-keepers. The Eddy-stone was the first lighthouse to be built on an isolated rock constantly washed by the waves. The modern lightship is a vessel built of wood, about 33 metres in length and 7·5 metres beam.

(*e*) The force of the waves on Bishop Rock lighthouse in a storm is perhaps more terrible than upon any other lighthouse. On one occasion a bell weighing 250 kg, which was fixed 33 metres above sea-level, was torn away by a monstrous wave. That the keepers in this lighthouse can live and retain their reason through the winter gales is almost beyond belief.

2. State the theme of each paragraph in the exercises on Summary-writing on pp. 143–147.

Orderly Sequence of Paragraphs

We have already mentioned that a writer's train of thought can often be traced by noting the themes of his paragraphs throughout the essay.

He does not usually achieve this orderly progression of paragraphs by considering and writing each paragraph as a separate unit, and then putting them all together. The normal process is for the writer first to see his essay as a whole with its own main ideas, and then to consider how this whole can best be divided into progressive stages.

Paragraphs can come into being when related ideas in the rough notes are collected into groups, each group being the skeleton of a paragraph. Thus in the plans discussed on pp. 25–27 each number would probably introduce a fresh paragraph.

In the actual writing of the essay the writer may find that a paragraph is developing more fully than he expected, and needs to be divided into two (each with its own theme); but he should not lose sight of his original paragraphing scheme or he is likely to lose the thread of his essay.

Let us consider an example of the orderly sequence of paragraphs:

A Summer's Day on the Farm

A. The long summer days begin very early at Wick. About half-past two on a morning in June a faint twittering under the eaves announces that the swallows are awaking, although they will not commence their flight for a while yet. At three o'clock the cuckoo's call comes up from the distant meadows, together with the sound of the mower sharpening his scythe; for he likes to work while the dew is heavy on the grass, both for coolness and because it cuts better. He gets half a day's work done before the sun grows hot, and about eight or nine o'clock lies down under the hedge for a refreshing nap. Between three and four the thrushes open song in the copse at the corner of the Home-field, and soon a loud chorus takes up their ditty as one after the other joins in.

B. Then the nailed shoes of the milkers clatter on the pitching of the courtyard as they come for their buckets; and immediately afterwards stentorian voices may be heard in the fields bellowing "Coom up! ya-hoop!" to which the cows, recognizing the well-known call, respond very much in the same tones. Slowly they obey and gather together under the elms in the corner of the meadow, which in summer is used as the milking-place. About five or half-past another clattering tells of the milkers' return; and then the dairy is in full operation. The household breakfasts at half-past six or thereabouts; and while breakfast is going on, the heavy tramp of feet may be heard passing along the roadway through the rickyard —the haymakers marching to the fields.

C. For the next two hours or so the sounds from the dairy are the only interruptions of the silence. Then come the first wagons loaded with hay, jolting and creaking, the carter's lads shouting "Woaght!" to the horses as they steer through the gateway and sweep round, drawing up under the rick.

D. Between eleven and twelve the wagons cease to arrive—it is luncheon-time: the exact time for luncheon varies a quarter of an hour or twenty minutes, or more, according to the state of the work. Messengers come home for cans of beer, and carry out also to the field wooden "bottles"—small barrels holding a gallon or two. After a short interval work goes on again till nearly four o'clock, when it is dinner-time. One or two labourers, deputed by the rest, and having leave and licence to do so, enter the farmhouse gardens and pull up bundles of onions, lettuces, or radishes—sown over wide areas on purpose—and carry them out to the cart-house, or wherever the men may be. If far from home, the women often boil a kettle for tea under the hedge, collecting dead sticks from the trees. At six o'clock work is over: the women are allowed to leave half an hour or so previously, that they may prepare their husbands' suppers.

E. As the sunset approaches, the long, broad, dusty road loses its white glare, and yonder by the hamlet a bright glistening banner reflects the level rays of the sun with dazzling sheen; it is the gilding on the swinging wayside sign transformed for the moment from a wooden board rudely ornamented with a gilt sun, all rays and rotund cheeks, into a veritable oriflamme.

F. There the men will assemble by-and-by, on the forms about the trestle table, and share each other's quarts in the fellowship of labour. Or perhaps the work may be pressing, and the wagons are loaded till the white owl noiselessly flits along the hedgerow, and the moon rises over the hills. Then those who have stayed to assist find their supper waiting for them in the brewhouse, and do it ample justice.[1]

[1] Richard Jefferies, *Wild Life in a Southern County.*

The themes of the paragraphs could be expressed as follows:

A. "The long summer days begin very early at Wick." (*Topic sentence.*)

B. Farming activity from milking-time until breakfast.

C. A period of quiet until the hay-wagons arrive.

D. From luncheon till six—feeding arrangements during the day's work.

E. Sunset embellishes the local inn.

F. Refreshment at the inn after the day's labour.

It might be thought at a quick reading that unity of theme in paragraph *A* was destroyed by the fourth sentence ("He gets . . . refreshing nap"). This is not really so. This sentence is in effect a parenthesis, explaining how the mower is able to work so very early. The steady time-sequence which distinguishes this paragraph is continued in the next sentence.

It would be possible to divide paragraph *D* into two— (i) luncheon-time and (ii) dinner till six o'clock. But this paragraph so stresses the day's feeding arrangements that the unity of theme is best preserved by leaving the paragraph as it stands, even though it is longer than the others.

This illustrates the point that paragraphs in an essay need not be of uniform length. Indeed, variety in paragraph length is a good thing, provided that it arises naturally and is not artificially contrived at the expense of unity.

EXERCISES

1. Divide the following passage into four paragraphs, under the headings below:

(*a*) Greenland's inhabitants.

(*b*) Popular misconceptions.

(*c*) Actual characteristics.

(*d*) Danish help.

It is not necessary to write out the whole passage. The first and last few words of each paragraph should be enough. Express the theme of each paragraph a little more fully than in the above headings:

Since the extinction of the Norse colonists in the fifteenth century the population of Greenland has been exclusively Eskimo, save the few score whites—officials and missionaries. It is the impression of many people, slightly modified by recent visiting expeditions, that the Eskimo of Greenland are a primitive, ignorant, unchristianized race, unprogressive and decadent through casual contact with a superior civilization. Snow-huts in winter, rock *igloos* in summer for shelter, and seal oil as a luxurious food are fanciful pictures, often presented. As a matter of fact, they are Christians, live comfortably, and are literate and to a certain extent artistic. They are a peaceful, law-abiding, self-supporting people. They hold fast to their racial heritage, retain their language, and at the larger settlements have, during the past century, had a literature, expressed in Eskimo text in pertinently illustrated books and pamphlets. Every settlement from Cape Farewell north to Upernivik, about a thousand miles, presents evidence of the fostering care of Denmark for the mental and spiritual welfare of the inhabitants in the shape of churches and schools. For these purposes Denmark spent more than £19,000 during 1927. These educative facilities are highly valued by the natives, who as a community or nation stand high in literacy.

A. W. Greely, *The Polar Regions in the Twentieth Century*

2. Arrange the following passage in six short paragraphs, under the following headings: (*a*) the threatening storm, (*b*) the rain holds off, (*c*) making for water, (*d*) Elmore reached, (*e*) spasmodic winds show the storm is at hand, (*f*) the rain advances, heralded by thunder, (*g*) the storm bursts suddenly:

The day was sultry, but it became worse after lunch. Dark clouds were gathering, and we could see lightning on the horizon. There were rumbles of thunder. In the east a strange, dark cloud streaked earthward as if tipping tons of water on the bush away across the flat paddocks. The storm swung around us, and, save for a few drops, we had no rain. But it was still unbearably close. We entered each town hoping for a brimming trough, but those towards which the horses thrust their eager heads contained only dry flakes of mud. We were told that the nearest water was at Elmore, so we made for there. It got very black ahead of us. We drove in a sunny circle surrounded by a black curtain. The thunder became louder. I wanted to camp before the storm broke, so urged the horses to a faster trot. We reached Elmore just after sunset, and watered the horses at a trough. We then hurried out of the town and pulled on to a flat patch that lay at the foot of a bank beside the road. It was dry and hard and criss-crossed with tiny sun-cracks. Gusts of wind sprang up. They were spasmodic and powerful. They roamed like wolves across the plain, skirting the caravan in moments of calm, then turning and racing up to us in a fury. They leaped as if to bear us down, then raced away again. Across the paddocks I could see the advancing rain like an enormous dust cloud. Behind it, in some bitter arena, explosive cracks and dull, thunderous blows heralded a conflict we could not see. We got the horses out, the nosebags on, the carts covered, when the storm struck us. In a moment we were wet through. There was no pattering of drops. Some shattered reservoir of the sky had tipped its contents on us. Breathing was difficult. We blundered to the caravan and fell through the door as if saved from drowning.   ALAN MARSHALL, *These are my People*

[The storm described is in Australia.]

3. Arrange the following passage in five paragraphs, making sure that each paragraph has its own theme or topic. The themes should be somewhat as follows, but not in the same order: (*a*) ingenuity, (*b*) religion, (*c*) women's needlework, (*d*) primitiveness, (*e*) head of the family. Do not make any alterations in the writing or arrangement of the passage itself.

Give a brief but precise statement of the theme of each paragraph. This statement should be just a little fuller than those given in (*a*) to (*e*) above:

In some respects the Chucunaques are as primitive as any people on earth. They have no metal or any idea of it. More than that, they do not even use stone, all their weapons being made of wood. Yet in many ways they are extremely ingenious. All use bows, arrows, and spears. The bows, made of black palm, are strung with vegetable fibres, and the five-pointed arrows are barbed like fish-hooks. They make blowpipes from hollow reeds, and the darts blown through these are dipped in a virulent poison which is made by soaking rotten liver in the venom of serpents. They cultivate sugar-cane, and have devised an ingenious press for extracting the juice from the cane. They not only drink the pure juice, but pour it into the pots in which all their food is cooked, boiling it up with lizards, yams, pineapples, bananas, and all sorts of stuff, into a regular witch's brew. The women spend a great deal of their time in working the most extraordinary and intricate designs in needle-work on cloth. During their stay with the Chucunaques the travel-lers were presented with a large number of these strips, and some, when examined in London, were found to consist of a velvet-like material of great age. Several pieces were trimmed with Spanish lace at least three hundred years old, thus proving that at some period the ancestors of the tribe must have been in touch with the Spanish conquerors. These embroideries form a sort of pictorial record or history of the tribe, and prove that the Indians who made them understand, among other things, the length of the solar year. Among these people the wife rules the family. True, the chief and the medicine-men are supreme, but in all smaller matters the woman is more powerful than the man. It is she who orders the building of a new house, the getting of firewood or food, and the husband does none of these things unless his wife first orders him to do so. Each family has its own god carved out of wood. The carving is done partly by the use of fire and partly with the aid of the teeth of sharks or wild animals. (There are no flints such as most savages possess.) These wooden *ju-jus* are most curious. Some have wings, and several show the figure of a man wearing what appears to be a top hat and frock-coat. Yet most certainly none of these people had ever seen either of these garments.

T. C. Bridges and H. Hessell Tiltman,
Heroes of Modern Adventure

4. Arrange the following passage in four paragraphs, stating the theme of each:

In the end the crew became so used to sharks that they would play a game of tail-pulling with them. To the conventional landlubber, and perhaps also to the conventional seaman, this does not seem a suitable sport for anyone but a Colossus; but the *Kon-Tiki* party found it quite practicable. They would first offer the shark some tit-bits of fish, and then, as it began to dive under the water again, they would take a firm grip on the upper part of its rough tail where there was a little dent for the fingers to grip, and heave sharply before the shark realized what was happening. Often they could pull it half-way over the logs, where, if they let go and skipped out of the way, it would either thrash itself helplessly on deck or else tumble overboard. The commonest of all visitors were pilot fish and dorados. Pilot fish are normally about six inches long, and swim in a group just ahead of a shark, which they appear to be piloting, and which does not appear to resent their presence. When sharks were caught and pulled on board the raft the bewildered pilot fish would attach themselves to the *Kon-Tiki*, supposing it to be a kind of giant shark. Some of these pilot fish accompanied the raft for hundreds of miles over the sea, and the crew respected their trust in the vessel and forbore to touch them. The dorado, a brilliantly coloured fish about three to four feet long, was often caught, however, and proved good eating. There was no lack of food during the journey, and even without the rations they had brought it would have been difficult to starve. There was an abundance of fish always to be had. Sometimes they did not even have to bother to catch it: the fish obligingly landed on deck and waited to be picked up. Not all the supplies that were brought with them remained edible. They had to be stored in boxes under the deck, stacked upon the lowest logs, in the spaces between the cross-beams. The sea was playing round them continuously. Many hermetically sealed tins proved unable to stand up to this treatment, and the sea-water somehow penetrated the tin.   G. F. LAMB, *Modern Action and Adventure*

5. Divide the following into four or five paragraphs, stating the theme of each paragraph:

Providence meant the week-end for rest and relaxation; but every one knows that it is now the time to be up and away. A man will take the week calmly, dictating a thoughtful letter here and signing a reluctant bank draft there; but every Saturday he seizes his golf-clubs, and pants from tee to tee. It is the same with the ladies. A girl will spend the days from Monday to Friday in a steady round of crochet and typing; but on Saturday she cuts herself sandwiches and is off on a frenzied hike. Even so, the week-end does bring moments for quiet thought. There are the book reviews to read and the library list to complete. A man then may take his ease as he weighs the merits of a tome on Balkan politics against one on the flora of Zanzibar; and if he looks sometimes at the novels or notes the title of some music-hall memoirs he has many authorities from Horace onwards that the world cannot always be serious. It is, however, this business of titles that is likely to give him some bother. Time was when the words on the cover were a safe sort of guide to the contents. *Bangalore Days*, said the dust-jacket, and it added for good measure, 30 *Years in the I.C.S.* Such directness nowadays is frowned on. The title must be bizarre, allusive, or quaint. Footballers, recording their views on life for posterity, queue to use the title of *Muddied Oaf*. The dog-breeder penning his memoirs will call them *Royal Dane*; and no one knows until he opens *Down on the Range* whether it is a saga of cow-punching or a treatise on how to cook duck. Up to now the school books have stood immune. *Arithmetic, Parts I and II*, is what the name implies. *A Revision Course in Geography* says starkly what it is. Even here, however, the tendency is afoot. *Modern Geometry, Progressive Science, The New Algebra*, are all titles that contain the witch words of flattery; and *Talk of the Town* might well be a bright sort of title for some new text-book of civics. Yet the warning must be sounded. The pill can be sugared too richly, for on the whole the young student likes his medicine straight. As an inducement to learning, *Middle-school French* for a title may seem a trifle dull. But it will be an angry day for the schoolboy when he welcomes *A Trip to Paris* as his text-book only to find that it starts with the usual stuff about *avoir* and *être*.

The Times Educational Supplement

OPENING THE ESSAY

Students are sometimes under the impression that they must lead off with a special introductory paragraph before starting what they really have to say, and often they waste time racking their brains in search of one.

To think of the opening as something to be tacked on to the real essay is an error which results in feeble and artificial writing. Some essays need an introductory paragraph to make clear the angle from which the writer intends to approach his subject. But where such explanation is unnecessary, the best thing to do is often to plunge into the subject without any waste of words. An introductory paragraph which contributes nothing essential to the main theme had far better be omitted.

A common fault, especially in essays of the narrative type, is to include an account of irrelevant preliminaries. Consider the following openings (taken from students' actual work) to essays on "A street accident you have witnessed."

EXAMPLE 1

There are many street accidents every year. Most of the victims are children.

This is an unnecessary introduction to an essay on "A street accident," which should be a piece of vivid description. It would be more suitable (though rather commonplace) as a way of beginning an essay on "Street accidents" in which the writer proposed to lay particular stress on the dangers to children. When you are asked to describe a particular incident it is a mistake to begin with a vague general statement.

EXAMPLE 2

It was a beautiful afternoon in midsummer. The scent from the rose-trees and the steady buzz of insects gave an atmosphere of drowsiness which hung over the whole valley. Having lunched, it was decided that the four of us should take a stroll into the town to fetch some potatoes.

We all went out and began to walk down the narrow country lane which led to the main road and thus on to town. On arrival in town we walked placidly along the streets, first looking into this shop and then into that, for we were in no hurry, and anyway it was too hot to walk fast. After some time we bought the potatoes, and then decided to visit the nearest milk-bar for an iced drink before going back home. Whilst we sat there I noticed that some little boys were playing with tops on the pavement, and thought to myself how dangerous it was for kiddies to play in the street.

Suddenly it happened. A car had turned the corner without any warning. . . .

This is a bad opening, because the first paragraph and part of the second are quite irrelevant. They do not even give the background to the scene of the accident. The drowsy valley where "the four of us" lunched is not where the accident took place. The fact that they were going to buy potatoes has no significance; the same accident would have occurred in the same way if they had been going to buy plums, or pen-nibs, or parachutes. They were not even buying the potatoes when the accident occurred; the purchase had been completed, and they were seated in a milk-bar.

The reference to "the four of us" is a further irrelevance, bearing an apparent significance which is entirely misleading. The group played no part in the subsequent scene, and is not mentioned again in the essay. The number could have been five, or fifteen, or even fifty without affecting the accident in any way. The author of the essay is the only one of them with whom the reader is concerned, and then only because it is he who is relating the story.

It may be that the student was trying to make his opening offer a peaceful contrast to the sudden shock of the accident.

If so the idea was sound enough, but he took too long in getting to the point, and missed it when he got to it. He drew the wrong comparison. The contrast should have been between the drowsy street *before* the accident, and the hubbub and excitement in the same street *after* the accident occurred.

The essay might have begun after this fashion:

> It was a drowsy afternoon in midsummer. As I lolled in my seat in the window of the milk-bar it seemed to me that the village street was half asleep. The sun-blinds were drawn over the shop-windows, and hardly a soul was stirring. The only animation was shown by a group of little boys playing with tops on the glaring pavement, and even they were lackadaisical in their game. In a lazy, absent-minded way I thought to myself how dangerous it was for kiddies to play in the street.
>
> Suddenly it happened. A car had turned the corner without warning. . . .

From what has already been said the student will realize that the opening of an essay cannot really be considered in isolation. It must be closely connected with what follows; and sometimes, indeed, the ending may be decided on first. None the less, it may be useful to consider some common ways of beginning an essay.

Some Types of Opening

1. The *apt quotation* or anecdote. This can be useful if it leads directly to the main topic. But beware of dragging in a quotation which has only a vague bearing on the theme.

> "It's an infernal mountain, cold and treacherous," wrote George Mallory the second time he came face to face with Everest.
> *The Observer*

This opening leads to an essay on "Mount Everest" discussing the formidable difficulties which the mountain has presented to all those who have attempted to climb it. The tone of the essay is effectively indicated.

"Time and tide," said the ignorant proverb-monger, "wait for no man." He reckoned without the spirit of progress and the march of civilization, ever moving onward to better and nobler things.

E. V. Knox

This is the opening to a semi-humorous essay on the introduction of official summer-time, when clocks are put forward an hour. The author light-heartedly considers some of the advantages and disadvantages of what he calls "this practice of playing fast and loose with Time."

2. The *direct opening*, in which the writer starts straight away on the first aspect of his subject without any pre-liminaries. The following is an opening for a factual essay such as the one planned on p. 25 (*A*):

When we look at the source of the Thames it is not easy to picture the great river which carries sea-going ships from the docks of East London to the North Sea. We see a rivulet flowing from the Cotswold Hills, a gentle stream over which a boy can easily jump, passing quietly through lonely meadows. Not until Lechlade, where we meet the highest lock, can it be said to become a river.

This opening makes it clear at once that the writer is dealing with the Thames; it indicates the general line of thought which he is going to develop (the growth from rivulet to mighty river); and it gives a simple description of the river's source.

A writer who proposed to develop his essay on the lines suggested by plan *C* (p. 26) could begin at once with the first topic, *boating*:

The Thames is the largest and most famous river in England; but to most people in the southern counties its name suggests not a great commercial waterway, but a source of delight. For these people it is the holiday river. In the summer months thousands of pleasure-seekers throng its banks and cover its surface with punts, skiffs, and sailing-craft, while steamers thrust their way up-river as far as Oxford.

On a fine Saturday or Sunday river-picnics are the order of the day. Richmond is the picnicker's favourite haunt; and it was here that I enjoyed my first encounter with the Thames. . . .

3. A paragraph *indicating the angle* from which the author is going to deal with the subject.

In the last example the writer's brief personal experience was to be used merely to illustrate one of several aspects of the river (see plan *C*). But a student whose personal experience of the river was sufficiently wide to enable him to make this experience his main theme would be wise to indicate in his opening paragraph the approach which he intended to adopt. This might be done in the following way:

> To me the Thames is not merely a famous river, replete with historical association and notable as the largest in England. It is a source of personal happiness. The name conjures up in my mind recollections of lazy afternoons on Cliveden Reach, of camping week-ends between Maidenhead and Windsor, of picnics by the tow-path at Runnymede and Richmond, of twinkling lights reflected from the London Embankment, and of exciting steamer journeys from Westminster Bridge to the widening mouth of the river as it flows past Greenwich and Woolwich and approaches Tilbury.
>
> My first experience of the Thames was . . .

The above is a *necessary* introductory paragraph. It reveals the main theme of the essay (the writer's personal delight in the Thames), indicates at once which river is to be described, and endeavours to whet the reader's appetite by hinting at the pleasures that are about to be depicted.

If the writer had decided to tackle the subject on the lines indicated in plan *B* on p. 26 it would be sensible to begin the essay with an introductory paragraph indicating this special line of approach. For example:

> In some ways a river resembles a human life. It has its birth, its infancy, its period of growth; and at length, as it reaches its strength, it goes out into the wider world of the sea just as a youth goes out from the classroom into the wider world outside the school.
>
> From this point of view the River Thames offers a fascinating study. . . .

4. The opening which refers to *topics which are to be dealt with* in the essay. An introductory paragraph of this

kind is often a useful preliminary to the Discussion type of essay. The example which follows is for an essay on "The aims of education."

> There are four main functions which any adequate education must in some degree fulfil. The pupil must be given an opportunity to reach a reasonable standard in those attainments, such as reading and writing, which most people need in order to earn a living; he must be encouraged to use his leisure wisely; he must be equipped to carry out his duties as a useful and well-informed citizen; and, not least, he must be helped to develop a standard of moral and artistic values.
> Let us consider each of these functions in turn. . . .

This type of opening should not be allowed to develop into a mere catalogue of names. Note that in the above example just enough of each topic is hinted at to give the reader a clear idea of what the essayist is going to drive at. The opening would have been far less satisfying if the topics had been merely catalogued as follows: "The main functions of education are vocational training, the use of leisure, citizenship, and the development of standards of values."

5. The *provocative opening*, which challenges the reader to pay attention to the essay by presenting him at once with an unexpected point of view. Here is an example for an essay on "Road accidents, and how to prevent them."

> "Fifteen people murdered last night!"
> What a sensation would be caused if we were all to open our morning papers one day and read these words! Yet it is a horrifying truth that fifteen murders are committed every day of the year. Every death due to a road accident is in effect a murder.

This opening presents a too familiar fact—the number of fatal accidents on the roads—in a new and challenging light, and whether the reader is startled into agreement or provoked into disagreement, he is probably constrained to consider what the essayist has to say about the problem.

Compare this opening with Example 1 on p. 39.

EXERCISES

1. Consider the following essay subjects. (a) Suggest for each subject the type of opening that you think you would find most satisfactory. (b) Set out brief plans for *two* of the subjects, and write an opening for each. (c) Write another opening, for a different type of essay, on one of the subjects chosen in (b).

(i) How I spent (or hope to spend) my Christmas holidays.

(ii) Hills.

(iii) If you had the choice, would you prefer to live in the town or in the country? (Suppose that your parents are undecided, and you are trying to present a convincing argument to sway them to one side or the other.)

(iv) School life in fiction and in fact.

(v) Have we progressed during the last fifty years? Give reasoned arguments and illustrations to support your opinion.

(vi) The modern aeroplane.

2. Here are the openings to some actual essays. Say briefly what kind of opening the author has adopted, what you think the author's approach to the subject would be (*e.g.*, light-hearted, broadly humorous, factual, persuasive, etc.), and what kind of material you would expect to find in the essay itself. Does one of the openings strike you as unsatisfactory? If so, why?

(a) *The oldest joke.* Many investigators have speculated as to the character of the first joke; and as speculation must our efforts remain. But I personally have no doubt whatever as to the subject-matter of that distant pleasantry: it was the face of the other person involved. . . .

(b) *Arctic explorers.* The desire to know what is at the northern end of the earth is an old one, and few regions have been the scene of more persistent effort. Many distinguished explorers have shared in these efforts, but in a brief essay there is space to consider only a few. Among these we must include Frobisher, one of the first Elizabethan seamen to sail to the North; Franklin, the pioneer of North American coastal discovery; Amundsen, first conqueror of the North-West Passage, and Larsen, its most recent and only other conqueror; Peary, the only leading explorer who has stood at the North Pole; and Nansen, whose voyage in the *Fram* was one of the most remarkable of Arctic journeys.

Frobisher's voyages were instigated by commercial enterprise. . .

(c) *The Girls' Training Corps.* When elderly grey-heads shake foreboding pates and say that they don't know what the girls and boys of to-day are coming to—when they were youngsters there was none of this mad rush for pleasure and so on—the present-day youngster is apt to make a rude gesture and say pertinently and impertinently, "So what?" "What" being precisely what grey-head is quite unable to define. the prophet of gloom generally retires, muttering.

Each generation after the days of Adam probably having said the same about its girls and boys (and tried to do something about it according to its lights), it has fallen to the present generation of youth to be the first to come under real official discipline. . . .

(d) *Walking tours.* It must not be imagined that a walking tour, as some would have us fancy is merely a better or worse way of seeing the country. There are many ways of seeing landscape quite as good; and none more vivid, in spite of canting dilettantes, than from a railway train. But landscape on a walking tour is quite accessory. . . .

(e) *Popular superstitions.* Going yesterday to dine with an old acquaintance, I had the misfortune to find his whole family very much dejected. Upon asking him the occasion of it, he told me that his wife had dreamt a strange dream the night before, which they were afraid portended some misfortune to themselves or to their children. At her coming into the room, I observed a settled melancholy in her countenance, which I should have been troubled for had I not heard from whence it proceeded. . . .

ENDING THE ESSAY

An essay should arrive at a definite finishing-point. The reader is left with a feeling of dissatisfaction when the essay just stops because the writer cannot think of anything more to say or because he is pressed for time. Too many students' essays leave the reader wondering whether he has actually reached the end or whether there is a page missing! They do not reach a terminus: they merely fail to continue the journey.

It is often useful when you are planning the essay and gathering your ideas into paragraph-groups to decide first of all on your final paragraph and let your preceding paragraphs lead up to this conclusion. If this can be done it will ensure that your essay has a firm finish.

The ending, like the opening, must be an integral part of the essay. For this reason it is difficult to offer formal rules

A good ending is almost meaningless without reference to what has gone before. None the less, there are two broad rules worth bearing in mind:

(i) A short paragraph, ending with a crisp sentence, is more likely to be satisfying than a long paragraph, ending with a long-winded sentence.

(ii) A definite statement is more satisfying than a qualified one.

Some Types of Ending

1. The *straightforward conclusion*, announcing that we have reached the end of the episode or journey. This is often used in an essay with some narrative content.

> I did not leave the ground until twenty minutes to seven, and even then there were still a few stragglers left.
> Thus ended the bloodless battle of Footerloo. ROBERT LYND

[From *The Battle of Footerloo*, a narrative description of the scene at a Wembley Cup Final.]

> Passports and customs at Ramadi. Fallujah's bridge of boats, a run over the flat land between the rivers, and then Baghdad with all but its sand-coloured minarets hidden in palm groves. It seems incredible but we are there. FREYA STARK

[From a descriptive essay, *The Desert Route*, on a motor-journey across the desert from Beyrout to Baghdad.]

2. The ending which rounds off a descriptive essay with a *reflective comment*:

> But the squalor of that march! What she had done I have no notion, but she was well punished for it long before Vine Street was reached. I hope that magistrates sometimes take these distances into consideration. E. V. LUCAS

[From the essay *A London Thrill*, describing the arrest of a young woman, and the crowd that followed her on the journey to the police-station.]

3. A *summary* of the impressions or opinions conveyed in the body of the essay:

> Thus you carry away from New York a memory of a lively air, gigantic buildings, incessant movement, sporadic elegance, and

ingenuous patronage. And when you have separated your impressions, the most vivid and constant impression that remains is of a city where the means of life conquer life itself whose citizens die hourly of the rage to live.

CHARLES WHIBLEY

[From a descriptive and reflective essay entitled *New York*.]

4. *Repetition* (sometimes with a new significance) *of the title or opening words* of the essay:

The garden has lost its smiling mistress; the greyhounds their kind master; and new people, new manners, and new cares have taken possession of the old abode of peace and plenty—the great farm-house.

M. R. MITFORD

[From an essay entitled *A Great Farm-house*, a reminiscent description of a farm which the author used to know. The essay begins with a reference to the fact that she suddenly came upon it "the other day" after an absence of ten or twelve years.]

5. A *look into the future* of the subject under discussion:

We must hope, without much confidence, that the graceful and gentle art of letter-writing may have another flowering time among us.

[From an essay, *Letter-writing*, referring to a number of famous letter-writers of the eighteenth and nineteenth centuries.]

SUMMARY OF CHIEF POINTS

Choice

1. Look first for topics which suit your own interests.

2. Cross out any subjects which definitely do not interest you.

3. Consider carefully the *exact* significance of the title.

4. Make sure you have enough material before finally choosing your subject.

5. Use the 'tin-opener' only as a last resort.

Arrangement

6. Jot down ideas on the chosen subject as they occur to you.

7. Arrange these ideas in groups, letting each group form the basis of a paragraph. The final paragraph may be decided upon first.

8. Have clearly in your mind the main theme (or angle of approach) which will give your various groups coherence.

9. Do not spend more than about a third of your time on the planning of your essay.

Writing

10. Avoid an irrelevant introduction.

11. See that you keep a unity of theme in your paragraphs.

12. Aim at a conclusion that leaves your essay satisfactorily rounded off.

CHAPTER II

TYPES OF COMPOSITION

THE following list of subjects, taken from various examination papers, will illustrate some of the ways in which prose composition may be broadly classified:

1. A day in the life of a worker in your district.	NARRATIVE
2. Tell the story of a play (or film) that you have recently seen.	NARRATIVE
3. The village policeman.	DESCRIPTION (Person)
4. The changing sky.	DESCRIPTION (Scene)
5. A morning's wait on a country railway station.	NARRATIVE and DESCRIPTION
6. Explain how you would make a model, a toy, a garment, or a favourite dish.	EXPLANATION
7. "All work and no play makes a dull life."	DISCUSSION or ARGUMENT
8. Superstitions.	REFLECTION

It would be wrong and confusing to overstress the importance of these classifications. An essay remains an essay in whatever category it may be put; and a student could write a very good one without stopping to find out under which heading to place it. Some essay subjects, moreover, are hard to classify; they combine features of more than one category. Thus some of the Sir Roger de Coverley essays by Addison and Steele are partly narrative, partly descriptive, and partly reflective.

None the less it is useful to consider separately certain distinctive types of composition, and to note some of the special points relating to each.

NARRATIVE

An essential part of good narrative is logical sequence of events. You should take care in planning your essay to see that this sequence is kept. Where the story to be related is at all complicated this planning is doubly important. You must select the main thread of events, ruthlessly disregarding most other matters, otherwise you will be led into endless side-tracks and irrelevancies, and your narrative will become confused or even chaotic.

This selection is particularly important where you are asked to tell the story of a film, play, or book. There will necessarily be a great deal that you must leave out. Get the right sequence of events in the main story, and either leave the rest or make it fit unobtrusively into your main theme. Similarly with an account of a journey or expedition. You cannot possibly include every detail in a short account, so make sure that you keep in mind the main objectives of the journey, and the incidents which relate to these objectives.

Points to Remember

1. Aim at simplicity in writing. Let the story unfold itself naturally.

2. Avoid using the words 'then' and 'next' as far as you can. The over-use of these words, and their equivalents, is a common fault in students' narrative composition. They can nearly always be omitted with advantage to the smooth reading of the composition; they are nearly always unnecessary.

Example 1

The Story of a Play (or Film)

In the essay below, certain words and phrases which students tend to employ unnecessarily in narrative composition have been put in square brackets. You will see that if these words are omitted the essay loses nothing in clarity, while it gains in smoothness and freedom from monotonous repetition.

1. *Strife*, generally regarded as one of John Galsworthy's most

notable plays, deals seriously and sincerely with the theme of
struggle between two unyielding forces and reveals the harm
arising from stubborn fanaticism.

2. The play is concerned with a strike at a tin-plate works in
Wales. It opens with the directors holding a board meeting in
the manager's house where they are discussing the policy to be
adopted at a coming interview with the men's representatives.
[It is now shown that] the strike has been going on for some time,
and the directors are getting anxious about loss of dividends and
about the stability of the company. But the chairman of the
company, Mr Anthony, is inexorable in refusing to consider
yielding to the men's demands.

3. [At this point Harness, a trade union official, arrives.] The
arrival of Harness, a trade union official, introduces the theme of
conciliation. He suggests that such disputes always end in compromise in the long run, and that the sensible thing to do is to
reach agreement without further delay. Anthony rejects the
advice; and the attitude of Roberts, the leader of the men's
representatives, shows that he is as intransigent.

4. [Then] the scene shifts to Roberts's home, where his wife is
dying of starvation, typifying the hardships being endured by the
strikers' families. [Next] at a meeting of the strikers we see the
differences of the men among themselves. Several speakers put
forward conflicting viewpoints, in which, however, a tendency to
throw Roberts over gradually becomes evident. [Then] by a
diatribe of fiery eloquence he brings the crowd round to his point
of view; but at the very moment of his triumph a message is
brought that his wife is dead. [Then] the harsh realities of the
strike being brought home to them, the men decide to abandon
Roberts's leadership and let the trade union make terms for them.

5. Meanwhile the directors are growing increasingly uneasy at
the deterioration of the company's financial position. Stirred to
action by the news of Mrs Roberts's death, Anthony's son throws
his weight against his father's obdurate policy; and despite a grim
and powerful speech by the old chairman, his fellow directors go
against him. [Then] he immediately resigns from his position as
head of the company which he founded and to which he has
devoted his life.

6. Thus the two inflexible leaders are overthrown; and the
dispute is settled by a compromise which is identical with one
which had been proposed by Harness and the company's secretary
before the strike began.

7. The unforced moral of the play is that we must be prepared
to make an effort to understand each other's point of view if our

finest energies are not to be wasted in useless conflict. It is a truth interpreted by Galsworthy with vision and sympathy, and quickened with warm human feeling.[1]

The following plan will show how the sequence of main events has been traced:

1. Main theme—struggle between unyielding forces.

2. Setting—inexorable attitude of chairman at directors' meeting.

3. Conciliation efforts rejected by leaders of both sides.

4. Hardships force men to give way, despite Roberts's eloquence—Mrs Roberts's death.

5. Directors throw over Anthony.

6. Compromise reached.

7. Unforced moral—need for mutual understanding.

EXAMPLE 2

The Story of a Well-known Journey of Exploration

1. In the year 1879 an American yacht named the *Jeanette* was frozen in the ice in latitude 71° 35′ North and longitude 175° 6′ East. While frozen in she drifted with the ice to a point to the north of the New Siberian Islands. It was this drift of the *Jeanette* which put it into the head of Dr Fridtjof Nansen to make his great attempt at drifting across the North Pole.

2. His idea was to build a ship so strong and of such a shape that instead of being crushed by the ice she would rise above it, just as an orange-pip rises when pinched between the fingers. The result was the famous *Fram*. She was built of wood, her sides being of enormous strength and thickness. She was fitted with engines and a screw, and rigged as a schooner. With a crew of thirteen men, and with every inch packed with stores, the *Fram* sailed on the 24th of June, 1893.

3. On the 4th of August she reached the Kara Sea, and by the 10th of September had forced her way as far as Cape Cheluyski, the most northerly point of Europe. This was the point for which Nansen had been making, for here he hoped to pick up the Arctic current. Very soon the ship was frozen in, but to the disgust of every one aboard, instead of drifting to the north-east, they found themselves going south-east.

---

[1] Adapted from Galsworthy's "*Strife*": *A Commentary and Questionnaire*, by G. F. Lamb.

4. Soon the ice was thirty feet thick, and presently came the nip. Like a frozen billow the crushed ice pushed forward against the ship in a huge roll. The *Fram* groaned and trembled, and even Nansen's heart was in his mouth. Then with a mighty wrench she broke from the bonds that held her, and rose upward until she was safe.

5. The course of the current changed, and the *Fram* drifted northward. During the following summer the drift turned to the west, and preparations were made for a dash by sledge towards the North Pole. On the 14th of March, 1895, Nansen, with one companion, Lieutenant Johansen, three sledges, and twenty-eight dogs, left the ship on his desperate venture. The ice was very rough, but on the 7th of April the two had reached a point within two hundred miles of the Pole. Here the temperature averaged 40° below zero.

6. Their clothes and sleeping-bag were frozen stiff, and Nansen decided to turn back. The difficulties were appalling. May passed and found them still struggling over rough ice. It was not until August that they reached open water, in which they saw several islands, on one of which they made their winter quarters.

7. Few men could have survived a winter under such terrible conditions. But these two men not only did so; they kept their health and were able to start away again in the following May.

8. Fresh adventures befell them. After climbing an iceberg to get their bearings, they found their canoes adrift, and Nansen was forced to swim in his heavy furs through the icy water to retrieve them. Later a huge bull walrus attacked Nansen's kayak (canoe) and nearly destroyed it. He and Johansen camped to repair it, and after supper got into their sleeping-bag and rested peacefully.

9. In the morning Nansen got up first. To his utter amazement he heard the bark of a dog, and looking across the ice saw a man approaching. This was Mr F. G. Jackson, leader of the Jackson-Harmsworth expedition, which was making a detailed survey of Franz Joseph Land. A few hours later the two bold explorers enjoyed the amazing luxury of a wash, clean clothes, and a real dinner in the comfortable quarters of the English expedition.

10. As for the *Fram* herself, in the middle of July 1896 she reached open water, and sailed safely back to Norway, reaching Vardo just a week after Nansen and Johansen.[1]

Exercise

Supply a plan showing the main sequence of events.

[1] Adapted from *The Book of Discovery*, by T. C. Bridges.

EXERCISES IN NARRATION

1. Tell the story of a play or film you have seen (other than *Strife*).

2. Give an account of any exploratory journey or expedition (other than Nansen's in the *Fram*).

3. Tell the story of a life-boat rescue. You may refer to:

> (a) The distress signal; (b) the setting out of the lifeboat: (c) the condition of the sea and the journey towards the wreck; (d) the sighting of the wreck—her position and state; (e) the first attempt at rescue—difficulties; (f) eventual success; (g) return to safety.

You are not obliged, however, to keep to this plan if a different plan suits your story better.

4. Give an account of some person distinguished for labours in the relief of human suffering, or similar humanitarian work, such as Sir Wilfred Grenfell, Florence Nightingale, Father Damien, Louis Pasteur, or Albert Schweitzer. First gather your material from a biography, or some work of reference, and arrange it according to a suitable plan.

A plan for the first-named character is suggested as an example, though it need not be rigidly followed:

> (i) Descended from Sir Richard Grenville—love of sea as child.
>
> (ii) Decision to become doctor—London Hospital—help with boys' club in East London.
>
> (iii) Doctor with North Atlantic fishing fleet off Labrador—hospital ship.
>
> (iv) Attends cases on Labrador coast—need for medical help—hospitals started.
>
> (v) Care for neglected children—homes added to hospitals.
>
> (vi) Other activities in Labrador.
>
> (vii) Fame—International Grenfell Association—knighthood—books.
>
> (viii) Death in 1940—but work lives on.

5. A summer holiday.

6. The happiest day in your life.

7. Give an account of a conjuring performance you have seen.

8. A cricket-match.

9. Tell the story of any novel you have recently read.

10. An escape by a prisoner-of-war from a prison camp.

11. After a severe snowstorm two boys living in the country have been put on their honour to make their way along the snow-bound roads to school, two kilometres away, unless they genuinely find the snow is too deep. Half-way to school they find themselves up to their waists. One boy wants to turn back, the other persuades him to go on,

as it was left to their honour. Describe the incident, adding any details you think fit.

12. Six men set out from Peru on a raft made of balsa logs to sail across the Pacific Ocean to the South Sea Islands, 6,400 kilometres away. They have plenty of stores aboard, and also rely on catching fish. The raft is fitted with a single sail, and has a crude hut, open on one side, erected on deck. During the voyage one man falls overboard in a shark-infested sea, and is rescued in the nick of time by a comrade who has dived after him, holding a lifebelt attached to a line. Tell the story.

13. A detective has to track down a murderer. The only clue is an old felt hat. Inventing any details you please, describe how he succeeded in his task.

14. The story of a famous battle, at sea, on land, or in the air.

15. You are on a bus which collides with a small car coming out of a side-turning, and then careers across the road, mounts the pavement, and crashes into a shop-window. The bus was travelling about fifty kilometres an hour at the time of the incident. You were sitting in the left-hand front seat at the time. Write out a careful statement for the benefit of the police, sticking to facts as far as you can. (You may invent any necessary factual details.)

DESCRIPTION

There are two important mental processes necessary as a preliminary to good descriptive writing, whether the description is that of a place, a person, or an object. The first is careful observation; the second is intelligent selection of detail. Imagination plays an important part in both processes.

In the examination room imagination is doubly important, for opportunity for immediate observation is obviously ruled out—unless you are to describe the examination room or the supervisor. You will have to conjure up a clear recollection of whatever you are describing.

In drawing upon your recollections of a scene or person you should try to discover the main impressions which have been made in your mind. Jot these down on rough paper as the basis of your description, and let the various details as they occur to you fit into place to support one or other of these main impressions. One of the commonest faults in poor descriptive writing is to give a list of unrelated features from which no clear impression can be gained.

There are two kinds of description—objective and subjective.

In *objective* writing the author describes a scene or person without obtruding his own viewpoint: he writes down what he sees without indicating the impression upon himself. In *subjective* writing the author allows his own personality to be reflected in his description, and often to give colour to the description: he presents a picture of what he has seen in such a way that his feelings about it are also revealed.

There is a place for both types of writing; but a strong subjective element is usually to be found in the most interesting descriptions.

Description of Place or Scene

EXAMPLE 1

(The following is *not* to be taken as a model.)

The Isle of Wight is easily reached by travellers, being accessible by plane or by boat. It is 38,850 ha in area. Though large enough to offer every facility to the holiday-maker, it is not so large that it cannot easily be seen in a day. Attractive excursions are run from seaside resorts on the mainland, including sea-voyages and motor-coach tours round the island.

The chines are a feature of particular interest. Ornamental foot-bridges cross deep ravines, which are overhung with trees and great ferns.

There are numerous villages with charming cottages and old churches. The seaside resorts, including Ventnor, Sandown, Shanklin, and Seaview, offer sunshine and extensive stretches of sand to youthful holiday-makers. Among the other attractions of the island are the cliffs of Alum Bay, the Needles, Osborne House, Carisbrooke Castle, the famous Cowes Regatta, and many delightful downs. On the hills above Ryde pleasant views of the shipping in Spithead and Southampton Water can be obtained.

The Isle of Wight is a truly delightful spot.

This sort of essay, written in conventional guide-book style, has a few good points. The facts are to some extent sorted out, and they are expressed in reasonably correct English. There is a main theme running through the description—namely, that the Isle of Wight is a pleasant place—and this theme is directly stated in the concluding sentence (though both this sentence and the opening sentence are tame and weak). The essay can at least be said to hang together.

None the less it is rather a colourless piece of work. Several of the chief features of the island are mentioned, but no vivid impression is given. There is a tendency to 'catalogue' names. Though the essay is not entirely objective—the general tone of praise, and phrases such as "attractive excursions," "charming cottages," "other attractions," indicate that the writer has a point of view—the note of personal experience is kept very much in the background. As a whole the essay is an indifferent example of third-person objective writing.

Here is an essay on the same theme, in which the author is frankly subjective, and deliberately portrays the island by revealing the impressions made by it on himself:

EXAMPLE 2

The Isle of Wight's only fault is its accessibility. You can fly there from London in an hour and a half, and cross to it from the mainland in about twenty minutes.

It is too large for a single man to own, but it is just the right size to cope with a summer invasion. I have been all round it in much less than a single day, for the motor-coach excursion on that occasion started at eight o'clock in the morning from Brighton and by eight o'clock in the evening we were in Brighton again. It was an admirably varied excursion, for it included two sea-voyages, a visit to at least twenty crowded sandy bays, miles of high-banked lanes, a tremendous run along Ryde Pier (surely the longest in the world), and a steep climb up and down a number of chines.

Chines are to the Isle of Wight what cream is to Devon, something rich and rare and unobtainable in quite the same form elsewhere. They are deep green ravines with tumbling waters, crossed by ornamental foot-bridges and overhung with trees and giant ferns.

Isle of Wight villages are cosy, compact places with white-washed thatched cottages and grey-towered medieval churches; and the Isle of Wight summer resorts, Ventnor, Seaview, Sandown, Shanklin, and the rest, are cheerful places open to the sun, with miles of sands, and every opportunity for vigorous youth to take the sort of exercise that vigorous youth most likes.

But what I like best about the Isle of Wight is not Alum Bay with its multi-coloured cliffs, nor the pure white razor edge of the Needles, nor the fact that Tennyson and Queen Victoria lived there and Charles I was imprisoned there, nor even Cowes Regatta, that pageant of unforgettable beauty: but the chalk down of Arreton, Mersley, and Ashey above Ryde, where I have lain through a long summer afternoon with the smell of wild June roses mingling with the scent of wild thyme, and watched the slow stately procession of transatlantic liners entering Spithead, the white excursion steamers from Bournemouth and Brighton, and hundreds of small craft running into and out of Southampton Water as if they were bees at the entrance of a hive.

I like the Isle of Wight because it is a delightful chunk of the garden of England that has drifted far enough away to make believe that it is an island on its own.[1]

Readers will probably agree that the description gains a great deal from the personal element, and that the resulting picture of the Isle of Wight is warmer and more vivid than the third-person description in Example 1. Point out some of the differences between the two descriptions.

An effective description is sometimes achieved by the use of the second person singular, the reader being button-holed, as it were, and persuaded to feel that he is himself looking at the scene.

EXAMPLE 3

Strand-on-the-Green

You would never imagine that this quaint unspoilt little village could exist so near London, yet it lies just below Kew Bridge. As you reach the bridge from Chiswick, turn to the left, and walk along the road for a little way, and then you will find Strand-on-the-Green: just a line of old houses, inns, and boat-builders' yards, perched on the river-bank.

[1] S. P. B. Mais, *Isles of the Island.*

Trees edge the tow-path, and children play in the old barges that lie derelict here. Through the open doors of the boat-sheds come the clanging of hammers, and if you look inside you will see the half-finished boat that is in the making. A tiny row of pretty cottages bears a tablet that says, "Two of these houses built by H. Thomas Child, one by A. Solomon Williams, and one by William Abbott, Carpinter on [h]is own charge, for the use of the poor of Chiswick for ever, 1724."

The old inns are quaint, with their low doorways and oddly-shaped windows. Many of the houses have little built-out rooms, with wide windows overlooking the river, and nearly all of them are covered with wistaria. You see a little entry in a wall, and peep inside, and it is like a sudden view of a picture, for hidden away here are several little cottages, with gardens full of flowers.

At Zoffany House lived the artist, Johann Zoffany, and he died here in 1810. You must notice, too, the old Ship House, with its wonderful old brass door-knocker.

Strand-on-the-Green is a fragment of London which has stood still through the centuries, untouched by the busy traffic of the town. It is a favourite place of artists and of those who love the lazy, peaceful life of the river.[1]

EXERCISE

Give a brief numbered plan for the compositions in Examples 2 and 3.

Description of Person

The simplest form of personal description merely enumerates factual details concerning a person's appearance, habits, or profession. This is the type of description which is found in notices about persons wanted by the police, or missing from their homes.

The example below is a "Wanted" notice relating to the distinguished author of *Robinson Crusoe*, Daniel Defoe, who was in trouble with the Government over his political activities:

He is a middle-aged man, about forty years old, of a brown complexion, and dark-brown coloured hair, but wears a wig; a hooked

Mary Fox-Davies, *London*.

nose, a sharp chin, grey eyes, and a large mole near his mouth: was born in London, and for many years was a hose factor in Freeman's Yard in Cornhill, and now is the owner of the brick and pantile works near Tilbury Fort in Essex.

This gives the sort of details which might enable a person who did not know Defoe to spot him, or which might enable some one who had known him at Cornhill or Tilbury to be certain that it was the same man who was now wanted by the Government. But the description is purely utilitarian. No one could read it for pleasure; and after reading it no one would have much idea of Defoe as a person. The details given are correct, but they do not bring the man to life.

To bring a person to life the facts must be presented to the reader in such a way that they are seen to have significance. In a good description it is not enough merely to mention details: the details must be carefully selected and arranged around a main theme if a vivid representation of a living person is to be built up. (The processes of selection and arrangement are not necessarily deliberate: many good writers achieve them instinctively.)

There is no formula for such writing, but a careful study of examples by good writers will reveal something of the way in which the selection of one or two salient points can be made the basis of a convincing character-sketch.

EXAMPLE 1

An Elderly Man of Masterful Disposition

In the centre of the room, under the chandelier, as became a host, stood the head of the family, old Jolyon himself. Eighty years of age, with his fine, white hair, his dome-like forehead, his little, dark grey eyes, and an immense white moustache, which drooped and spread below the level of his strong jaw, he had a patriarchal look, and in spite of lean cheeks and hollows at his temples, seemed master of perennial youth. He held himself extremely upright, and his shrewd steady eyes had lost none of their clear shining. Thus he gave an impression of superiority to the doubts and dislikes of smaller men. Having had his own way for innumerable years, he had earned a prescriptive right to it.

It would never have occurred to old Jolyon that it was necessary to wear a look of doubt or of defiance.[1]

Comment. There are three salient features of the portrait: Jolyon's age; his haleness; his unaffected and unconscious domination. Name the details which help to build up each of these three features.

EXAMPLE 2

An Old Bookworm

The old gentleman was a very respectable-looking personage, with a powdered head and gold spectacles. He was dressed in a bottle-green coat with a black velvet collar; wore white trousers; and carried a smart bamboo cane under his arm. He had taken up a book from the stall, and there he stood, reading away, as hard as if he were in his elbow-chair in his own study. It is very possible that he fancied himself there, indeed; for it was plain, from his abstraction, that he saw not the book-stall, nor the street, nor the boys, nor, in short, anything but the book itself; which he was reading straight through, turning over a leaf when he got to the bottom of a page, beginning at the top line of the next one, and going regularly on, with the greatest interest and eagerness.[2]

Note how the character is described by his *actions* as well as by details of his appearance.

Which details here do you think are particularly effective in making the portraiture vivid?

EXAMPLE 3

A Child

It was in the neighbourhood of Berkeley Square, and I had come out of a drawing-room, warm, scented, and full of "portable property". The hall door was closed behind me, the East wind caught me in the face, and I walked into a child.

She may have been five years old. With a scanty red petticoat widespread over her humped-up knees, she was sitting on the pavement and beating it with a bit of withered branch decorated with three or four brown leaves. In time to the beating she chanted a song. Blackish-brown curls hung all about her round, smutty little face; the remains of a hat rested beside her on the pavement; and two restless little black devils looked out of her eyes. She was so delightful a contrast to the "portable property" that it was impossible not to stare at her.

[1] John Galsworthy, *The Man of Property.*
[2] Charles Dickens, *Oliver Twist.*

So I went down the street crabwise.

She knew I was going crabwise, she knew the position of the 'bobby' at the corner, she knew everything all round her. And when she saw me vanishing she began to flirt with me. She put her head on one side like a terrier asking for cake, and looked up through her tangle of curls. She smiled—I smiled, and went round the corner.

There was a little patter of hobnails, and *she* came round the corner. If she was queer on the ground, she was queerer on her feet; she had clapped her hat—the last bit of a large girl's hat—on the back of her bare head; her short red petticoat gaped, her bare brown legs were thrust into a woman's boots. She shuffled along behind, beating the railings with her branch. Sometimes she ranged up alongside, shot a shy glance at my top-hat, and fell back again.

People passed and stared at her, but she paid no attention.

In Oxford Street we stopped and held a conversation. It began and ended thus:

"Would you like some sweets?" I left her sucking a sixpence, staring after me with her great black eyes, and beating a shop window with her branch.

But when I looked round again she was dancing to a barrel-organ with some other children, her petticoat a little red *tee*-totum in the crowded street.[1]

Comment. This attractive little sketch of childhood was originally entitled *Joy of Life*. Note the effective use of contrast: Berkeley Square drawing-room—street waif; ragged clothing—carefree disposition.

The author builds up his picture by giving us the details in the order in which we should notice them. First—approximate age, red petticoat, action of beating with withered branch. Next—the face, and the hat lying on the ground.

Note the way in which the child's *actions* reveal her: the careless beating with a branch; her 'flirtatious' following of the passer-by; her swift changes of activity.

But the charm of the description cannot be fully dissected and analysed, for it arises naturally from the author's personality as well as from his quick perception of contrasts, his keen eye for significant detail, and his sympathy with the child's spontaneity. The passage is a truthful record of a personal contact.

What is the effect of deliberately irregular paragraphing?

---

[1] John Galsworthy, *A Motley*.

EXERCISES IN DESCRIPTION

1. Give a precise description in about 100 words of an object in your pocket or handbag.

2. Choose an object in the room in which you are sitting and describe it carefully in about 200 words.

3. You are writing to an intelligent native of an Arctic district; he understands English well, but has never been out of his own area. He is puzzled by the following words that he has come across in his reading: lawn-mower, bicycle, typewriter, gramophone.

Describe each of these, showing (a) what it is used for, (b) its structure, (c) the materials from which it is made, and (d) how it works.

4. Describe the following to a person who is colour-blind: (a) an automatic traffic signal, (b) the American flag.

5. Here are the opening words of a passage describing a detective's first view of a school where a murder has been committed:

> Travers never forgot his first sight of Woodgate Hill School in that weird light, through the drizzling rain, and against the background of the empurpled sky. The building reared itself above the sprawling indeterminate villas like something grimly forbidding. . . .[1]

Imagine a murder has been committed in your school. Write a description of the building from the viewpoint of the detective.

6. A friend wants to know what your garden is like. Write a detailed description of it for him. (Begin with a general impression, and then pass on to the separate features.)

7. The editor of the local newspaper in the district where you spent your holiday would like to have your honest impressions of the place. Write an article for him.

8. Describe a park or recreation ground in your town on a Saturday afternoon or a Sunday evening.

9. Describe the scene on the beach or at a bathing-pool, (a) on a crowded Saturday, (b) on a wet Sunday.

10. Describe the scene at a cricket or football match or a sports meeting. (Do not relate the course of the game.)

11. The school magazine requires a word-portrait of the school captain, cricket captain, football captain, or some other prominent member of the school. There is space for about 250 words. Write the description.

12. Describe one or more of the following: a postman, a bus conductor, a policeman, a shopkeeper, a window-cleaner. Go out and find one before you write your description.

---

[1] Christopher Bush, *The Case of the Dead Shepherd.*

13. Give a description of any well-known sportsman or sportswoman.

14. Write a character-sketch of any elderly person known to you.

15. Describe a young child (*a*) from the point of view of a person sympathetic towards children, (*b*) from the point of view of the disagreeable old gentleman next door.

EXPLANATION

Under this heading we may include the giving of information, the giving of instructions and directions, and the exposition of ideas. No type of expression enters more fully into our daily lives. In no type of expression are accuracy and clarity of greater importance.

It will be obvious that no simple formula can be offered to cover the writing of all types of explanation by all types of people. Good writing cannot be achieved in this mechanical way. But the following points may be useful as indicating a general method.

Points to Remember

1. Consider to whom the explanation is to be given, for this must influence your approach to the task. You will not explain to your little sister how to make a paper hat in the same way that you explain to a friend interested in model aeroplanes the special points of the one you have just bought.

2. Consider what preliminaries may need to be made clear before you embark on the explanation proper. Thus if you are going to explain to a friend how to make a three-valve wireless-set you should begin by stating exactly the kind of set you are going to deal with. Your preliminary statement might also include a mention of the materials you propose to assume your friend already has in his possession, and of the tools it will be necessary to use.

3. Arrange in logical order the chief stages of the process you are going to explain, and build up your explanation around this framework.

4. Decide whether it will be best to make your explanation personal, directional, or impersonal. (See below.)

5. Put yourself in the place of the reader and ask yourself what points you would need to have clarified.

6. Be careful not to make casual reference to some point or process which needs explanation and which you have not yet dealt with.

7. See that you give the *purpose* for each stage in a process. For example, if you are explaining how to mend a puncture it would be unsatisfactory merely to tell the reader to insert the inner tube in a bowl of water without giving him the reason for this. Your explanation might run:

> If you cannot locate the puncture, partly inflate the inner tube and insert it, one portion at a time, in a bowl of water. The pressure of the air escaping from the puncture will cause a stream of bubbles to rise to the surface from the hole in the tube.

Similarly, you might continue, again giving the reason for the process:

> Begin by inserting the valve, so that, as you work your way round the tube, you will know, by reaching the valve again, when you have examined the whole of the tube; in which case you may need to make a second and more careful examination.

8. See that each stage of the explanation leads naturally to the one which follows. If the explanation is a fairly long one it is often a good plan, after three or four paragraphs, to recapitulate the main points, as far as you have gone, before proceeding to the next stage.

9. When you find yourself using the pronouns 'it' and 'them' make sure that there is no uncertainty about their antecedents. (See Chapter VIII: Pronouns.)

10. Write simply.

Methods of Approach

In giving an explanation your approach to the reader may be personal (1st person), directional (2nd person), or impersonal (3rd person).

The *personal* form is most suitable where the explanation to be given is closely linked with your own experience. (*E.g.*, "Explain how you made a model in a Woodwork lesson, or a frock in a Needlework lesson.") It may also be used when a writer wishes to reduce an exposition of more abstract ideas to quite simple terms. For example:

> I can still know exactly how Chaucer thought and felt, though the where and when of it are lost beyond discovery. This is because Chaucer was a poet, one who made himself such a master of words that as we of to-day read his words we know exactly what he wanted us to know.

The *directional* form is most naturally used where explanation consists in advice or directions on what to do. The use of the 2nd person gives the reader the impression that he personally is being shown how to carry out the instructions, even though in fact he may be one of a multitude of readers. A subtle suggestion is implied that the writer is interested in the reader's success in following the explanation. Compare the friendly intimacy of

> When you come out of the station, turn to the right and follow the footpath across the green until you reach the golf-course. . . .

with the impersonal indifference of

> When the station has been left, a footpath on the right should be followed across the green until the golf-course is reached. . . .

The *impersonal* form is used when the writer does not wish or require to associate himself personally with the explanation, or where the reader is not required to follow directions. The form is often used for official instructions, for the explanation of a game or process to some one whose interest is theoretical and not practical, for the exposition of ideas, and for scientific explanations. The personal or directional forms, however, could correctly be used in these cases if the writer wished to achieve a friendlier tone, or to make his explanation particularly simple.

EXAMPLE 1

In the following example of impersonal explanation a plan of the composition is first given to show how the explanation is logically built up.

The Electric Bell

1. *Preliminary* comment—common use of electric bell explained.

2. *General principle* explained—application of electro-magnet —device to break circuit.

3. *Apparatus*—how it is fixed. Armature explained.

4. Actual *working* of apparatus in 'trembler' type of bell explained.

5. How bell is *kept in use* for long periods.

1. The electric bell is probably the best-known of all domestic appliances, and, since it draws its current usually from a Leclanché cell (which produces electricity by chemical action) or from a dry battery, it is to be found in use even in houses where a mains supply of electricity is not available. Where there is a mains supply the current for the bell is often obtained from this source through a small transformer.

2. The operation of an electric bell is a practical application of the electro-magnet. As long as current is passing through the magnet it will attract a piece of iron to itself; when the current ceases the iron will be released. The mechanism of the bell therefore requires a device that will make and break the circuit automatically.

3. The apparatus consists of a gong, an electro-magnet, and a piece of soft iron, called the armature, which is pivoted at one end. To the free end of the armature is fastened a hammer which strikes the gong. The pivoted end is sprung to allow of its moving backward and forward easily. There is also a contact screw, the end of which touches the armature when the latter is at rest. All these parts are fastened to a baseboard.

4. The wire from one pole of the battery leads direct to the contact screw, which is adjustable. The other pole is connected through the bell-push to one arm of the electro-magnet. From the post which pivots the armature a wire goes to the other arm of the magnet. Pressure on the bell-push completes the circuit, and current runs from the battery through the magnet, down the armature, and along the contact screw back to the battery. The magnet attracts the soft iron to itself, and the hammer strikes the gong. This movement of the armature brings it away from the

contact screw and the circuit is broken. The arm is therefore released from the magnet and springs back to its original position, so completing the circuit again; this means that the armature is once more attracted to the magnet; and the process is repeated so long as pressure on the bell-push continues. Thus we get the continuous ringing in what is known as the 'trembler' type of bell.

5. It will be realized that current for electric bells is required for short spells only, with periods of rest between the times of use. Such conditions are ideal for the use of the Leclanché cell. This type of battery requires little attention other than a periodic charging with a solution of sal-ammoniac and an occasional renewal of the zinc rod. Where the battery is not needed, the current being obtained from the mains supply through a transformer, the bell will usually be in use for years without any attention whatsoever.[1]

EXAMPLE 2

Learning to Swim

If any ladies should chance to read how Bevis and Mark learnt to swim, when they are at the seaside will they try the same plan? Choose a smooth sea and a low tide (only to have it shallow). Kneel in the water. Place the hands on the sands, so that the water may come almost over the shoulders—not quite, say, up to them. Then let the limbs and body float. The pleasant sense of suspension without effort will be worth the little trouble it costs. On the softest couch the limbs feel that there is something solid, a hard framework beneath, and so the Sybarites put cushions on the floor under the feet of their couches. On the surface of the buoyant sea there is nothing under the soft couch. They will find that there is no pressure on the hands. They have no weight. Now let them kick with both feet together, and the propulsion will send them forward.

Next use one arm in swimming style. Next use one arm and kick at the same time. Try to use both arms, lifting the hand from the sand a little first, and presently more. Stand up to the chest in water, stoop somewhat and bend the knee, one foot in front of the other, and use the arms together, walking at the same time, so as to get the proper motion of the hands. Place the hands on the sand again, and try to use both arms once more.

Finally, stand up to the chest, face the shore, lean forward, and push off and try a stroke—the feet will easily recover themselves.

[1] Adapted from *English for Practical People*, by J. Barclay and D. H. Knox.

C

Presently two strokes will become possible. after a while three;
that is swimming.[1]

Comment. This was, of course, written in days when swimming
was not as common among ladies as it is to-day. The explanation
does not go into details about the arm and leg movements in swimming, as these were dealt with earlier in the book.

The directional and impersonal approaches are here mixed, perhaps to the disadvantage of the passage. Paragraph 1 begins imper-
sonally, becomes directional, and then slips back into the impersonal
again. It would be more in keeping with the tone of the passage if
the directional form were retained throughout, after the opening
sentence (*i.e.*, "You will find . . ." "Now kick with both feet . . .").

Note the simplicity of the style, and the effective comparison
between the buoyancy of the sea and the less perfect buoyancy of
a couch on solid ground.

The method of learning to swim is carefully arranged in logical
steps. Analyse it.

EXERCISES IN EXPLANATION

1. What is your method of boiling an egg?
2. Explain to a young friend how to begin riding a bicycle.
3. A foreigner is puzzled about the functions of the umpires at
cricket. Explain them to him.
4. How did you make your last woodwork model? *or* What garment
have you made in a recent Needlework class and how did you set
about it?
5. A friend who has just started gardening finds that his garden is
infested with slugs. What advice would you give him?
6. Explain the working of one of the following: a vacuum-cleaner;
a sewing-machine; an electric torch; a bicycle-pump.
7. Explain to a young brother how to do a simple equation, *or*
how to turn Direct Speech into Reported Speech, *or* how to find
Wellington (New Zealand). the River Amazon. and Mt Everest in
an atlas.
8. Say how you would carry out again some experiment that you
have done in a science lesson.
9. Explain what is meant by one (or more) of the following: jazz,
concerto, lyric, musical comedy, swing music. melodrama, slow foxtrot,
crooning, ballet, opera.
10. How do you spend your leisure time. and why do you use it in
the way you do?

[1] Richard Jefferies, *Bevis.*

11. You are enabled, by a time-machine device, to meet William Shakespeare. You mention to him that you have recently seen one of his plays on television. He is completely bewildered. Explain your meaning fully.

12. Why is coal so important in modern life?

13. Explain the public-library system to a friend from abroad who is quite unfamiliar with it.

14. A friend a little younger than yourself has been advised to take up dancing. Explain in detail how to set about it.

15. How would you run your ideal school if you had the chance?

DISCUSSION AND ARGUMENT

The ability to discuss a controversial theme intelligently is a valuable one, for discussion helps to keep us mentally alive. The ability cannot altogether be learnt; we must have a natural gift for clear thinking, and we need to have factual knowledge upon which to base our thinking. Without facts, indeed, we are in no position to form a worthwhile opinion, let alone to try to convince other people. But we can to some extent develop the thinking-power that Nature has given us; and we can certainly learn to acquire some familiarity with the facts of a case before we begin arguing about it, either in speech or on paper. We can also learn to suspend our judgment when our knowledge of the facts is limited.

Controversial topics often appear in examination papers. Here are a few points to bear in mind:

1. The subject-title is often a quotation (*e.g.*, "The surest way to lose happiness is to pursue it"). The quotation is not necessarily meant to be accepted as a complete truth; and it may even have been chosen to goad you into disagreement. Make your own decision, after reflection.

2. In dealing with controversial subjects it is usually best to decide exactly how you are going to end your essay before you begin it. You must know what you are going to try to prove before you set about proving it.

3. Be consistent. Having decided on your conclusion,

keep this firmly in your mind. A quietly reflective essay may legitimately ramble a little (though not in an examination room), but an argumentative essay should go steadily towards its goal. Arguments which do not really help your conclusion should be scrapped; and the scrapping should be done during the roughing-out stage of the essay.

4. Be fair. It would, agreed, be foolish to deny a place in literature to one-sided argument, to vigorous denunciation, even to whole-hearted invective. But the place for this kind of writing, generally speaking, is not the examination room. Although one can admire a writer's handling of words without agreeing with his views, style cannot be considered quite apart from the ideas which it reveals; and to ask an examiner to assess your abilities on a piece of writing which is violently partisan is not sensible. This applies particularly to political and to religious topics. An examiner will not hesitate to give very good marks to a reasonable essay which puts forward viewpoints that he does not share; but he is most unlikely to give high marks to an essay that is ill-balanced and prejudiced, even though the writer is not without literary ability.

I am not suggesting that you should write tepidly on a subject about which you feel strongly. If you feel indignant, say, about cruelty to animals or about road accidents, do not stifle your feelings; but do not let your feelings stifle your judgment. Remember that those who do not entirely share your views are not necessarily fools or knaves.

5. Be sincere. That is not to say that an interesting essay cannot be written in which the writer puts forward views which he does not altogether agree with, in order to consider, on a particular matter, possible lines of thought or possible courses of action. This is not insincerity, but detachment. But do not simulate a strong feeling that you do not possess. The artifice is likely to betray itself. You will probably get rather low marks, and you will deserve no marks at all, for your writing will be worth nothing.

6. Textbooks sometimes advise students to deal with a controversial subject by first stating the *case for* and then the *case against* (or *vice versa*). This advice seems to me bad, unless the method represents how you feel about the subject; it leads, I believe, to many dull and artificial essays. Do not misrepresent a case that you do not agree with; but, on the other hand, do not simulate an impartiality that you do not feel. Say what you think. But remember that before you do this it is necessary *to think*.

EXERCISES IN DISCUSSION AND ARGUMENT

1. Do we spend too much time watching games instead of playing them?

2. "Football pools should be prohibited. They waste time and they waste money, while the people they employ would be better employed on more useful work." Do you agree with this?

3. Should homework in your school be increased, decreased, or abolished? Your headmaster is anxious to know your views, and you are invited to submit a statement. Bear in mind the differences in the lower school, middle school, and upper school.

4. Owing to lack of money a certain school can have only one of the following: a television-set; a radiogram; a ciné-projector. In order to help the school to arrive at a decision, present a reasoned argument in favour of the one you would choose.

5. "Don't call athletics a sport. It is merely a boring way of obtaining exercise." What is your opinion? You may consider the matter from the point of view of the spectator as well as of the athlete.

6. Professionalism in sport.

7. Do you agree that boys ought to learn needlework and ballroom dancing at school, and that girls ought to learn woodwork and cricket?

8. Do you think that boys and girls ought to be taught together in the same school? Make clear whether your arguments are based on factual experience or supposition, and say whether or not your views would differ according to differences in age.

9. This century is often termed "The Machine Age". Attempt a reasoned estimate as to whether we have gained more than we have lost or lost more than we have gained by the development of the machine.

10. Should we be proud or ashamed of our treatment of animals to-day?

LETTER-WRITING

For practical purposes we may consider letter-writing from two aspects: (1) business letters, (2) private letters. It is on the former type of letter that advice and examples are most likely to be useful, for private letters are often too intimate to come under rules and conventions.

All letters, including business letters, are basically just a form of English composition, and all general advice that applies to the writing of essays applies also to letter-writing. Every letter should be written in good, clear English; it should be sensibly paragraphed; it should be correctly punctuated; and there should be no mis-spellings.

There are, however, two points which make the letter different from other types of composition. One is the formal setting-out of the letter; the other is the fact that a letter, unlike most other types of composition, is normally addressed to a particular person on a particular occasion, and the effect the letter is going to have on the reader is more immediately important than in less personal writings. This psychological aspect of letter-writing makes it especially important to consider the *tactful* presentation of ideas.

Business Letters

THE SETTING-OUT. Unless you have printed notepaper **your address** should be written at the top *right*-hand side of the notepaper, the first letter of each line being placed a little to the right of the first letter on the line above. (Some business firms have their name and address printed across the top of the notepaper: there is no rule in this matter.) It is customary to put a comma at the end of each line, but these commas serve no useful purpose, and many firms now omit them. Similarly, the comma after the number of the house, formerly regarded as necessary, is now generally omitted. *In an examination*, however, the omission of such commas may possibly be taken as the result of ignorance rather than as deliberate choice.

The **date** should be written under the address-heading on the right-hand side, usually beginning rather to the left of the last line or two of the address. The logical way of setting down the date is: day—month—year. It should be written **in full** (16th October, 1963), not in brief (16/10/63), **the latter** form being suitable only for a brief postcard message. Many people omit the *th*, *rd*, *st*, or *nd* after the day, and the omission is legitimate, just as it is on a calendar or newspaper. It is customary to put a comma after the month.

The **name and address of the receiver (addressee)** of the letter are written on the *left*-hand side, a line lower than the date. This is partly so that, when the envelope is discarded (as it usually is at once), there can be no inconvenient doubt for whom the letter is intended; and also as a precaution should any legal dispute arise on this matter. (The name and address of the addressee are occasionally written at the bottom instead of at the top, but nothing is gained by this.) If there is a reference number to quote, it should be placed above the addressee's name, opposite the writer's own address. The addressee's name and address should appear on the letter in exactly the same form as they appear on the envelope, except that it is usual, to prevent 'sprawling,' to put the first letter of each line directly under the first letter of the line above.

If you are writing to an individual member of a business firm you may include his position as well as his name. If the addressee is a man you should follow the convention of using the title *Esq.* (for *Esquire*), and not *Mr.*
Thus:

> Arthur Jones, Esq..
> Secretary,
> Messrs Geo. G. Hallock and Co., Ltd,
> 128 Low Tyburn,
> Clerkenwell,
> London EC1M 3AB

If the title of the firm includes a personal name, such as Hallock above, it is usual to address the company as *Messrs* (= *Messieurs*), but you should not use the title otherwise. (E.g., *NOT* Messrs Oxford University Press.)

For the **salutation** the accepted formula for business and other formal letters is *Dear Sir* if your letter is addressed to a single person (*e.g.*, the Secretary), and *Dear Sirs* if it is addressed to a company (*e.g.*, Messrs A. Smith and Co.). It would be illogical to write to Messrs A. Smith *and Co.* as *Dear Sir*. If you know the member of the firm to whom you are writing it is natural to write to him as *Dear Mr* ——, though some firms indicate on their notepaper that replies should be addressed to the firm, and not to individuals.

The usual **subscription** to a letter beginning *Dear Sir(s)* is *Yours faithfully*, or, less often, *Yours truly*. If your letter begins *Dear Mr* —— your subscription may be either *Yours truly* or *Yours sincerely*, the latter being the more friendly. *Yours respectfully* should generally be avoided, except perhaps by an applicant for a junior position in a firm, or by a junior member of a firm writing to his employer. The words *I am, dear Sir(s)*, are occasionally inserted before *Yours faithfully*: they should be written on the previous line, beginning more to the left, and should invariably have a comma after *am* and *Sir(s)*. *Yours faithfully* (always with capital *Y* and small *f*) should begin about the middle of the page, and be followed by a comma. The writer's signature (hand-written) should come underneath.

THE BODY OF THE LETTER. The letter should begin by making clear what you are writing about. If your letter is a reply to a previous communication, for instance, you might begin:

> In reply to your letter of the 28th April, stating that the text-book *Icelandic for General Certificate*, by G. Flam, is temporarily out of stock, I am writing to say . .

or

> With reference to our telephone conversation of this morning about the textbook *Icelandic for* . . .

Sometimes the main topic is typed and underlined directly above the body of the letter, but on the line below the salutation:

DEAR SIR

73 Parsley Road

> With reference to this property, we regret to say . . .

In applying for a post many candidates begin, "I beg to apply for the post of . . ." There is nothing incorrect here; but unless you are applying for a rather humble position it is perhaps more dignified to write, "I am writing to apply for . . ." or, "I wish to make application for . . ."

A fresh paragraph should be taken for each fresh topic. If there are several separate topics they are sometimes numbered.

Any facts in a letter should be clearly stated; a vague reference may either waste the time of the receiver in compelling him to hunt up information, or it may be actually misleading. Be precise.

The letter should be written in plain English, not in 'literary' English or in 'commercialese'. Phrases such as "Yours of the 15th inst. to hand", or "I beg to acknowledge receipt of your esteemed favour of the 16th ult.", which some students imagine to be business-like, are merely pseudo-business jargon. A reputable firm nearly always avoids them, and the correspondent says what he means in decent English: "Thank you for your letter of the 15th April (*or* April 15). . . ."

Be courteous and tactful. Remember that a critical comment that can safely be made over the lunch-table may have an entirely different effect if set down in black and white in a letter. "I think that's a very bad suggestion" can be said without offence when there is a pleasant smile to take the edge off the remark. But "Dear Mr ——, With reference to your letter of April 17, I think your suggestion is a very bad one," could easily alienate a correspondent. A tactful comment should compensate for the missing smile (*e.g.*, "I am afraid that there are many difficulties which prevent us from adopting your suggestion").

EXAMPLES

A Letter of Application

MELCHESTER,
12 CROSSROADS AVENUE,
BARCHESTER,
SUSSEX.
18*th March*, 197–

THE MANAGER,
MESSRS STONES AND STIGGINS,
PECK STREET,
LONDON SE29 6BA

DEAR SIR,

With reference to the advertisement in to-day's issue of "The Daily Megaphone," I wish to make application for the post of junior assistant in the Book Department of your Central Stores.

I am seventeen years of age, and have recently left the Leybury Grammar School, where I was a pupil for five years. In my last year I sat for the General Certificate of Education examination, and was successful in passing at Ordinary Level in English, English Literature, Mathematics, History, and French. Since leaving school I have been attending evening classes in Typewriting. English, and Book-keeping.

I am deeply interested in books, and during my last year at school acted as one of the school librarians, my duties being to help in arranging and cataloguing the library, to take charge of the issue and return of books, and to encourage school pupils to make full use of the library facilities. In my spare time I have also helped to run the hospital library at the Nelson Cottage Hospital, Barchester, where I have attended one evening a week for the last six months, and have endeavoured to interest the patients in reading and to find suitable books for them.

The secretary of the hospital, Mr J. Harding, C.B.E., has kindly consented to allow me to use his name as a reference.

You will see from my headmaster's testimonial, a copy of which I enclose, that mathematics was one of my best subjects at school, and I am hoping to continue the study of accountancy in my spare time.

Should you be so good as to offer me the vacancy I would use every effort to fill the post to your satisfaction.

Yours faithfully.

GEORGE SMITH

Letter of Instructions to a House Agent

101 ODDITY ROAD,
WYETOWN,
ESSEX.

21st September, 197–

MESSRS SELHAM AND BYERS,
ESTATE AGENTS,
202 LONG ROAD,
WYETOWN.

DEAR SIRS,

re 3 Threefold Road

I understand from my solicitors, Messrs Alfa and Beta, that they have still not received the contract from Mr Cratchit's solicitor, and it appears that he is backing out from the purchase of the above property.

In the circumstances I must ask you to regard the property as still open for sale, and I shall be glad if you will find another purchaser as soon as possible. As you know, I am leaving the district very shortly, and I am anxious to settle the sale of the house in Threefold Road before I go.

I have to ask you not to hand over the key of No. 3 Threefold Road to Mr Cratchit or his representative without the written consent of Messrs Alfa and Beta, who will let you know at once if the contract is after all received from Mr Cratchit's solicitor. On their advice, I must also ask you not to let anyone view the house without being accompanied by your representative, who will keep the key in his possession.

The price I am asking for the property is still £8500, though I should be prepared to come down to £8350, say, for a quick sale.

Yours faithfully,

C. DEEKES

EXERCISES

1. Write to a house agent asking him to include your house in his list of properties for sale. Give some necessary details (*e.g.*, number and kind of rooms, type and size of garden, convenience for shops and buses).

2. You have ordered by post a new book (or gramophone record) from a firm of booksellers (or music-dealers). When it arrives you discover that they have sent the wrong article and enclosed a bill for double the proper amount. Write and point out the mistake, making clear that you need the article urgently.

3. Write to the secretary of a hospital or other charitable organization offering your services in any capacity you think fit. Make clear in what ways you think you might be of service, and what spare time you have available.

4. Write to the secretary of a local cricket, football, tennis, or other sports club, asking for details of the subscription, etc., and mentioning that you would like to join the club. State your qualifications and standard.

5. Write to the B.B.C. *either* pointing out, in a reasoned letter, some deficiency or deficiencies in the quality or arrangement of the programmes, *or* congratulating them upon some feature or features that you admire.

6. Write to a firm of theatrical costumiers giving details of costumes and equipment wanted for a school or club play, and asking for terms.

7. Write to the editor of a local or national newspaper with reference to an article (or report of a speech) which has criticized young people of to-day for their casual attitude towards things that matter and their lack of the spirit of adventure. You may either oppose or support his point of view.

8. You have left an attaché-case containing several articles of importance to yourself in a bus on your way home from school or work, and do not discover the loss until you have reached home. You are feeling unwell at the time, and are confined to bed for the next two or three days, and hence cannot take any active steps in the matter. Write to the bus company's lost-property department giving full details concerning the loss.

9. Write a short letter as from a farmer to campers who have inquired about the possibility of using one of his fields. Give brief details of amenities and stipulate conditions, limiting the body of the letter to 80 words. Include the full layout of a formal letter, and invent appropriate names and addresses.

(London)

10. Write a letter of application for one of the following posts:

JUNIOR CLERK (male or female), aged 15–16, for accounts office. Good salary and prospects. Apply Personnel Dept., Mullins Mechanics Co., Ltd, 2, Ethel Street, London SE6 5BC.

A VACANCY OCCURS in the ADVERTISEMENT DEPT. of a national newspaper for a Junior Young Lady, age 16–17. Knowledge of typing an advantage. Write, giving details of education, experience, if any, to A.V. 6883, "Daily Megaphone," London EC4X 6LR.

LEADING WEST END furnishing house has vacancy for Youth as trainee, commencing in carpet dept. Excellent prospects for keen, ambitious lad. Write, stating age, etc., to W.L. 14684, "Daily Megaphone," London EC4X 6LR.

SMART, INTELLIGENT YOUNG LADY required for Counting House, gown manufacturers. Able to type, and with aptitude for figures. Apply R. C. Fordwell and Co., Ltd, 42/43, Gt. Mansion Street, London W2 1AA.

If there are no posts which appeal to you in these advertisements, choose one from a recent issue of a local or national newspaper.

11. Write a letter to the editor either supporting or opposing the opinion given below. Your letter should present reasoned arguments.

We should make it an offence for dogs to appear in built-up areas without a leash—offenders to be impounded and their owners fined. Such a piece of legislation would not be difficult to administer, and would effectively reduce the two thousand or more accidents due to dogs each year.

From a letter to *The Guardian*

12. You have promised to help in a function for a charity in which you are interested. Just before the function is to take place you find that you are unable to undertake the duty. Write a letter of explanation to the organizer.

(*Southern Universities*)

Private Letters

It is difficult to give general advice on the writing of private letters, for the personal relationship between the two correspondents, and the particular occasion for writing, must determine the tone and contents of the letter. However, here are a few points to consider:

1. If you are writing to a friend in reply to a letter of his you should begin by answering any definite queries he may have put. Incidentally, you should see that you do not have to begin (as too many of us have to do) with an apology for not writing sooner!

2. In *sending* a letter of *invitation* to a party, outing, or holiday give your friend enough information to enable him (or her) to know what to wear or bring. Make sure that you give precise details of the date, time, and place.

3. In *replying* to an *invitation* repeat the date, time, and place as given to you, just in case your correspondent has made a mistake. Do not forget to thank him for the invitation; and, unless he is a comparative stranger, add at least a comment or two of a personal kind. Rigid formality is out of place between friends.

4. In writing a letter of *thanks* do not confine yourself to a bare general expression of gratitude. Try to pick out some special point or points about the gift or hospitality that you particularly appreciated, and stress this. You should aim at being cordial without being fulsome.

5. In a *persuasive* letter, in which you attempt to convince your friend of the need for some course of action that seems to you advisable, be careful to keep in mind his personal disposition. Some people need a good deal of persuasion before they can accept an idea; others, if they suspect that some one is trying to push them, tend to go in the opposite direction. In general, do not over-argue your case.

6. In writing to really intimate friends and relations you will, of course, conclude your letter in any way that you please. It is natural to send love to parents, brothers, sisters, and other close connexions. *Yours affectionately* may be used to less intimate relations (*e.g.*, uncles and aunts, or cousins). To friends *Yours sincerely* is an accepted formula, sometimes varied to *Very sincerely yours*, *Sincerely yours*, *Yours very sincerely*, or (informally) just *Sincerely*.

EXERCISES

1. You receive a letter from a friend asking for particulars of a well-known holiday camp. As the letter begins *Dear Sir* you assume that he has written to you and to the organizer of the holiday camp at the same time, and then put the letters in the wrong envelopes. Write a reply to him (or her).

2. Write to a friend inviting him (or her) to stay with you for a week-end, and indicating the kind of activities you are proposing to engage in.

3. Write to a friend or relative giving news of a theatre party, dance, or evening party which you have recently attended, and commenting on an account of a similar activity described by your friend.

4. Your parents, after you have left home and bought a house of your own, are wondering whether to sell their house and come and live near you. Write and advise them. You are a little concerned at the idea of their moving house at their time of life, but you feel it would be a good thing if they were near enough for you to keep in touch with them easily. They are inclined to be touchy at any suggestion that they are getting on in years.

5. A friend has written to ask you to stay for a few days during the holidays, and makes some suggestions as to how you might spend your time. You would like to stay with him (her), but would prefer to occupy your time in some other way. Write a tactful letter.

6. You receive an invitation to a party or other outing that you would very much like to go to. Unfortunately you have a standing arrangement with another friend to go out with him (her) on that day or evening. Make a decision what to do, and then write a letter to each of your friends. (The first would like an early reply.)

7. Write to a friend who has gone to live abroad, giving news of yourself and your family, and describing any interesting happenings in your town or village, where he or she also used to live.

8. You have become very interested in some hobby or pastime (*e.g.*, stamp-collecting, acting, cycling, conjuring). A well-to-do acquaintance of your father sends you by post a parcel of three or four books relating to your hobby. Write and thank him. (From your own knowledge of your hobby decide which books are in the parcel, and make a note of them before writing the letter.)

9. Write a letter (in not more than 100 words) to your grandmother in which you try to dissuade her from taking a journey by air.

(London)

10. Suppose that you have just decided on your future occupation. Write a letter to a friend describing the advantages that it offers to you and telling why you prefer it to other occupations which you might possibly have chosen. *(Royal Society of Arts)*

THE SHORT STORY

The short story is a form of narrative either wholly or partly fictitious. It may be based upon a character, an incident, a connected series of incidents (*i.e.*, a plot), an idea, or an atmosphere.

A whole book could easily be written—and many have been written—on the art of the short story. For our present purpose a few brief points must suffice.

1. The story must hang together. As with some other types of composition it may be best to decide on your ending first, and let the rest of the story lead up to this. It need not be a surprise ending—such endings are often cheap and mechanical—but it should leave an impression of completeness in the reader's mind.

2. The story must have unity of theme. Do not ramble from one point to another. Try to concentrate on one essential idea around which your story can grow, and beware of irrelevancies.

3. You will have little time to spend on preliminaries. Plunge into your story quickly.

4. Beware of writing a kind of potted novel. Do not try to give the whole family history of your characters. Select only those points which are significant to your theme.

EXERCISES IN STORY-WRITING

1 Write a story with the title *A Narrow Escape*.

2. Here is the opening sentence of a short story: "Scowling blackly, muttering to himself, he strode along the rough lane which led to the open moor." Continue the story.

3. Write a story ending with the sentence: "Neither of them ever went there again."

4. Tell the story of an adventure suggested by the following:

> By fits and starts they rode apace,
> And very often was his place
> Far off from her; he had to ride
> Ahead, to see what might betide
> When the roads cross'd.

5. Write a story in which a ghost (real or supposed) is a central figure.

6. While out for a country walk you (or some fictional character) call at a farmhouse or country cottage to obtain a drink or ask the way. The farmer or cottager mistakes you for an escaped convict for whose capture a reward is being offered. Tell the story.

7. Write a story which takes place at night, either in the country or in town, and in which the darkness or the night atmosphere plays a part.

8. Write a story suggested by the statement: "Danger always brings out either the best or the worst in a person's nature."

9. Write a short story beginning with the words "The sound was gradually increasing," and ending "Then there was silence."

(*London*)

10. "Dogs hunt boys lost in caves." Tell a story about six boys who were lost while exploring some old quarry workings.

(*Associated Examining Board*)

11. Write a short story suggested by *one* of the following:

(*a*) "All is not gold that glitters."

(*b*) "It was a narrow escape, but a miss is as good as a mile."

(*Oxford and Cambridge*)

ESSAY SUBJECTS

Write a composition on **one** subject in each of the following groups, paying due attention to subject-matter, arrangement, and style:

1. (*a*) The career you hope to choose, and your reasons for choosing it.

(*b*) A famous explorer, living or dead.

(*c*) English rivers.

(*d*) "Where there's a will there's a way."

(*e*) School and class libraries.

(*f*) Camping out.

(*g*) How would you seek to convince a student who disliked mathematics that the study of this subject was valuable both from the practical standpoint and as an intellectual exercise?

2. (*a*) The fascination of shop-windows.

(*b*) Monday.

(*c*) You are left one day to look after a house where you are staying as a visitor. Recount your experiences.

(*d*) Crowds.

(e) A pageant *or* a procession through a town or village.

(f) Castles in the air.

(g) You have recently attended an auction sale as a spectator. Give an account of what you saw and heard while you were there.

(h) During your holidays you consented to make a selection of books for the bookshelf of a younger brother or sister, or of a young visitor staying in the house. Describe how you set about your task, and how you succeeded in explaining your selection and in persuading the child to read the books.   (*Cambridge*)

3. (a) Explain to a friend how you would make a model, a toy, a garment, *or* a favourite dish.

(b) Describe to some one of your own age, who is moving into your own district, its main features.

(c) Write, as an article for your school magazine, an interesting account of a match away.

(d) Explain to your next-door neighbour how to look after your cat *or* dog *or* bird for you while you are away on holiday.

(e) Write a letter to a friend living abroad, describing a visit to a famous building in the British Isles.

(f) Make clear to a beginner the finer points of an active game in which you show some skill.   (*London*)

4. (a) Street noises in former days and in modern times.

(b) Interesting occupations.

(c) "The modern daily newspaper contains something to appeal to every one in the family." How far do you think this is true?

(d) Railway travel.

(e) Our dog (*or* cat).

(f) Explain how you would endeavour to keep physically fit if you were engaged in an indoor occupation in a town during the daytime on weekdays.

(g) Modern farming methods.

(h) An imaginary dialogue between Queen Elizabeth I and Queen Elizabeth II.

5. (a) A Sunday-morning stroll in the heart of an industrial or commercial city.

(b) Imagine you are a painter; describe the picture you would like to paint.

(c) A morning's wait on a country railway station. Say why you were there and what you did and saw.

(d) Which activities of a youth organization do you consider essential to its success? Give your reasons and describe some of the activities in detail.

(*e*) The advantages and disadvantages of being one of a large family.

(*f*) Opportunities in the professions for women to-day.

(*g*) Speed: its advantages and disadvantages in holiday travel.

(*h*) "It is the little things of life, not the great things, that make life what it is." How far do you find this statement true?

(*i*) Write a story based on the following lines:

> The hinges whined to the shutters shaking
> When clip-clop-clep came a horse-hoof raking
> The stones of the road at Caesar's gate;
> The spear-butts jarred at the guard's awaking.
> "Who goes there?" said the guard at the gate.
> "What is the news that you ride so late?"
> "News most pressing, that must be spoken
> To Caesar alone, and that cannot wait."

(Cambridge)

6. (*a*) A journey you would like to make, and why you would like to make it.

(*b*) A visit to a cathedral or abbey.

(*c*) The fields in summer.

(*d*) Is the importance of sport exaggerated in schools?

(*e*) If you were invited to choose, for a present, four or five books by a single author, which author would you select? Give some account of his work, explaining what qualities in it appeal to you. (You need not specify which *books* you would choose.)

(*f*) The modern aeroplane.

7. (*a*) Amateur theatricals.

(*b*) A storm.

(*c*) Your ideal television programme.

(*d*) Your favourite holiday resort.

(*e*) Discuss which of the following has made the greatest contribution to civilization—the statesman, the scientist, the writer.

(Oxford and Cambridge)

8. (*a*) Which foreign country would you most like to visit if you had the opportunity? Explain why you would like to visit it and how you would spend your time there.

(*b*) The conquest of the air.

(*c*) A holiday under canvas.

(*d*) Should boys and girls be educated at the same school?

(*e*) Collecting autographs *or* collecting postage-stamps.

(*f*) A short story illustrating the adage "A stitch in time saves nine".

(*g*) The prevention of accidents on the road and in the home.

9. (a) Describe your first day at your present school.

(b) You are paying your first visit to a pen-friend abroad. Write a letter home telling your parents about the house where you are staying and your friend's family.

(c) Describe *either* the procedure you would adopt as chairman of a dramatic-club committee at the first meeting after the play had been chosen, *or* the arrangements you would make for preparing and serving refreshments at a small private dance.

(d) You have witnessed an accident to a fellow-pupil at school and are asked by your headmaster or headmistress to write an account of what happened. Pay attention to order and accuracy of detail.

(*London*)

10. (a) Unwelcome visitors.

(b) Do you consider that Physical Training in the gymnasium should take the place of school games?

(c) Write an answer to the person who asks, "Why waste your time reading poetry?"

(d) Describe the making of a new road or the widening of an old road which you have seen taking place.

(e) You have been asked to make a speech about your own school to a party of foreigners who understand English. Write the speech you would make.

(*Oxford*)

11. (a) Discuss how science benefits you personally.

(b) Give the main arguments for *and* against compulsory military service for young people of your own sex.

(c) Describe a market.

(d) Write about a fight against overwhelming odds.

(e) "It is a glorious thing to be alive in the world to-day." Discuss.

(f) Give a character-sketch of an old soldier or an old sailor.

(*London*)

12. (a) The power of the Press.

(b) The best month of the year.

(c) Gipsies.

(d) The scientific preservation of food.

(e) The essentials of a good School Magazine.

(f) If you could replan the town in which you live, what are the chief alterations that you would make?

(g) Cycling for pleasure.

13. (a) The wonders of the sea or the seashore.

(b) The best occupations for women.

(c) Do you think boys should be taught Domestic Science?

(d) Assuming that you have power to transfer yourself from this century to another, which century would you choose? Why do you think you would find it attractive?

(e) A country holiday.

(f) The influence of the internal-combustion engine on civilization.

(g) What have you taught yourself that is not taught at your school?

14. (a) "School summer holidays are much too long." Give your reasons for agreeing or disagreeing with this opinion.

(b) The British climate.

(c) What are the chief things that a good housewife ought to do?

(d) Your favourite living author.

(e) The work of famous scientists and their achievements in promoting health and comfort.

(f) Write a short story or dialogue entitled *either* "The Race" *or* "Lost in the Jungle."

15. (a) Do girls employ leisure time more profitably than boys?

(b) The relative merits of handwork and machine-work.

(c) A day in the life of a worker in your district. (Any type of occupation or profession may be dealt with.)

(d) The Great Fire of London.

(e) The keeping of pets.

(f) Is it better to go for a walk alone or with companions?

(g) Clocks and watches.

(h) Write a story beginning with the words: "I must get rid of it," said the man in the corner of the carriage.

16. (a) The empty house.

(b) The pleasantest surprise of my life, *or* the biggest disappointment.

(c) A local celebrity.

(d) Should wild animals be kept in captivity?

(e) A visit to another planet.

(f) Tunnels.   (*Northern Universities*)

17. (a) Exploration.

(b) A description of a seaside resort in winter *or* an industrial town or city on a Sunday afternoon.

(c) Should Britain adopt the decimal system?

(d) "All that glisters is not gold."

(e) Advertising.

(f) The advantages and disadvantages of a predominantly scientific education.

(g) First impressions.   (*Southern Universities*)

CHAPTER III

PUNCTUATION

WHEN we are speaking we help to indicate the relationship between one idea and another by pauses, changes of tone, gestures, and facial expression. In writing we have no such aids to expression. Their place is taken by the various signs and symbols which we know as punctuation marks.

The correct use of these symbols is of great importance to clear and effective writing. The rules relating to the use of punctuation marks are not rigid, for people no more write alike than they speak alike. Writing cannot be brought under the sway of fixed rules, for it is the expression of the human mind, which is full of infinite variety. A skilful writer, for instance, will sometimes use punctuation symbols in an unusual way in order to express a subtle shade of meaning.

Nevertheless, there are certain punctuation practices that are commonly followed, and the student should be familiar with them. A hazy knowledge of punctuation is one of the commonest causes of muddled writing. Careful attention to punctuation, moreover, can assist clear thought, for you cannot punctuate correctly without considering what you wish to say.

The rules of punctuation, as I have indicated, are not rigid, and they cannot be learnt by heart like an algebraic formula. Careful reading of good writers is the best guide to punctuation. But such reading needs to be supplemented by a study of the punctuation system, and we will deal in detail with some of the main points to note in the use of stops. (Note that the word 'stop' is a general term covering all punctuation symbols, though it is also used in telegraphic English as an abbreviation for 'full stop.')

THE FULL STOP

This is the basic essential of all punctuation. Failure to use it where it is needed is one of the commonest faults in composition, and is perhaps the most serious punctuation error.

The two main rules for the use of the **full stop** are:

1. It must be used after a complete statement.
2. It marks a stronger break between ideas than the comma, semi-colon, or colon.

Example in these matters is more helpful than precept, so let us examine a piece of straightforward writing simply from the point of view of its punctuation. Here is a passage in which the author is describing the return of himself and his wife from England to his farm in Wales after an unexpected and violent snowstorm.

This is how he did *not* punctuate it:

> In the Southern papers there was no hint of the severe weather, and one Monday morning we telegraphed that we were coming home for a couple of nights to see that everything was all right, it took us a day to cover the last thirty miles, after many attempts we reached Bettws-y-Coed at midday on the Tuesday. In answer to our inquiries no one could give us news of Capel Curig, the snow had come without warning during the Saturday night, the roads were lost under drifts, the telephone wires were down over several counties, we knew about the wires, I had lifted the tangled masses time and again while Esmé drove the car under them.

Try to judge for yourself where full stops are required instead of commas.

This is how the author *did* punctuate the passage:

> In the Southern papers there was no hint of the severe weather, and one Monday morning we telegraphed that we were coming home for a couple of nights to see that everything was all right. It took us a day to cover the last thirty miles. After many attempts we reached Bettws-y-Coed at midday on the Tuesday. In answer to our inquiries no one could give us news of Capel Curig. The

> snow had come without warning during the Saturday night. The
> roads were lost under drifts; the telephone wires were down over
> several counties. We knew about the wires. I had lifted the tangled
> masses time and again while Esmé drove the car under them.[1]

It will be seen that a full stop is used after each complete
statement which is not definitely linked to another statement. In the first passage the commas after "right,"
"miles," "Curig," "night," "counties," and "wires" are
clearly wrong. A comma is correctly used after "weather"
in the first sentence, however, as the second statement ("one
Monday morning we telegraphed . . .") is closely linked by
the conjunction "and" to the first statement ("In the
Southern papers . . .").

It would have been possible, without altering the wording,
to have used semi-colons in some places instead of full
stops. (*E.g.*, "The snow had come without warning during
the Saturday night; the roads were lost under drifts . . .")
The author has correctly used full stops, however; the
shorter, swifter sentences help to intensify the swift unexpec-
tedness of the snowfall, the shock to the author and his wife
of meeting it so suddenly, and the dramatic strangeness of
the world in which they found themselves.

The Full Stop in Abbreviations

Note that the *full stop* is also used to indicate certain
abbreviations. For example:

Mon. = Monday, etc. = et cetera, M.A. = Master of Arts,
Esq. = Esquire, H.M.S. = Her Majesty's Ship.

This full stop may be followed by a comma (*e.g.*, George
Brown, Esq., B.A.); but where an abbreviation ends the
sentence one full stop only is used. For example, we should
write: "He was awarded the O.B.E."

Where the abbreviation is formed by using the first and

Thomas Firbank, *I Bought a Mountain.*

last letters of a word some writers do not use a full stop.
Thus it is correct to write:

Mr *or* Mr.   Thos *or* Thos. (Thomas)
Dr *or* Dr.   1st *or* 1st.
St *or* St. (Saint)

Note that although we write Yorks., Cambs., Worcs., and
Leics. (abbreviated county names), Hants and Notts are
regarded as variants, not abbreviations, and require no stop.

EXERCISES (*A*)

1. Change commas to full stops where necessary:

We abandoned the car at Bettws-y-Coed, and reached our valley
in the cold half-light of evening, the frozen lakes lay dead in a
shrouded world. Our lost domain was silent as the grave, the virgin
drifts covered the buried road. and nowhere was there a spark of
life, we ploughed up the valley, waist-deep in the soft snow, when
at last we reached the cottages we were received with exclamations
of surprise, Davies had seen no one but our own people since
Saturday.

2. Insert the full stops in the following passage, and change commas
to full stops where necessary. The passage describes a mountaineer's
adventure with his guide in the Alps.

We found ourselves separated from the next rocks by a gap about
twenty yards across, the ridge was here narrowed to a mere wall,
upon the wall of rock was placed a second wall of snow, which
dwindled to a pure knife-edge at the top, it was white, of very fine
grain, and a little moist how to pass this snow ridge I knew not,
for I did not think a human foot could trust itself upon so frail a
support Bennen's practical sagacity, however, came into play, he
tried the snow by squeezing it with his foot, and to my astonishment
began to cross it even after the pressure of his feet the space he had
to stand on did not exceed a hand-breadth I followed him, exactly
as a boy walking along a horizontal pole, with toes turned outwards,
right and left the precipices were appalling we reached the opposite
rock, and an earnest smile rippled over Bennen's countenance as he
turned towards me, he knew that he had done a daring thing, though
not a presumptuous one

3. Insert full stops in the following passage, and change commas to
full stops where necessary. The passage describes the experience of a

salvage diver who is investigating a submarine lying at an angle on the ocean bed.

Cold fear suddenly gripped me a stream of bubbles was pouring upward through the water from my hand the jagged steel to which I clung had cut open my watertight glove, and from the highest point in my suit I was rapidly losing all my air, frantically my lead-soled boots beat the sides of the *S4*, trying to get a foothold on something to support me, to allow me to drop that arm below my helmet and save my air, it was useless, on the sheer side of the submarine there wasn't the slightest toe-hold I felt the sea pressing in on my chest as the air went out, and breathing became more difficult

QUESTION MARK (?) AND EXCLAMATION MARK (!)

These stops have the same force as the full stop in marking the end of a sentence. Note that each of them contains a full stop (? !) and that it is therefore incorrect to write a full stop, colon, semi-colon, or comma immediately after ? or ! (Thus ?, !. are *wrong*.)

A **question mark** is used:

(i) At the end of a direct question:

"Where are you going?" he asked.
Where would be much of the glory of inspiring love, if there were no contempt to overcome?

(ii) Where a question is implied, even though the sentence is not cast in question form:

"These gentlemen travel for their pleasure?" asked the landlady, observing our drenched forms.

(Cast in question form, the sentence would run: "Do these gentlemen travel for their pleasure?")

Note that no question mark is used for an *indirect* question:

He inquired where we were going.
The landlady asked if the gentlemen were travelling for their pleasure.

(These sentences are not questions, but statements about questions.[1])

An **exclamation mark** is used:

(i) After exclamations or exclamatory sentences:

> What a piece of work is man! How noble in reason! How infinite in faculty! In form and moving how express and admirable! In action how like an angel! In apprehension how like a god!
>
> SHAKESPEARE, *Hamlet*

> You want to marry my daughter? God forbid!

> "That's him that killed the boy!" I cried.
> "Look to your window!" said Alan; and as I turned back to my place, I saw him pass his sword through the mate's body.
>
> R. L. STEVENSON, *Kidnapped*

(ii) After interjections, or words or phrases used as interjections, such as: "Alas!" "Oh!" "Heavens!" "By Jove!" "My sainted aunt!" "Ten thousand curses!" "My dear chap!"

Sometimes a brief exclamation or interjection and the words following it are together regarded as forming a single exclamatory sentence, and the exclamation mark is delayed till the end of the sentence. Thus

> No! No! A thousand times no!

could also be written

> No, no, a thousand times no!

The first form would imply a greater stress on each expression of the word "No."

(iii) To indicate that some *special* emotional emphasis is to be placed on the words. Compare the following:

> (*a*) Open the door. My hands are full.
> Open the door! The room's on fire!

[1] See Chapter IV, p. 126.

(*b*) He's a fine fieldsman. [Words used in ordinary sense to express admiration.]

He's a fine fieldsman! [Words used ironically about cricketer who has just dropped a catch.]

(*c*) "This is the end," said Margaret as the curtain fell.

"This is the end!" said Margaret as she flung back the engagement-ring.

You should be sparing in your use of exclamation marks. Do not use them whenever you wish to suggest emotion or excitement (your choice of words should do this), or to indicate an ordinary wish or command. Thus exclamation marks are not required in the following:

The sudden jog upon my nerves made me leap up. I had my pistol in my hand. I flung it up swiftly, roughly levelled at the head. I fired one barrel at the head, and one a little lower down. The bullet scattered the bark in all directions.

JOHN MASEFIELD, *Lost Endeavour*

I wish I had more money. But who cares?

Put your books away, and lead on quietly.

A piece of writing littered with exclamation marks drawing attention to facetious or strongly felt comments does not commend itself to the judicious reader. If you find yourself using exclamation marks rather freely, go through your work and strike them out wherever possible.

The use of the double or triple exclamation mark and similar eccentricities ("I wish I had more money!!! But who cares?!"), though perhaps pardonable in a personal letter to an intimate friend, is quite out of place in more formal writing, and should be avoided in the examination room.

FURTHER EXAMPLES OF THE CORRECT USE OF EXCLAMATION MARKS

1. "A miss-fire, by God!" said Danvers.

The seconds crowded round them.

"Give me those pistols!" said Masters, taking them from the weak hands that held them. "The loaded one might be hanging fire, and we don't want it to go off now."

C. S. FORESTER, *Mr Midshipman Hornblower*

2. "Hold your tongue, sir!" said Mr Fang peremptorily.

"I will not, sir!" replied the old gentleman.

"Hold your tongue this instant, or I'll have you turned out of the office!" said Mr Fang. "You're an insolent, impertinent fellow. How dare you bully a magistrate!"

CHARLES DICKENS Oliver Twist

3. From Loanda I could fairly expect to be home by July the 20th. Home, friends, decent meals, a real bed, and security! It was one of the radiant moments of life.

H. W. NEVINSON (after a journey of several months in
the interior of Africa)

Suggest in each case the function of the exclamation mark.

EXERCISES (*B*)

Insert full stops, question marks, and exclamation marks *where necessary* in the following:

1. "These gentlemen are pedlars" asked the landlady

2. HAMLET. My excellent good friends How dost thou, Guildenstern Ah Rosencrantz Good lads, how do you both

3. They wanted to know whether we were going away

4. "Appears against the boy, does he" said Fang, surveying Mr Brownlow contemptuously from head to foot. "Swear him"

5. She began by asking me if I were single

"Yes," said I

"And your friend who went by just now"

"He also is unmarried"

6. "God bless my soul" said the chief constable "You mean to say his body was carried up there"

"I shall say at the inquest that he wasn't killed where you found him"

"What's the sense of that" The Inspector frowned

"My dear fellow Oh my dear fellow You supply the sense I only supply the facts" Mr Fortune bent again over the map

H. C. BAILEY, Mr Fortune, Please

THE COMMA

The **comma** marks a shorter break than the full stop, semi-colon, or colon. It does not stop the flow of the sentence. Note that the comma indicates a grammatical relationship or a *pause in sense*; it does not necessarily indicate a breathing pause.

Main Uses of the Comma

(i) To mark a slight change of direction, as it were, in the thought expressed by a sentence:

> Wales ended the Rugby season triumphantly by beating France at Cardiff, although the losers put up such a gallant fight that the issue was in doubt until the end.

> If you consider yourself affronted by what I have felt it my duty to tell you, I apologize.

> Alcock had little more than 1000 feet of runway in which to take off the overloaded biplane, and a cross-wind to contend with as well.

The first two examples illustrate the use of the comma to mark off an adverbial clause from the main clause. Where such clauses are short and the relationship between them is close the comma is often omitted:

> Wales won the game although they were a man short.

> If you don't like it you must lump it.

The modern tendency is to omit the comma in many instances where earlier generations would have used it. Although we should avoid over-using the comma, if the omission of it would cause even a momentary confusion it is wiser to insert it. This situation often occurs, for example, when a clause (or phrase) *ending* in a noun is linked by 'and' to a clause (or phrase) *beginning* with a noun; if the comma is omitted it may appear at first glance that the two nouns are naturally associated:

> The motorist was so drunk that he ran over *a pedestrian and a policeman* arrested him.

Here are one or two further examples where a comma is needed to prevent a false train of thought being momentarily started in the reader's mind:

> I knew that fifty-one years before, Livingstone himself had emerged at Loanda from the interior of Africa.

Once upon a time everybody recognized that print was a form of frozen sound, and reading was then a form of listening.

As soon as you see him, go indoors.

(ii) To mark off a phrase or noun in apposition:

Professor Piccard, *the famous Belgian scientist*, was now ready to make his ascent into the stratosphere.

On the Monday, *July 6th*, a little Alsatian boy, *Joseph Meister*, was brought by his mother to Pasteur's laboratory.

How Hambledon, *a Hampshire village*, became the capital of cricket is unknown.

(iii) Frequently to mark off a qualifying clause or phrase:

The fast bowlers, *who had been toiling all the morning in the blazing sun*, were at last given a rest.

Realizing that the batsmen were set, the new bowlers tempted them to hit out.

Note that a single adjective, when it is placed *after* its noun for emphasis, follows the above rule.

The bowler, exhausted, collapsed in the pavilion after the match. (*But:* The exhausted bowler collapsed . . . match.)

Careful attention to the use of the comma in qualifying clauses and phrases is particularly important, for its omission may completely alter the meaning of the sentence. Consider the following:

A. The police gave chase to the car, which had no number-plate.
B. The police gave chase to the car which had no number-plate.

In sentence *A* the main clause ("The police gave chase to the car") is complete in itself; "which had no number-plate" is a qualifying clause giving some extra information about the car. In sentence *B* the clause "which . . . number-plate" is absolutely necessary to the main clause, which would be incomplete without it. This sentence states that the car which the police chased was the one with no number-plate (as distinct from other cars which were about); the clause "which . . . number-plate" *defines* which particular car is being referred to. This type of clause is known as a *defining clause*.

A defining clause is never separated by a comma from the noun which it is defining. Thus to leave out the comma before a qualifying clause may have the effect of turning that clause into a defining clause.

Consider these sentences:

As soon as you see him, arrest the man, who is wearing a blue raincoat.

As soon as you see him, arrest the man who is wearing a blue raincoat.

Explain the difference in meaning between them.

(iv) To separate items in a list or series:

And now abideth faith, hope, charity, these three.

The chief editor wore a ruffled shirt, a large ring, a collar of obsolete pattern, and a check tie with the ends hanging down.

MARK TWAIN

Suppose Shakespeare had been knocked on the head some dark night in Sir Thomas Lucy's preserves, the world would have wagged on better or worse, the pitcher gone to the well, the scythe to the corn, and the student to his book; and no one been any wiser of the loss.

R. L. STEVENSON

Note 1. It requires at least *three* items to make a list. Where there are only *two* items, joined by 'and,' no comma is used.

Women and wine led to his downfall.

But: Wine, women, and gambling led to his downfall.

Note 2. Some writers omit the comma before the 'and' in such a list. (*E.g.*, "Wine, women and gambling . . . downfall.") On the whole, however, it is better to retain it, for the word 'and,' without a comma, tends to link words together, whereas the comma tends to separate them. Thus the omission of the comma before the 'and' leaves the last two items in the series apparently more closely connected with each other than with the preceding items.

Where the series consists of phrases, not single words (as in the above examples from Twain and Stevenson), the omission of the last comma would be particularly unfortunate.

(v) To separate interpolations or asides such as 'however,' 'moreover,' 'none the less,' etc.:

Hydrophobia was a disease which, *to say the least*, was very much dreaded a century ago, for doctors could not cure it.

However, a French scientist, Louis Pasteur, at length found the answer.

His name will always be regarded as one of the greatest in the history of medical science, *without any doubt*.

Note that 'however' is not always an interpolation. There is a difference between

(a) I do not think, *however*, that you will succeed.

and

(b) I do not know *however* you are going to manage.

The word 'however' could be omitted from sentence (a) without destroying the sense of the sentence, and is thus an interpolation. It could not be omitted from sentence (b), where it is not an interpolation, but a conjunction introducing a noun clause. It would be wrong to insert a comma or commas in this sentence.

(vi) To mark off the nominative of address:

Play the game, *you cads*, play the game!
Wake up, *you at the back*!
Jones, give out these books, please.

EXERCISES (C)

1. Insert necessary commas in the following sentences, and be prepared to explain why the comma is necessary:

(a) One of the pioneers of lifeboat construction Lionel Lukin designed the earliest British safety ship.

(b) His purpose however was merely to produce an unsinkable ship.

(c) It would be misleading therefore to call him the originator of

D

the lifeboat for a lifeboat is a vessel designed for the specific purpose of rescuing shipwrecked persons.

(d) The pig I found was a grossly maligned animal. [This could be punctuated in two ways. What is the difference in meaning?]

(e) When I went into the dining-room to look for my brother I found a pig under the table.

(f) *Treasure Island* which is sometimes loosely referred to as if it were a horn-book for young pirates hardly touches the main problems of pirate life at all.

(g) Beware of the elderly man who sits in the corner of the carriage and says that the train is two minutes behind time for he is the Ancient Mariner of railway travellers and will hold you with his glittering eye. [No comma is required after *carriage*.]

(h) Mr Williams was greatly respected by the boys who all knew his tall handsome figure by sight and he frequently stood near the playground a pleased observer of their games.

(i) As the tide slowly rises the masts which have been lying over on one side in a sleepy stillness begin to stir then to sway until with each new impulse of the sea all the boats are dancing.

(j) Call trade sport and give gold cups and championship belts to the man who sells the largest number of shirts or neckties over the counter and business would become a pastime at once.

2. In which of the following sentences are commas required before the words *who*, *which*, *when*, and *where*? (Study Rule (iii) carefully before attempting this exercise.)

I do not know when I shall recover from the shock of being chased by an armed robber. This was the fellow's weapon which he dropped as he ran. I hurried to the police station where I blurted out my story to the sergeant in charge. Together we went to the place where I had last seen the robber. After a fruitless search we were just turning away when we heard a rattle from behind a dustbin. The dustbin was one which was large enough to form a screen. We dashed over to it when we heard the noise. There was the man who had been chasing me! He was promptly arrested by the sergeant who took him off to the police station.

EXERCISES (D)

Insert necessary commas, full stops, and question marks in the following:

1. If you can wade through a few sentences of malice meanness falsehood treachery and cant you will perhaps be repaid by a laugh at the style of this ungrammatical twaddler.   DICKENS

2. If you look back on your own education I am sure it will not be the full vivid instructive hours of truancy that you regret. [Indicate two possible ways of punctuating this passage.]

R. L. STEVENSON

3. For fifteen mortal hours or so with few and brief intervals I have been making myself agreeable saying the right thing asking the apt question exhibiting the proper shade of mild or acute surprise smiling the appropriate smile or laughing just so long and just so loud as the occasion seemed to demand.   SIR MAX BEERBOHM

4. How now young fellow what dost thou here
   Truly sir I take mine ease
   Is not this the hour of the class
   Nay but thus also I follow after Learning by your leave.

R. L. STEVENSON

5. The costume of the Hambledonians was elegant indeed equipped for a match they wore velvet caps knee-breeches and stockings while as for their shoes some realist or another declares that he has seen Walker tear his finger against a silver buckle in picking up a ball. [In this passage "indeed" is an adverb of degree.]

6. Father Damien went steadily forward to the end instructing his fellow outcasts receiving their confessions binding their sores even feeding them putting the food into their mouths when the leprosy had eaten away their hands.   ARTHUR QUILLER-COUCH

7. Father Damien was a priest who went to a leper colony in the Hawaiian Islands to help the native sufferers in the course of time he caught the disease himself suffered with it for six years at length took to his bed and shortly afterwards died sixteen years after his first arrival on the island.

8. Sainte-Beuve as he grew older came to regard all experience as a single great book in which to study for a few years ere we go hence; and it seemed all one to him whether you should read in Chapter XX which is the differential calculus or in Chapter XXXIX which is hearing the band play in the gardens.   R. L. STEVENSON

9. For many people in England the first sight of "moving pictures" as they were then called was a film depicting life in the Navy it was shown at the Polytechnic Regent Street London in 1900 even before this in 1889 a scene in Hyde Park had been photographed by William Friese-Green a native of Bristol after official inquiry in

the United States Friese-Green was declared to be the true inventor of the moving-picture camera.

10. One February in 1895 about three o'clock in the morning some policemen on duty heard loud shouts coming from a building in Hatton Garden London they rushed to the scene only to find that Robert Paul another early pioneer of the cinema had just succeeded in throwing a clear moving picture on the screen for the first time and was rejoicing at his success.

If you can use the full stop and the comma accurately and intelligently you have mastered the essentials of punctuation. Other stops, such as the semi-colon, the colon, and the dash, are refinements which are less often required by the ordinary person who is not aiming at a subtle literary style. At the same time, you should know when they can be used; and a few examples of their use are given here, as their function is best explained by illustration.

THE SEMI-COLON (;)

This is used when a comma does not seem to offer a sufficient break, and yet where the connexion between two clauses is so close that a full stop appears to make too decided a break. It is often used to link two clauses where the idea expressed in the second clause balances that which is expressed in the first.

It may sometimes be a matter of personal preference whether a comma or a semi-colon is used. No rigid rules of right and wrong can be offered.

Note that the semi-colon is normally used only between clauses, not between a clause and a phrase.

1. We commenced washing down the decks. This operation, which is performed every morning at sea, takes nearly two hours; and I had hardly strength to get through it.

R. H. DANA

A comma could be used instead of a semi-colon in this sentence; but the extra pause given by the semi-colon gives the reader time to appreciate the length of time taken in washing down the decks, and helps to emphasize the heaviness of the operation and the writer's difficulty in accomplishing it.

2. You get another chance at football if you foozle a kick; but Hobbs in all his majesty must pass out of the scene for hours if for a second he should fall into the error that hedges all mortal activity.
NEVILLE CARDUS

Again, a comma could be used here; but the semi-colon is used because two contrasting ideas are balanced against each other. The reader is given time to assimilate the first idea before being presented with the contrasting one. Is it necessary to add that J. B. Hobbs was one of the greatest *cricketers* of all time?

3. A man generally makes a small scene if he finds salt in his coffee; if he doesn't, he has some reason for keeping quiet.
G. K. CHESTERTON

A comma could *not* be used here, as the two statements are made without any link-word to join them. Yet the second statement follows so closely from the first that the author rightly prefers a semi-colon to a full stop.

4. A pilot sucked at a final cigarette; a mechanic lifted the cowling, peered underneath, and nodded to his chief; a light steel ladder was drawn into the fuselage; the door closed.
ALAN SULLIVAN

Semi-colons are here used to separate the items in a list. Note that commas could not be used to separate these items, for commas are needed to separate the closely connected items between the first and second semi-colons.

EXERCISES (*E*)

Comment on the use of the semi-colons in the following:

1. The great delight of the railway journey was the obvious light-heartedness of my father; his method of counting the luggage to

see that it was all there; the tones in which he announced the stations which were passed, which would not have seemed real if anyone else had spoken them; and it was part of the ritual, all unknown to him, that as we approached our port of embarkation he should let down the window and make some remark on the state of the weather or the sea.

FILSON YOUNG

2. It did not appear to be blowing hard, and looking up through the scuttle, we could see that it was a clear day overhead; yet the watch were taking in sail.

R. H. DANA

3. It is doubtful if the Spanish people feel the heat so much as our reapers; they have their siesta; their habits have become attuned to the sun, and it is no special strain upon them.

RICHARD JEFFERIES

4. The sun spares not; it is fire from morn till night.

RICHARD JEFFERIES

5. Monday brings a feeling of revolt: Tuesday, the base craven, reconciles us to the machine.

E. V. LUCAS

Insert necessary commas and semi-colons in the following three passages:

6. Castiglione became a kind of centre for the reception of the wounded after the battle of Solferino but any arrangements that had been made for their care soon completely collapsed. Suffering men lay mutilated and unattended in and around the town their wounds black with flies. Some were taken into private houses others were brought or staggered on their own to the shelter of the churches yet others just lay in the roads.

7. Sometimes a discovery comes like a flash of lightning more often it is the reward of infinite patience of sheer dogged persistence which takes no thought of time difficulties or sacrifices.

8. A walking tour should be gone upon alone because freedom is of the essence because you should be able to stop and go on and follow this way or that as the freak takes you and because you must have your own pace and neither trot alongside a champion walker nor mince in time with a girl.

THE COLON (:)

This stop is most commonly used, in modern English, as follows:

(i) As an alternative way of introducing a passage in Direct Speech:

> I was suddenly called back by the harsh voice of the turnkey, crying as before:
> "What are you doing? Have you found nothing?"
>   J. MEADE FALKNER

(ii) For introducing an amplification of an immediately preceding statement:

> National Red Cross Societies sprang up in country after country: there are now more than sixty of them.

(iii) For introducing quotations, lists of words, or exercises:

> When I am tempted to air my limited knowledge, I remind myself of Pope's line: "A little learning is a dangerous thing."

> Give adjectives corresponding to each of the following words: technique, futility praise, ability.

(iv) As a substitute for *namely*:

> Galsworthy's *Strife* reveals many of his finest qualities as a dramatist: his profound pity, his feeling for character, his mastery of dialogue, and his sense of tragic irony.

In addition to acting as an introducer, the colon is sometimes used in the body of the sentence to separate contrasted statements, though its function here can hardly be distinguished from that of the semi-colon:

> Speech is silver: silence is golden.

THE DASH (—)

This stop is often used too freely by careless writers. It should not be used merely as a lazy substitute for the full stop or the comma. It has its own punctuation value.

The chief uses of the **dash** are:

(i) To separate a parenthesis from the main part of the sentence. Two dashes are used here, and they serve the same purpose and are put in the same place as brackets:

> How could Percy (a marked man if ever there was one) go from prison to prison to inquire about Jeanne?
> OR How could Percy—a marked man if ever there was one—go from prison to prison to inquire about Jeanne?

> He looked up at the cliff—the leper settlement lay under the shadow of a cliff—and wondered how to obtain a supply of water.
> OR He looked up at the cliff (the leper settlement lay under the shadow of a cliff) and wondered how to obtain a supply of water.

(ii) To mark a sudden breaking off in thought or—more usually—conversation:

> "I shall not fail you. My lodgings are—"
> "Oh! do not trouble," interposed Chauvelin with a polite bow; "we can find that out for ourselves."

(iii) To give special emphasis to the end of a sentence, especially an end which is particularly pointed or unexpected:

> The guard had been bribed, the keeper corrupted, everything had been prepared save the reckoning with the one irresponsible factor —chance.

> The Africans accompanying us always carried spears and bows and arrows as a protection against wild animals. The arrows are sold locally—sixpence plain and one shilling poisoned.

> Before that felling blow could be delivered, Uncle Jim's ear had caught a footfall, and he turned. Mr Polly quailed, and lowered his broom—a fatal hesitation.

> With the year 1886 we approach one of the major biographical problems of Watson's career—the date of his marriage.

(iv) To mark hesitation in dialogue:

> "Not quite so straight a shot as you used to be, Sir Percy." Chauvelin said mockingly.
> "No, sir—apparently—not."
> The words came out in gasps.

MISS HARDCASTLE. But you have not been wholly an observer, I presume, Sir: the ladies, I should hope, have employed some part of your addresses.

MARLOW (*relapsing into timidity*). Pardon me, madam, I—I—I— as yet have studied—only—to—deserve them.

QUOTATION MARKS (INVERTED COMMAS) (" ")

1. Quotation marks are used to mark off dialogue in a sentence or passage containing words that are not dialogue. Only words actually used by the speakers are enclosed within the quotation marks.

Normally it is customary to put the closing quotation marks *after* other punctuation marks. (But see 3, *Note*, on p. 112.) The following examples will illustrate the usual procedure.

(i) When the speech comes first:

(*a*) "There's a policeman over there," said Jack.
(*b*) "Can you tell me the right time?" he asked.
(*c*) "Go to blazes!" answered the policeman unexpectedly.

Note the small letters (*he*, *a*nswered) in (*b*) and (*c*). This is because the question mark and exclamation mark here indicate not the end of a full sentence but the end of only the quoted part of it. The words *he* and *answered* are thus in the middle of a sentence.

(ii) When other words precede the speech:

(*d*) Turning round he said quietly, "You're standing on my foot."
(*e*) Mr Willoughby sat up as well as he could in the hammock-chair and said sternly:
"Am I to understand that you regard any lie as justifiable if it serves its purpose?"

Note that a capital is always used for the first word of a quoted speech (*Y*ou're, *A*m). After a colon used thus, the quoted speech often begins, as here, on a new line; but this is not essential. If the quoted speech consists of more than a few words, a colon and not a comma is most often used to introduce it.

(iii) Broken quotation:

(*f*) "Either you or I," said Mr Willoughby feebly, "must be going mad."

Note that there is a small *m* for *must*, as this word is not the *first* word of a quoted speech. Contrast with *You're* in (*d*).

(*g*) "I am a parson," said Meldon; "but you can't expect me to wear a dog-collar on a ten-ton yacht."

(*h*) "I came up here to have a chat with you," said Meldon. "Perhaps you wouldn't mind turning round. I always find it more convenient to talk to a man who isn't looking the other way."

Note that in (*g*) there is a small letter for *but*, as this word follows a semi-colon. In (*h*), however, the word *Perhaps* follows a full stop, and thus requires a capital letter.

Note that in each case the quotation marks have to be reopened after a piece of dialogue has been interrupted, no matter whether the interruption is followed by a comma, a semi-colon, or a full stop.

(iv) Explanatory words omitted.

In a passage containing more than one speech a fresh line should be taken each time there is a change of speaker. It is not necessary to explain who is speaking if this is clear from the context, especially in a piece of writing containing a good deal of dialogue. It would be tedious to keep repeating (for instance) *he said*, *answered the other*, *said Jones*, and similar explanatory phrases.

The Colonel appeared in the door with a dragoon revolver in his hand.

He said, "Sir, I have the honour of addressing the poltroon who edits this mangy sheet?"

"You have. Be seated, sir. Be careful of the chair; one of its legs is gone. I believe I have the honour of addressing that blatant scoundrel, Colonel Blatherskite Tecumseh?"

"That's me. I have a little account to settle with you. If you are at leisure we will begin."

"I have an article on 'The Encouraging Progress of Moral and Intellectual Development in America' to finish, but there is no hurry. Begin."

Both pistols rang out their fierce clamour at the same instant.

MARK TWAIN

2. Quotation marks are used:

(i) To indicate a word or passage quoted from a piece of writing:

Gilbert White brags of no fine society, but is plainly a little elated by "having considerable acquaintance with a tame brown owl." Most of us have known our share of owls, but few can boast of intimacy with a feathered one. . . . In 1770 he makes the acquaintance in Sussex of "an old family tortoise," which had then been domesticated for thirty years. It is clear that he fell in love with it at first sight. We have no means of tracing the growth of his passion, but in 1780 we find him eloping with its object in a post-chaise. "The rattle and hurry of the journey so perfectly roused it that, when I turned it out in a border, it walked twice down to the bottom of my garden."

J. R. LOWELL (discussing White's *Natural History of Selborne*)

(ii) As a substitute for italics in indicating the title of a book or the name of a ship:

One of the most delightful books in my father's library was White's "Natural History of Selborne".

The largest ship in the world is the "Queen Elizabeth".

(iii) To indicate that the writer is using a word or phrase in a sense quite different from that normally accepted:

Even though "progressive" schools perform a useful function in stimulating teachers to think about their own educational conventions, the methods employed in these schools would rarely be practicable in the ordinary school.

The quotation marks make it clear that the writer does not accept that the type of school under discussion is necessarily more progressive than other schools.

We had a very "jolly" evening.

The evening, though supposed to be jolly, was actually nothing of the kind.

Quotation marks should be used very rarely in this way.

3. A quotation within a quotation is indicated by the use of single quotation marks within the double ones[1]:

> Poe wrote: "Charles Dickens, in a note lying before me, says, 'By the way, are you aware that Godwin wrote *Caleb Williams*?'"

The stickler for logical precision would add a full stop after the last inverted commas; but most writers would regard this conglomeration of stops as clumsy, and would prefer to take this final full stop as being absorbed into the question mark after *Williams*.

It is possible to invent sentences which contain various artificial difficulties, but such exercises have little practical value.

Note, however, the logical position for the question mark in sentences such as the following:

> Did he say, "Tell me the time"?

WHEN NOT TO USE QUOTATION MARKS

(i) Some people make the mistake of supposing that a word or phrase in common use is a quotation, and must be put within inverted commas. This is quite wrong, and results in a very feeble style. Thus the following sentence (from a student's essay)

> It is unusual for the parents of "the modern girl" to be consulted before she is "invited out." [*NOT* correct]

should be written

> It is unusual for the parents of the modern girl to be consulted before she is invited out.

Similarly, words used in their secondary sense and words used metaphorically should never be placed within quotation

[1] Some printers use single quotation marks for the main quotation, in which case double quotation marks are used for an inner quotation.

marks. It is an accepted part of the English language that words can have more than one meaning.

(ii) Quotation marks are not used when speech is set out in the form of dramatic dialogue, for names of characters and other explanatory matter are sufficiently differentiated from dialogue by being printed in capitals or italics, or by being underlined.

SHE [*weakening a little*]. I implore you as a wife and a mother not to cut in front of that motor-lorry.

HE. Am I driving this car or are you?

EXERCISES (*F*)

Insert quotation marks and other necessary stops in the following:

1. *You* ought to be a good cricketer he said.
2. He shouldn't have tried it, anyhow I said to myself. A man who eats like a pig ought to look like a pig.
3. If anything gives way and you tumble down I said you'll break your neck Pyecraft
4. What is the name of this obliging youth asked Sherlock Holmes
5. What are you going to do then I asked
To smoke he answered it is quite a three-pipe problem and I beg that you won't speak to me for fifty minutes
6. Both detectives stared and Father Brown added won't you tell them about it sir
7. Jeeves I said we want some tea
8. Precisely sir said Jeeves if I might make the suggestion sir I should not continue to wear your present tie the green shade gives you a slightly bilious air
9. Poirot asked curiously what did he answer
Meredith Blake replied with distaste:
He said: Caroline must lump it
10. I shall have to gag you of course he continued open your mouth
No! said Nelly desperately

THE APOSTROPHE (')

The **apostrophe** is used:

(i) To indicate possessive case:

barber's pole; boy's head [*singular*]
babies' rattles; spectators' rattles; children's games [*plural*]

Note St James's Park, Keats's poetry, Dickens's novels; *but* Moses' money, Ulys*s*es' adventures to avoid the ugly repetition of *s* or *z* sounds.

(ii) To indicate the omission of a letter or letters from a word:

> I'm = I *a*m, I've = I *ha*ve, I'll = I *wi*ll, don't = do *no*t, it's = it *i*s, we'd = we *shoul*d.

Note that the apostrophe is put where the missing letters would be. Such abbreviations are better avoided in formal composition, except when the writer is reproducing conversation.

(iii) In the plurals of figures and letters:

> How badly you write your 5's!
> How many *s*'s are there in 'Mississippi'?

The first of these examples is not very common, for it is usual to write numbers up to one hundred in words (*e.g.*, five orange pips; fifteen men on a dead man's chest; *The Thirty-nine Steps*).

Note (*a*) The following uses of the apostrophe:

> for pity's sake, *but* for goodness' sake
> everyone else's (*NOT* everyone's else)

(*b*) That *no* apostrophe is used for the possessive pronouns *yours*, *ours*, *its*, *hers*, *theirs*.

(*c*) That *no* apostrophe is needed at the beginning of curtailed words which have passed into the language as complete words in common use:

> bus, plane (aeroplane), phone.

EXERCISES (*G*)

Insert necessary apostrophes in the following:

1. Give the girls book to the ladies and the ladies books to the girl.

2. I dont think its any use collecting the childrens exercises until Ive had time to mark the fifth forms papers. and I shant see theirs for two days.

3. "Fancy Erbert avin is name in the papers," said Holly. "Theyll ave is photograph next."

4. "Ill get my razor now," ses Bill, in an awful voice: "dont let im go, Bob. Ill ack is ead orf."

5. Georges sisters gone to Jones to ask if hes any of his friends packs of cards to lend, for its his Mens Clubs ladies night, and its reputation for whist drives mustnt be lost.

6. Lets ask Masters to see if his masters mark registers been put among the headmasters books or if its in the boys common room with the others.

Insert necessary commas, quotation marks, and apostrophes in the following:

7. Weve been the wictims of a cruel outrage sir ses Bill doing all e could to avoid the mates eye which wouldnt be avoided.

8. Well Sam said Mr Pickwick all alive to-day I suppose?
Reglar game sir replied Mr Weller; our peoples collectin down at the Town Arms and theyre hollering themselves hoarse already.

SUMMARY OF CHIEF POINTS

1. Punctuation rules are not rigid, but there are many commonly accepted practices.

2. Careful reading of good writers is a useful guide, particularly to the correct use of full stops.

Full Stop

3. The full stop (or its equivalent ? !) must be used after a complete statement.

4. The full stop marks a stronger break than , ; :

Question Mark and Exclamation Mark

5. These normally have the same force as a full stop in marking the end of a sentence.

6. Do not use another stop (except inverted commas) with either.

7. A question mark should not be used with an indirect question.

8. An exclamation mark is used after exclamations, exclamatory sentences, interjectory comments, or for special emphasis.

9. Do not use an exclamation mark for ordinary wishes or commands, or to suggest emotion or excitement which is already indicated by the sentence or context.

10. Avoid double or triple exclamation marks.

Comma

11. The comma marks a shorter break than the full stop.

12. It indicates a pause in sense or a syntactical construction, and not a breathing pause.

13. Avoid over-using the comma, but insert it where its omission would cause even momentary confusion.

14. The comma is used to mark a change of thought-direction, a phrase in apposition, a qualification, the separate items in a list, an interpolation, and a nominative of address.

15. Do not use a comma with a defining clause.

Other Stops

16. The *semi-colon* offers a less complete break than a full stop, but a stronger break than a comma. It is often used between two balanced clauses.

17. The *colon* is mainly used for introducing quotations, lists of words, or the amplification of a statement, or as a substitute for *namely*.

18. The *dash* should not be used as a careless substitute for other stops; it should be used only to mark a parenthesis, a breaking-off or hesitation in dialogue, or to give special emphasis to the end of the sentence.

19. *Quotation marks* (inverted commas) should be used around words actually used by a speaker, around words quoted from a piece of writing, or around words used in a special sense.

20. The *apostrophe* is used to indicate possession, the

omission of a letter or letters, or the plural of letters or figures.

GENERAL EXERCISES ON PUNCTUATION

1. Punctuate each of the following sentences in two different ways, and explain the differences in meaning:

    (a) Only students who have tickets will be allowed to see the play

    (b) I cant think whatever will happen

    (c) This is the playing-field where we hold our Sports

    (d) Those people who live in glass houses should not throw stones

    (e) The captain is talking on the steps that may help us to win the match this year

    (f) He was not cheerful because he fell in the river

    (g) The captain says Jackson is the best batsman in the team

    (h) I dont care if she tries to swim the Channel why should I

    (i) Ive been overworking perhaps I need a holiday.

    (j) The book I discovered was worth a hundred pounds

2. Punctuate and set out the following passage, inserting all necessary capitals:

to get into this church of tytherington where there was nothing but damp naked walls to look at i had to procure the key from the clerk a nearly blind old man of eighty he told me that he was a shoemaker but could no longer see to make or mend shoes that as a boy he was a weak sickly creature and his father a farm bailiff made him learn shoemaking because he was unfit to work out of doors i remember this church he said when there was only one service each quarter but strange to say he forgot to tell me the story of the dog locked up in the church between one service and the next and still alive what didn't he tell you about the dog exclaimed everybody there was really nothing else to tell w h hudson a shepherds life

3. Punctuate and set out the following passage inserting all the necessary capitals:

im afraid gentlemen you will not have a very grand dinner observed the captain as the steward removed the plated covers off the dishes but when on service we must rough it how we can mr o'brien pea-soup i recollect faring harder than this through one cruise we were thirteen weeks up to our knees in water and living the whole time upon raw pork not being able to light a fire during the cruise pray captain kearney may i ask where this happened to be sure it

was off the bermudas we cruised for seven weeks before we could
find the islands i presume sir you were not sorry to have a fire to
cook your provisions when you came to anchor said o'brien i beg
your pardon replied captain kearney we had become so accustomed
to raw provisions and wet feet that we could not eat our meals
cooked or help dipping our legs over the side for a long while
afterwards captain marryat peter simple

4. Paragraph and punctuate the following passages, inserting all
necessary capitals:

(*a*) a visiting preacher at a public school noticed during the
sermon a curious clicking noise at intervals when he asked the
headmaster at supper what the noises were the latter said they were
the hats the boys have hard straw hats which hang on pegs in front
of them when they get a bit tired of the sermon one boy will dislodge
his hat then another follows suit and so on we can almost measure
the interest of a sermon by the number of clicks good heavens
ejaculated the preacher they must have been fed up i heard four or
five clicks dont worry said the headmaster your score was quite low
we had the bishop last sunday and he scored 27

(*b*) the rambling preacher seems long because he is discursive
he has been satirised in the advice given to a curate by a sardonic
dignitary when youve used up your material yet somehow still go
on for it shows a want of enterprise to stop because youve done dont
hunt around for subjects new or tax your weary brain just take what
someone else has said and say it all again the too fluent preacher is
often wearying because there is little cohesion in his message he is
like a deservedly popular b b c speaker who can talk about any
and every topic with equal facility one day the mayor of a provincial
town asked him to speak on behalf of a local charity he got up
genially surveyed the audience and put them at their ease with a
few chatty remarks then leaning over towards the mayor he said in
a whisper by the way whats the name of the charity for which im
supposed to be speaking

(*c*) youre late jack said mr benjamin allen been detained at
bartholomews replied hopkins anything new no nothing particular
rather a good accident brought into the casualty ward what was
that sir inquired mr pickwick only a man fallen out of a fourth floor
window but its a very fair case very fair case indeed do you mean
that the patient is in a very fair way to recover inquired mr pickwick
no replied hopkins carelessly no i should rather say he wouldn't
there must be a splendid operation though to-morrow magnificent
sight if slasher does it

[*Note* that it is the second speaker who says that nothing particular has happened and then goes on to describe the accident.]

(*d*) a clergyman was explaining to a sunday school the significance of the colour white why does a bride desire to be clothed in white he asked as no one answered he went on because white stands for joy and the wedding day is the most joyous occasion in a woman's life please sir piped up a little boy at the back why do all the men wear black

(*e*) but who wants to be foretold the weather it is bad enough when it comes without our having the misery of knowing about it beforehand the prophet we like is the old man who on the particularly gloomy morning of some day when we particularly want it to be fine looks round the horizon with a particularly knowing eye and says oh no sir i think it will clear up all right it will break right enough sir ah he knows we say as we wish him good morning and start off wonderful how these old fellows can tell and we feel an affection for that man which is not at all lessened by the circumstances of its *not* clearing up but continuing to rain steadily all day ah well we feel he did his best

(*f*) a lady from england staying with some friends in ireland thought to try her hand on the natives of limerick in the cause of temperance furnished with a list of names she proceeded to the poorer suburbs where she called on a mrs doherty good morning mrs doherty she said in a coaxing tone good morning maam replied the woman of the house taking her arms out of the washing tub what can i be doing for you im collecting for a drunkards home mrs doherty said the visitor you are maam replied the other then if you send round about ten oclock to night you can collect doherty

(*London*)

(*g*) twilight had already closed in when they turned off the path to the door of a roadside inn yet twelve miles short of portsmouth twelve miles said nicholas leaning with both hands on his stick and looking doubtfully at smike twelve long miles repeated the landlord is it a good road inquired nicholas very bad said the landlord as of course being a landlord he would say i want to get on observed nicholas hesitating i scarcely know what to do don't let me influence you rejoined the landlord *i* wouldn't go on if it was me wouldn't you asked nicholas with the same uncertainty not if i knew when i was well off said the landlord and having said it he pulled up his apron put his hands into his pockets and taking a step or two outside the door looked down the dark road with an assumption of great indifference (*h*) in this year lamb made his greatest essay in housekeeping by occupying colnebrook cottage at islington on the banks of his beloved new river there occurred the immersion of george dyer at noontide which supplies the subject of one of the last essays of elia and which is veritably related in the following letter of lamb to mrs hazlitt dear mrs h sitting down to write a letter is such a painful operation to mary that you must accept me as her proxy you have seen our house what i now tell you is literally true yesterday week george dyer called upon us at one oclock on his way to dine with mrs barbauld at newington and he sat with mary about half an hour the maid saw him go out from her kitchen window but suddenly losing sight of him ran up in a fright to mary instead of keeping to the slipway that leads to the gate he had deliberately staff in hand in broad daylight marched into the new river he had not his spectacles on and you know his absence of mind who helped him out they can hardly tell a mob collected by that time and accompanied him in send for the doctor they said and a one-eyed fellow dirty and drunk was fetched from the public-house at the end

(*i*) the landlady sat on a chair an inch or two higher than the rest gerard asked her if he could have something to eat she opened her eyes with astonishment supper is over this hour and more but i had none of it good dame is that my fault you were welcome to your share but i was benighted and a stranger and belated against my will what have i to do with that all the world knows the star of the forest sups from six till eight come before six ye sup well come before eight ye sup as pleases heaven come after eight ye get a clean bed and a stirrup-cup or a horn of kine's milk at the dawning gerard looked blank may i go to bed then dame said he sulkily for it is ill sitting up wet and fasting and the byword saith he sups who sleeps the beds are not come yet replied the landlady you will sleep when the rest do inns are not built for *one*

5. Read the following passage with careful attention to its punctuation, and then state *briefly* and clearly why the punctuation marks and apostrophes listed beneath the extract are used:

The speaker said, "The islanders' happiness is obvious to all. How do we account for this? It's clear that in this country there is a very general level of material prosperity; except among recent immigrants there is hardly anything that can be called poverty. Everybody is comfortable, and nobody is rich." It seemed to him, he continued, that the island had affinities with Gonzalo's ideal commonwealth in *The Tempest*.

(*a*) Inverted commas (lines 1 and 5).

(b) The apostrophe in *islanders'* (line 1).

(c) The question mark (line 2).

(d) The apostrophe in *It's* (line 2).

(e) The semi-colon (line 3).

(f) The comma after *comfortable* (line 5).

(g) The comma between *him* and *he* (lines 5 and 6).

(h) The comma after *continued* (line 6).

(i) The apostrophe in *Gonzalo's* (line 6).

(j) Why are italics used for *The Tempest* (line 7)?

(Oxford)

6. Punctuate the following passages without changing the order of the words:

(a) do you think its right he demanded to curtail the peoples liberty

(b) the idea that theirs is better than ours is absurd he exclaimed both cars are good

(c) he always said that his favourite play was macbeth his favourite poem miltons paradise lost and his favourite novel vanity fair by thackeray but i dont believe he had read any of them properly

(Cambridge)

7. Rewrite the following passages with correct punctuation:

(a) why i asked him do you always use the word disinterested when you mean uninterested theres no difference is there he replied what nonsense if you look them up in chamberss dictionary youll find youre wrong

(b) milton keats tennyson these were the poets i studied before writing my essay poetry i enjoy

(Cambridge)

CHAPTER IV

DIRECT AND REPORTED SPEECH

In making a summary of a piece of writing or a speech it is often necessary to change **Direct Speech** to **Reported Speech** —a process which we also carry out freely in our daily conversation.

Oral or written expression is said to be in Direct Speech when it comes to the reader in the form in which it was originally spoken or written. It is said to be in Reported Speech (or Indirect Speech) when the exact sense of the original expression is given, but not the exact words.

Note that inverted commas are required for Direct Speech only if other words in the same passage are *not* words actually spoken or quoted; if the passage is in dramatic form inverted commas are not in any case required.

Examples of Direct Speech

With inverted commas (words *not* in Direct Speech are here italicized):

  1. "I want you all to vote for me to-morrow," *said the candidate.*
  2. *The agent said quickly:* "Brown is the man to vote for."
  3. "Do you want our country to be ruined?" *the candidate asked.*
  4. "Vote for me and save England!" *Brown cried.*

Without inverted commas:

  5. BROWN [*persuasively*]. I want you all to vote for me to-morrow.
  6. I am writing to ask for your full support in the coming election.
  7. Brown is the most eloquent of the three candidates.
  8. Do not listen to the lies of our opponents!

Examples of Reported Speech

The above examples of Direct Speech might be put into Reported Speech as follows:

1. The candidate said that he wanted them all (*or* all of his hearers) to vote for him the following day.

2. The agent said quickly that Brown was the man to vote for.

3. The candidate asked his hearers whether they wanted the country to be ruined.

4. Brown begged (*or* ordered) his hearers to vote for him and save England.

5. Brown endeavoured to persuade all of his hearers to vote for him the following day.

6. In a written message the candidate said that he was asking the electors for their full support in the coming election *OR* The candidate wrote to ask the electors for their full support in the coming election.

7. Brown was stated to be the most eloquent of the three candidates.

8. The writer (*or* speaker) urged his readers (*or* hearers) not to listen to the lies of his party's opponents.

Changes in Form

A more detailed study of the first example will show some of the chief changes in form which are necessary in converting Direct Speech (D.S.) to Reported Speech (R.S.):

D.S. "*I* want *you* all to vote for *me* to-morrow," said the candidate.

R.S. The candidate said that *he* wanted *them* all (*or* all of *his hearers*) to vote for *him* the following day.

The changes fall under four main headings:

1. **Person.** If the reported version is made, as it usually is, by a third person (*i.e.*, neither the speaker nor the listener), then first- and second-person pronouns (or possessive adjectives) in Direct Speech are changed to third person in Reported Speech:

Direct Speech	*Reported Speech*
I; me; we; us	he *or* she; him *or* her; they; them
you (singular) nominative	he *or* she
you (plural) nominative	they
you (singular) accusative	him *or* her
you (plural) accusative	them
my; our; your	his *or* her; their; their

Note that it may sometimes be necessary in the Reported version to indicate to whom the Direct pronoun refers. Thus, in Example 1, "you" in Direct Speech may be converted to "his hearers" in Reported Speech for the sake of clarity.

Note also that if the report were made by the *speaker* himself the first-person pronoun would naturally be retained in Reported Speech. Thus, in Example 1, the candidate's own reported version would run:

> *I* said that *I* wanted them all to vote for *me*.

Similarly, a report made by the *listeners* would naturally retain the first-person pronoun:

> He said that he wanted *us* all to vote for him.

Unless you are specifically told otherwise, the exercises which follow should be written in the third person. If no indication of the author's (or speaker's) identity is given, you may begin: "The writer (or speaker) said that . . ."

2. **Verb.** Since the reported version must be given later than the original speech, it follows that what is present or future tense in Direct Speech will normally become past tense in Reported Speech. Thus, in the example, "want" in Direct Speech has become "wanted" in Reported Speech. Similarly:

Direct Speech	*Reported Speech*
shall, will	should, would
may	might
can	could
is, are	was, were
has, have	had

D.S. I *shall* go to Bournemouth at Easter if I *can*.

R.S. He said that he *would* go to Bournemouth at Easter if he *could*.

If the verb is already in a past simple tense in Direct Speech it may be necessary to put it into a past perfect tense in Reported Speech:

D.S. "I *played* football yesterday afternoon," said Jones.

R.S. Jones said that he *had played* football the previous afternoon.

But this rule is not rigidly applied throughout a passage where the frequent repetition of the past perfect tense would result in clumsiness of style. The auxiliary 'had' is sometimes left to be understood.

Note that infinitives are usually left unchanged:

D.S. "I wish *to make* a statement, inspector," said the accused man.

R.S. The accused man told the inspector that he wished *to make* a statement.

3. Time and Place. Just as verbs tend to move into the past in Reported Speech, so do adverbial expressions of *time*:

Direct Speech	*Reported Speech*
to-morrow	the following (next) day
to-day	that day
yesterday	the previous day
now	then

Adverbial expressions and demonstrative adjectives indicating *place* undergo a similar change from nearness to remoteness:

Direct Speech	*Reported Speech*
here	there
this	that
these	those

Note that words such as 'here' and 'now' cannot always be changed automatically into 'there' and 'then' if the Reported version is to be clear and exact. Nouns and phrases which are implied in the Direct version may have to be made explicit in the Reported version:

D.S. I want all of you *here* to join in *this* chorus.

R.S. The singer said that he wanted *everyone present* to join in the chorus *he was about to sing*.

NOT

The singer said that he wanted all of them there to join in that chorus.

4. Introductory Verb of Saying. Reported Speech is introduced by some verb indicating 'saying,' 'thinking,' or 'writing,' often followed by the word 'that.' Inverted commas are never used in Reported Speech. For examples see those at the beginning of this chapter.

Note that in *Indirect Questions* the word 'that' is usually unsuitable, and 'if' or 'whether,'[1] or the infinitive of the verb, may be used instead:

1. D.S. "Have you a driving licence?" asked the policeman.

R.S. The policeman asked the driver *whether* he had a driving licence.

2. D.S. "Will you help me across the road?" the little girl said to the policeman.

R.S. The little girl asked the policeman *if* he would help her across the road.
OR
The little girl asked the policeman *to help* her across the road.

In *Indirect Commands or Exhortations* the word 'that' is also unsuitable except after the word 'said.' The command or exhortation is more commonly introduced by a verb such as 'told,' 'ordered,' 'urged,' etc., followed by the infinitive:

1. D.S. "Get out before you're kicked out!" said the master angrily.

R.S. The master angrily ordered (told) the boy to get out before he was kicked out.
OR (*less effectively*)
The master said angrily that the boy was to get out before he was kicked out.

2. D.S. "Clear the court!" said the judge.

R.S. The judge ordered the court to be cleared.

EXERCISES (*A*)

Put the following into Reported Speech:

1. "I am going to ask you all to keep particularly quiet during the examinations this afternoon," the headmaster told the school.

---

[1] 'Whether' is generally used when there are two equally uncertain possibilities. The words 'or not' are usually understood.

[*A.* As reported by a visitor; *B.* As reported by a pupil; *C.* As reported by the headmaster himself.]

2. RADIO COMEDIAN. Can you hear me, Mother?

3. I suggest that if a time limit is placed on each innings it will do much to brighten the game of cricket. What do your readers think? [*Letter to the Press.*]

4. "You'll be quite safe here," said the guard to the old lady. "This is the rear carriage. In my experience it's the front carriage which is the most dangerous."

"Then why do you have it?" asked the old lady.

5. BOY [*pleadingly*]. Don't make me go to school to-day, Dad. I'm afraid to.

FATHER. Why?

BOY. Just as I was leaving school yesterday I saw Wilson bending down to do up his shoelace, and I gave him a jolly good smack with my plimsoll. Then I found it wasn't Wilson—it was the headmaster!

6. I sat down with the full intention of writing something clever and original; but for the life of me I can't think of something clever and original—at least, not at this moment. The only thing I can think about now is being hard up.   J. K. JEROME

7. I must break it to you, with such tact and tenderness as I can muster, that you who have for so long imagined yourself to be a single human personality are at your best a mob; and at your worst, in moments of indecision, you are a mere riot.   GERALD BULLETT

[Write from the point of view of one of his readers.]

8. "Girls!" said Ned, "put your dark shawls round you. It may be nothing, but it is better to be prepared. Dick, put a bottle of wine in your pocket; and let's all fill our pockets with biscuits."

Some Further Points

Tone. When converting Direct Speech to Reported Speech it is important to preserve the tone of the original passage. To achieve this it is often necessary to exercise care in the choice of main verb in the Reported version, especially with questions and commands; and it may also be necessary to paraphrase exclamatory statements.

EXAMPLES

1. D.S. "Save me, for pity's sake!" cried the drowning woman to the onlookers.

R.S. The drowning woman *implored* the onlookers to save her. [The exclamation "for pity's sake" has too immediate a force to be satisfactory in Reported Speech, and its sense is conveyed, therefore, by the use of the verb *implored*.]

2. D.S. Open the door, please, Jackson.

R.S. He *politely* asked Jackson to open the door. [The tone indicated by the word "please" is conveyed by the adverb *politely*.]

3. D.S. "Open the door, Sir Jaspar," she cried, "or I shall scream for Mother!" [This request to open the door is obviously different in tone from the previous example, and this should be indicated by the use of a stronger verb than 'asked.' Even 'told' would be rather weak. The tone of the sentence suggests a threat, so 'threatened' would be a very suitable verb.]

R.S. She *threatened* Sir Jaspar that if he did not open the door she would scream for her mother.
OR
She *threatened* that if Sir Jaspar did not open the door she would scream for her mother.

4. D.S. HAMLET. Unhand me, gentlemen:
By heaven, I'll make a ghost of him that lets me.

R.S. Hamlet commanded the men to release him, threatening *with an oath* to make a ghost of anyone who detained him. [The full force of "By heaven" is hardly conveyed by the verb "threatening" alone, so *with an oath* is added. Note that "lets" here means 'hinders, detains.']

Ambiguity. When two or more people of the same sex are concerned in a passage which is to be converted to Reported Speech some danger of ambiguity arises in the use of 'he,' 'him,' 'his,' etc. To make a sentence clear some other words, such as 'the former,' 'the latter,' may have to be used (they should be used sparingly, however); or, if necessary, the noun should be repeated.

EXAMPLES

1. D.S. "Just look at your lettuces," said Mr Robinson to Mr Smith; "they are bigger than mine. You have beaten me this time."

R.S. (*ambiguous version*). Mr Robinson told Mr Smith to look at his lettuces and said they were bigger than his. He had beaten him that time.

[It is by no means clear whether the first "his" refers to Mr Robinson and the second "his" to Mr Smith, or vice versa. There is a similar confusion in the use of "he" and "him" in the second sentence.]

R.S. (*improved version*). Mr Robinson invited Mr Smith to look at the latter's lettuces, and acknowledged that they were bigger than his own. He added that Mr Smith had beaten him that time.

[Here "the latter's" relates clearly to Mr Smith and is contrasted with "his own," which must therefore relate to Mr Robinson. In the second sentence the pronoun "him" is contrasted with "Mr Smith" and must therefore refer to Mr Robinson. All ambiguity is thus removed. Note also the use of "invited" and "acknowledged" to convey more accurately the tone of the original passage.]

2. D.S. "I shall tell my friend that I have passed my exam," said Frank.

R.S. (*ambiguous version*). Frank said that he would tell his friend that he had passed his exam.

[It is not clear whether it is Frank or his friend who has passed the exam.]

R.S. (*improved version*). Frank said that he would tell his friend that he (Frank) had passed his exam.[1]

OR

When Frank had passed his exam he said that he would tell his friend.

Misinterpretation. The conversion of a verb in Direct Speech to past tense in Reported Speech (or some similar change) may occasionally misinterpret a speaker's meaning:

"There is no real happiness in this life," the philosopher maintained.

To report this as

The philosopher maintained that there was no real happiness in that life

[1] This is a somewhat clumsy method which should be avoided if possible.

would be very misleading unless the philosopher's statement was intended to apply to a particular type of life which no longer existed. If, as is more probable, the philospher was referring to life in general, including our own life to-day, then the reported version should read:

> The philosopher maintained that there is no real happiness in this life (*or* in life).

Nominative of Address. Conventional words or phrases such as 'Ladies and Gentlemen,' 'Mr Chairman,' 'My Dear Friends,' are useful as indicating whom the speaker is addressing, but they must not be used in Reported Speech. They may be either paraphrased or omitted:

EXAMPLES

1. D.S. I should be obliged, ladies and gentlemen, if you would move a little closer to the platform.

R.S. The speaker said that he would be obliged if *the audience* (or *those present*) would move a little closer to the platform.

2. D.S. JOHNSON. Why, Sir, till you can fix the degree of obstinacy and negligence of the scholars, you cannot fix the degree of severity of the master.

R.S. Johnson said that (*or* told his companion that) until you could fix the degree of obstinacy and negligence of the scholars, you could not fix the degree of severity of the master.

3. D.S. ANTONY. Friends, Romans, countrymen, lend me your ears.

R.S. Addressing his hearers as his friends and fellow Romans, Antony begged them to listen to him.

["Fellow Romans" includes the idea of "countrymen." The words "lend me your ears," though forceful and persuasive in Direct Speech, would be somewhat ridiculous if literally rendercd into Reported Speech: the eagerness of the plea is indicated by the word "begged." Note, however, that it is not usually necessary or desirable to paraphrase as much as this.]

EXERCISES (*B*)

Put the following passages into Reported Speech:

1. "Come on, chaps, play up!" cried the captain.

2. BRUTUS. Who is here so vile that will not love his country?

3. Show me a man's hat and I'll give you a good guess at his ideas; show me a woman's hat and I am utterly dumbfounded.

4. CASSIUS. Most noble brother, you have done me wrong.
BRUTUS. Judge me, you gods! Wrong I mine enemies?
And if not so, how should I wrong a brother?·

5. Dr Burney said to him, "I believe, Sir, we shall make a musician of you at last." Johnson with candid complacency replied, "Sir, I shall be glad to have a new sense given to me."

6. If a madman were to come into this room with a stick in his hand, no doubt we should pity the state of his mind; but our primary concern would be to take care of ourselves. We should knock him down first, and pity him afterwards.   JOHNSON

7. And lastly, my friends, I will ask you to bear in mind that each man's stay on this earth is, alas, a brief one.

8. YOUNG MAN. I understand, sir, that your senior clerk has just died.
MANAGER. He has.
YOUNG MAN. Then I'm the man you need to take his place. When shall I start?
MANAGER. As soon as you can fix it up with the undertaker.

9. The master became angry with the boy and said, "Why have you again disturbed the class in this way? I have told you before that when I am speaking you should be silent. Leave the class, and do not return again today."

(Oxford and Cambridge)

10. Lord Curzon was once travelling to a political meeting in a train which was much behind time. "What's the matter with this train?" he asked the guard during a long stop at a station.
The guard was a surly individual. "If you don't like the train, mister, you can get out and walk."
"I would," said Curzon; "only they don't expect me till this train arrives."

EXAMPLE OF LONGER PASSAGE

Direct Speech. "Have you any idea of sending your boy to school, Mr Easy?" said Dr Middleton.

"The great objection that I have to sending a boy to school, Dr Middleton, is that I conceive that the discipline enforced is in opposition to all sound sense and common judgment. I will teach him everything myself."

"I do not doubt your capability, Mr Easy, but you will always have a difficulty which you cannot get over. You must be aware as well as I am that the maternal fondness of Mrs Easy will always be a bar to your intention."

In the evening Mr Easy said to his wife. "I have decided to send Johnny to school this month."

"But he's a mere infant!" exclaimed Mrs Easy.

"Are you not aware, my dear, that at nine years it is time he learnt to read?"

Reported Speech. Dr Middleton asked Mr Easy whether he had any idea of sending his boy to school. Mr Easy replied [1]that his great objection to sending a boy to school was that he conceived that the discipline to be enforced was in opposition to all sound sense and common judgment. He added that[2] he himself proposed to teach his son[3] everything. Dr Middleton did not doubt Mr Easy's capability, but warned[4] him that he would always have a difficulty which he could not get over. Mr Easy, he suggested, must be as well aware as the doctor himself that the maternal fondness of Mrs Easy would always be a bar to her husband's[5] intention. That evening Mr Easy told his wife that he had decided to send their son[6] to school that month. Mrs Easy protested that the boy was a mere infant, but[7] her husband reminded[8] her that at nine years it was time the boy learnt to read.

[1] The fresh line, the context, and the words "Dr Middleton" make it clear that Mr Easy is replying to the doctor.

[2] These words could be omitted, but they are advisable here as the remark they introduce is in the nature of an afterthought.

[3] "your boy" in the first sentence justifies this inference.

[4] Better than 'said' or 'added' as it indicates the tone of the following remark.

[5] "his" would be ambiguous.

[6] Better than "Johnny," which has an immediate (present) suggestion.

[7] Note the combining of two closely connected speeches into one sentence in Reported Speech.

[8] "Are you not aware" is not really a question here.

The above examples should make it clear that the changing of Direct to Reported Speech cannot be regarded merely as a matter of automatically applying certain rules. Always read through what you have written to make sure that it forms a piece of sensible English prose.

EXERCISES (C)

Rewrite the following passages in Reported Speech:

1. We talked of living in the country. JOHNSON. No wise man will go to live in the country, unless he has something to do which can be better done in the country. For instance; if he is to shut himself up for a year to study science, it is better to look out to the fields than to an opposite wall. Then, if a man walks out into the country, there is nobody to keep him from walking in again; but if a man walks out in London, he is not sure when he shall walk in again. A great city is, to be sure, the school for studying life; and "The proper study of mankind is man," as Pope observes. BOSWELL. I fancy London is the best place for society; though I have heard that the very first society of Paris is still beyond anything that we have here.
BOSWELL, *Life of Dr Samuel Johnson*

2. "There are cases, of course," said Dr Borden, "in which we can save people's lives without their helping us. But those cases are rare. The strongest of all medicines is faith. And your job is to justify the faith in yourself and your colleagues. I'm afraid this sounds like a sermon, Mr Bradley, but when I see a young man like yourself beginning his medical career, I like him to feel that it's a serious moment. It isn't like any other career. It's full of tremendous responsibilities not only to your patients but also to yourself. Very well, Mr Bradley, that's all. I wish you good luck."
(Associated Examining Board)

3. Mark Twain was once sitting in the saloon bar of an inn listening to a group of men telling rather boastful stories of their adventures. Presently Twain said thoughtfully to one braggart: "Your adventure, sir, reminds me of one of my own—the first time I won a medal for life-saving."
"What happened?" said his hearers.
"A house was on fire, and there was a fellow trapped right up on the fourth floor. I dashed for a ladder and put it against the wall. It was twenty feet too short. The flames were beginning to lick round the window-frame where the poor chap stood, and he was yelling wildly for help. I was at my wit's end."
"Well, what did you do?"

E

"Suddenly I had an inspiration. I found a long coil of rope, climbed up the ladder, and flung one end up to him. 'Tie it round your waist,' I shouted. He did so, and I climbed down the ladder to the ground and braced myself for the appallingly difficult task before me."

There was a pause while the author struggled with his pipe.

"What then?" said a listener at last, impatiently.

"Then I pulled him down," said Twain.

4. Booksellers are Turks and Tartars, when they have poor authors at their beck. Hitherto you have been at arm's length from them. Come not within their grasp. I have known many authors for bread,[1] some repining, others envying the blessed security of a Counting House, all agreeing they would rather have been Tailors, Weavers, what not! rather than the things they were. I have known some starved, some to go mad, one dear friend literally dying in a workhouse. You know not what a rapacious, dishonest set these booksellers are. Ask even Southey, who (a single case almost) has made a fortune by book drudgery, what he has found them. O you know not, may you never know! the miseries of subsisting by authorship. 'Tis a pretty appendage to a situation like yours or mine, but a slavery, worse than all slavery, to be a bookseller's dependant, to drudge your brains for pots of ale and breasts of mutton, to change your free thoughts and voluntary numbers for ungracious task-work. Those fellows hate *us*.

CHARLES LAMB (in a letter to B. Barton)

5. The countenance of Nicholas fell, and he gazed ruefully at the fire.

"Does no other profession occur to you, which a young man of your figure and address could take up easily, and see the world to advantage in?" asked the manager.

"No," said Nicholas, shaking his head.

"Why, then, I'll tell you one," said Mr Crummles, throwing his pipe into the fire, and raising his voice. "The stage."

"The stage!" cried Nicholas, in a voice almost as loud.

"The theatrical profession," said Mr Vincent Crummles. "I am in the theatrical profession myself, my wife is in the theatrical profession, my children are in the theatrical profession. I had a dog that lived and died in it from a puppy; and my chaise-pony goes on in 'Timour the Tartar.' I'll bring you out, and your friend, too. Say the word. I want a novelty."

CHARLES DICKENS, *Nicholas Nickleby*

[1] *I.e.*, authors who write for a living.

6. PAUL. Now, Jack, let me introduce you to my sister.

SARAH. I am always glad to know any friend of my brother's.

JACK. And I'm always glad to know any sister of anybody's. [*Shaking hands with* SARAH] I wish I had a sister.

SARAH. Why?

JACK. I don't know; for many reasons. A sister is a sort of sweetheart, who doesn't require attention; a kind of agreeable housekeeper, whom you can't fall in love with; an agreeable spinster, whom you can't marry. In short, a sister is as nice as—as somebody else's wife, without being so dangerous. But that extraordinary old man. What is he?

PAUL. The Duke.

JACK. What duke?

SARAH. His Grace the Gamekeeper of the Castle.

JACK. The Castle?

PAUL [*pointing*]. You see it there. T. W. ROBERTSON, *Birth*

7. Turn the following passage into Reported Speech. Your version should read smoothly and be composed in such a way that no important fact is omitted.

MR HARDING. It's worth twice the money. I shall have the house and garden, and a larger income than I can possibly want.

ELEANOR [*She takes his arm and makes him sit on the sofa.*] At any rate, you'll have no extravagant daughter to provide for.

MR HARDING. No, my dear; and I shall be rather lonely without her; but we won't think of that now. As regards income I shall have plenty for all I want. I shall have my old house; and I don't mind owning that I have sometimes felt the inconvenience of living in a lodging. Lodgings are very nice for young men, but at my time of life there is a want of—I hardly know what to call it—a want, perhaps, of respectability, in being a lodger.

ELEANOR. Oh, no! I am sure there has been nothing like that. Nobody has thought so; nobody in Barchester has been more respected than you have been. (*Cambridge.*)

Reported Speech to Direct Speech

EXAMPLES

1. R.S. Johnson said that he was very unwilling to read the manuscripts of authors, and give them his opinion. If the authors who applied to him had money, he bade them print boldly without a name; if the authors had written in order to get money, he told them to go to the booksellers and make the best bargain they could.

D.S. Johnson said: "I am very unwilling to read the manuscripts of authors, and give them my opinion. If the authors who apply to me have money, I bid them boldly print without a name; if they have written in order to get money, I tell them to go to the booksellers and make the best bargain they can.

2. R.S. Oliver demanded to know what the matter was. The Dodger replied by hushing him, and asked if he saw an old cove at the bookstall. Oliver wondered if the Dodger meant the old gentleman over the way, and agreed that he did see him. The Dodger considered cryptically that the old man would do, and Master Charley Bates observed tersely that he was a prime plant.

D.S. "What's the matter?" demanded Oliver.
"Hush!" replied the Dodger. "Do you see that old cove at the book-stall?"
"The old gentleman over the way?" said Oliver. "Yes, I see him."
"He'll do," said the Dodger.
"A prime plant," observed Master Charley Bates.

EXERCISES (D)

Put the following passages into Direct Speech:

1. The narrator walked right up to the table and put his hand on the man's shoulder, asking him if he wanted to be killed. The man sprang to his feet. With an exclamation the narrator cried that they were all murderers there, and that it was a ship full of them. They had murdered a boy already. Now it was the turn of the man he was addressing. The man remarked that they hadn't got him yet, and looking at the other curiously, asked if he was willing to stand with him. The narrator said ardently that he would. He assured his companion that he was neither a thief nor a murderer, and repeated that he would stand by him.

2. At noon Lieutenant Masters sent for Hornblower and told him that the captain had ordered the lieutenant to make an inquiry into the duel. He added that he had also been instructed to use his best endeavours to compose the quarrel. Hornblower briefly acknowledged the statement. The lieutenant wanted to know why Hornblower insisted on such satisfaction, for he understood that there had been a few hasty words over wine and cards. Hornblower explained that Mr Simpson had accused him of cheating before witnesses who were not officers of that ship.

3. Paderewski, the great pianist, was once accosted outside a well-known hall by a loudly-dressed man who wanted to know if the pianist could help him to get a couple of tickets. He added

patronisingly that he had often thought of going to one of his recitals and that on this occasion the box office clerk had said that all tickets were sold. Paderewski replied politely that he was sorry that he had no tickets. The man persisted that he was sure that a famous pianist must keep a few seats for his friends. Suddenly Paderewski appeared to recollect that he had just one seat available. The other was mildly annoyed that there were not two, but thought one would be better than nothing, and drawing out his note-book asked how much it would cost. The pianist assured him that he couldn't think of charging for the seat, and with a satisfied smile the man put his note-book away. Then he wanted to know in what part of the hall the seat was situated. Paderewski explained quietly that it was at the piano.

EXERCISES (*E*)

Rewrite the following passages with proper punctuation, giving the conversation in the form of Direct Speech:

1. The vicar was on his way to church when he met the local gamekeeper the vicar wanted to know how it was that he never saw the other at church the gamekeeper looked thoughtful and then explained mysteriously that he didn't wish to make the congregation smaller so he stayed outside the church at this the vicar grew annoyed and said that the man was talking nonsense and went on to demand an explanation with a smile the gamekeeper suggested that if he went to church then half of the congregation would go poaching.

2. Throwing the newspaper on one side Mr Fang commanded the officer to tell him what the fellow before him was charged with the officer explained to the magistrate that he was not charged at all and added that the man appeared against the boy surveying Mr Brownlow contemptuously from head to foot the magistrate repeated the officers words in an inquiring tone and then ordered him to be sworn Mr Brownlow observed that before he was sworn he must beg to say one word which was that without actual experience he really never could have believed at this point he was peremptorily interrupted by an order from Mr Fang to hold his tongue which he indignantly refused to do he was again ordered to hold his tongue immediately on pain of being turned out of the office.

3. Sam begged Mr Moggridges pardon and asked whether he was aware that was Sams chair and paper the poet looked up and said that surely any member of that club was entitled to use the club furniture and read the club Sam interrupted saying that he had only that moment left them Mr Moggridge replied that by a singular

coincidence he had only that moment taken possession of them himself Sam requested him to give them up the poet with some heat said he would do nothing of the kind at that point Sam was seized with the unlucky inspiration of quoting a stanza from one of Mr Moggridges poems which ran forbid the flood to wet thy feet or bind its wrath in chains but never seek to quench the heat that fires a poets veins this drew from the poet an angry exclamation that Sam was no gentleman Sam retorted that he might or might not be a gentleman but he was dashed if Mr Moggridge was a poet.

(Cambridge General Certificate.)

SUMMARY OF CHIEF POINTS

1. Speech or writing is in Direct Speech when it comes to the hearer or reader in its original form.

2. Direct Speech does not necessarily require inverted commas. These should never be used in Reported Speech.

3. In Reported (Indirect) Speech the exact sense of the original passage is given, but not the exact words.

4. In changing Direct to Reported Speech four main alterations are usually involved:

(i) Change of *person*, from 1st or 2nd to 3rd.

(ii) Change of verb *tense*, from present or future to past.

(iii) Change of adverbial or adjectival expressions, from *nearness to remoteness*.

(iv) Inclusion of *introductory words* making clear who is speaking or writing, together with the elimination of any inverted commas which may be in the Direct version.

5. The tone of the original passage should be preserved by the choice of suitable verbs.

6. Ambiguity must be avoided in the use of personal pronouns; if necessary, the original noun should be repeated.

7. Present tense may be retained in the Reported version if a statement relates to a general truth which remains in force at the time of the report.

CHAPTER V

SUMMARIZING (PRÉCIS).

PRÉCIS OF A SENTENCE

A SENTENCE should have a central idea at the heart of it. In a simple, terse sentence this idea will be expressed as briefly as it can be put; but in many sentences additional ideas are attached to the central one, and sometimes all these ideas are heavily clothed in words. It should always be possible, however, to pick out the central idea and set it down briefly.

There are two ways in which this may be done:

(i) If the central idea is expressed in the actual wording of the sentence, then the appropriate words may be selected, the others being discarded.

(ii) Where the central idea is not actually expressed in so many words, it should be possible for the reader to express the gist of the sentence briefly in his own words.

A combination of these two methods may, of course, be used, part of the sentence-summary being expressed in the original wording, the rest having to be expressed in the reader's own words.

EXAMPLE OF (i)

There arrives a day *towards the end of October*—or with luck we may tide over into November—when the wind in the mainsail suddenly takes a winter force, and *we begin to talk of laying up the boat.*

Summary. Towards (*or* About) the end of October we begin to talk of laying up the boat.

[Note that the use of the word "about" covers the reference to November.]

EXAMPLE OF (ii)

I plead guilty to a strong partiality towards that unpopular class of beings, country boys; I have a large acquaintance amongst them, and I can almost say, that I know good of many and harm of none.

Summary. I know and like many country boys, whom I find inoffensive.

EXERCISES (*A*)

Express each of the following sentences more briefly:

1. Women, fortunately perhaps for their happiness and their virtue, have, as compared with men, so few opportunities of acquiring distinction, that it is rare to find a female unconnected with literature, or with history, whose name is remembered after her monument is defaced, and the brass on her coffin-lid corroded.

MARY RUSSELL MITFORD

2. A considerable degree of inducement is necessary to persuade young performers standing at the wicket to advance the left leg in line with the ball and at the same time maintain their bat in an upright position when they encounter the bowling of a player considerably above medium pace.

3. Last summer was, as most of my readers probably remember, one of no small trial to haymakers in general, the weather being what is gently and politely termed "unsettled," which in this pretty climate of ours, during "the leafy month of June " may commonly be construed into cloudy, stormy, drizzly, cold.

MARY RUSSELL MITFORD

4. There are not many situations more incessantly uneasy than that in which the man is placed who is watching an opportunity to speak, without courage to take it when it is offered, and who, though he resolves to give a specimen of his abilities, always finds some reason or other for delaying it to the next minute.

SAMUEL JOHNSON

5. If we clung as devotedly as some philosophers pretend that we do to the abstract idea of life, or were half as frightened as they make out we are, for the subversive accident that ends it all, the trumpets might sound by the hour and no one would follow them into battle —the blue peter might fly at the truck, but who would climb into a sea-going ship?

R. L. STEVENSON

6. Poetry is not a formula which a thousand flappers and hobbledehoys ought to be able to master in a week without any training, and the mere fact that it seems now to be practised with such universal ease is enough to prove that something has gone amiss with our standards.

SIR EDMUND GOSSE

7. The Minister of Education said that he would not in general regard it as the proper task of the schools to give specific training in agriculture, but he welcomed what was being done in many secondary schools, particularly those in rural areas, to give an agricultural background to the instruction, especially in the teaching of handicraft and science.

8. For when the schoolmaster is angry with some other matter, then will he soonest fall to beat his scholar: and though he himself should be punished for his folly, yet must he beat some scholar for his pleasure: though there be no cause for him to do so, nor yet fault in the scholar to deserve so.   ROGER ASCHAM

9. Monoculus—for so, in default of catching his true name, I choose to designate the medical gentleman who now appeared—is a grave, middle-aged person, who, without having studied at the college, or truckled to the pedantry of a diploma, hath employed a great portion of his valuable time in experimental processes upon the bodies of unfortunate fellow-creatures, in whom the vital spark, to mere vulgar thinking, would seem extinct, and lost for ever.
                CHARLES LAMB

[Do not miss the gentle irony here.]

10. If, despite all our efforts to find the way of peace—and God knows I have tried my best—if in spite of all that, we find ourselves forced to embark upon a struggle which is bound to be fraught with suffering and misery for all mankind and the end of which no man can foresee, if that should happen, we shall not be fighting for the political future of a far-away city in a foreign land; we shall be fighting for the preservation of those principles of which I have spoken, the destruction of which would involve the destruction of all possibility of peace and security for the peoples of the world.
                NEVILLE CHAMBERLAIN, *August* 24, 1939

PRÉCIS OF A SHORT PASSAGE

METHOD. 1. Read the passage and find the main theme, which may sometimes be expressed in a topic sentence or phrase (see p. 29).

2. Select the chief points bearing upon this main theme; details which merely illustrate or emphasize the chief points may be ignored for the purpose of the précis, whatever they may contribute to the passage as a piece of literature.

3. Using the points you have noted, write a summary of the passage *in your own words*. It may, of course, be necessary to repeat certain 'key' words from the original passage (*e.g.*, "country boys" in the example below); but for examination purposes it is important to avoid reproducing whole phrases and sentences.

EXAMPLE

I plead guilty to a strong partiality towards that unpopular class of beings, country boys; I have a large acquaintance amongst them, and I can almost say, that I know good of many and harm of none. In general, they are an open, spirited, good-humoured race, with a proneness to embrace the pleasures and eschew the evils of their condition, a capacity for happiness, quite unmatched in a man, or woman, or a girl. They are patient, too, and bear their fate as scape-goats (for all sins whatsoever are laid, as a matter of course, to their door), whether at home or abroad, with amazing resignation; and, considering the many lies of which they are the objects, they tell wonderfully few in return. The worst that can be said of them is, that they seldom, when grown to man's estate, keep the promise of their boyhood; but that is a fault to come—a fault that may not come, and ought not to be anticipated.[1]

Note that a summary of a passage containing several sentences does not consist in a summary of each separate sentence. The substance of a whole sentence may be put in a word or two: thus the second sentence is covered by the words "unmatchably cheerful." The first sentence states the main theme, and is therefore more fully dealt with; but it would, of course, be out-of-place merely to reproduce the summary of this sentence given in Example (ii) on p. 140. Here the sentence does not stand alone, but contributes to a larger unit.

Main Theme. The good qualities of country boys.

Chief Points. I like them—know many—inoffensive. Unmatchably cheerful. Patient under wrongful blame. Tell fewer lies than they are told. Later failure to keep promise of youth—irrelevant.

[1] Mary Russell Mitford, *Our Village.*

Summary. I like country boys, knowing many, and finding them inoffensive, unmatchably cheerful, patient even under wrongful blame, and truthful compared with their defamers. If they later fail to live up to youthful promise, that is irrelevant to the present.

EXERCISES (B)

Write a short summary of the following passages, giving the main theme, the chief points, and then writing the summary in your own words.

1. Feature programmes have played an important part in educational broadcasting, as the B.B.C. Schools Department has developed it. The subject-matter of feature programmes presented in broadcasts to schools varies almost as much as that of adult programmes. The broadcasts may carry up-to-date scientific information, comment on current affairs, reconstruct historical events, dramatize the classics of world literature, or stray into pure fantasy. But, whatever the subject, the feature programme for schools has certain characteristics of its own. This is because, thanks to the co-operation of the schools themselves, it is possible to study the audience of children closely—and children have very decided tastes as listeners. A feature for schools is seldom longer than twenty minutes. The writing is vivid, the appeal to the child's imagination is direct and strong. The treatment is more simple than in adult programmes; there are fewer characters, and the action, instead of being stream-lined, develops step by step in a series of closely linked scenes. This means that the programme may not be as free to range through time and space as an adult feature, but what it loses in sweep it often gains in dramatic intensity.

LAURENCE GILLIAM, *B.B.C. Features*

[Comprehension questions will be found in Chapter VI, Exercise *B*, 1.]

2. I turned out at 0655 and could just hear the shipping forecast above the roar of the wind. "Northwest gale for Biscay." There was no reason to doubt it. I hesitated to go on deck at first, then slid back the hatch enough for head and shoulders. The sight was stupendous and exceptionally impressive from that vantage point of sea level. It was blowing great guns, and a gigantic sea was piling Ossa on Pelion. When she was on the crests of the waves, the whole boat vibrated with the force of the wind, and then did a sickening plunge into the trough before being wrenched upwards like a lift, ready to be assaulted by the following mountains. The odd avalanche

bursting on the topsides did not encourage me to remain long in admiring the pretty view, and the hatch was soon closed.

EDWARD ALLCARD, *Single-handed Passage*

3. In June 1963 Russian scientists accomplished another double space flight. Although this probably added nothing in particular to the technique of space exploration, it created two new records The most striking of these was the inclusion among the cosmonauts
5   of a woman—the first woman ever to venture into space. She was Valentina Tereshkova, 26 years old, and a former textile worker. She had had no experience of piloting an aircraft, but she was a keen amateur parachute jumper who had been training with the other cosmonauts since March 1962, and was a popular member of the
10 team.

The two spaceships were in radio contact with each other as well as with the earth during their flight. At one point they were only three miles apart, but the distance tended to increase. Both cosmonauts returned to earth at about the same time, landing by parachute
15 in Kazakhstan, though about 400 miles from each other. Valentina was on her 49th orbit.

G. F. LAMB, *Modern Adventures in Air and Space*

4. Some people do indeed ask what all this pother is about. If you want to get to the top of Mount Everest why not get an aeroplane to dump you down there? A similar question might be asked of a University crew. If they want to get from Putney to Mortlake why
5   not go in a motor-boat: they would reach there much quicker and more comfortably than by rowing themselves there in a boat. Or the runner in a mile race might be asked why he did not call a taxi-cab.

Man means to *climb* Mount Everest—climb it on his own feet.
10 That is the whole point. Only so does he get that pride in his prowess which is such a satisfaction to his soul. Life would be a poor affair if we relied always on the machine. We are too prone already to trust to science and mechanics instead of exerting our own bodies and our own spirit. And we thereby miss much of that enjoyment
15 in life which exercising our faculties to the full brings with it.

SIR FRANCIS YOUNGHUSBAND, *The Epic of Mount Everest*

5. There was never any intention that Mr Shipton's party, of four English climbers and two New Zealanders, should attempt this year the conquest of the great peak itself. Mount Everest is the inner keep or donjon of a gigantic system of fortifications, in which ward
5   beyond ward, each most formidably embattled, has to be successively reduced. Even the outermost ramparts have to be approached

through many miles of rugged and trackless country, so that the
whole attack must be planned with the strategic elaboration required
in a great military operation—and with the same impossibility of
precision, since the enemies' dispositions are imperfectly known. 10
Victory cannot be expected in a single campaign. Repeated expeditions, conducted with high spirit by some of the finest climbers of the
age, including Mr Shipton himself, have been launched from Tibet,
only to be thrown back from the grim battlements of the north face.
Little attention was paid in those days to the approaches from the 15
south-western side, partly because there the outer obstacles of rock
and ice seemed even more forbidding, partly because for a long time
political difficulties frowned upon any advance through the kingdom
of Nepal. These latter difficulties, however, have now been overcome.

The Times, "Mount Everest Reconnaissance Expedition, 1951"

[Comprehension and Vocabulary questions in Chapters VI, Exercise
B, 2, and VII Exercise B, 1.]

6. As our principal object in coming so far was to see an eruption
of the Great Geyser, it was of course necessary that we should wait
his pleasure; in fact, our movements depended entirely upon his.
For the next two or three days, therefore, like pilgrims round some
ancient shrine, we patiently kept watch; but he scarcely deigned to   5
vouchsafe us the slightest manifestations of his latent energies.
Two or three times the cannonading we had heard immediately
after our arrival recommenced—and once an eruption to the height
of about ten feet occurred; but so brief was its duration, that by
the time we were on the spot, although the tent was not eighty yards 10
distant, all was over. As after every effort of the fountain the water
in the basin mysteriously ebbs back into the funnel, this performance,
though unsatisfactory in itself, gave us an opportunity of approaching the mouth of the pipe, and looking down into its scalded gullet.
In an hour afterwards, the basin was brimful as ever.   15

LORD DUFFERIN, Letters from High Latitudes

[The above passage deals with a famous Geyser in Iceland.]
[Vocabulary question in Chapter VII, Exercise B, 2.]

7. They had gone to bed at the Log Inn, which was the only house
of entertainment in the place, but soon answered to our knocking,
and got some tea for us in a sort of kitchen or common room,
tapestried with old newspapers, pasted against the wall. The bed-
chamber to which my wife and I were shown was a large, low,   5
ghostly room; with a quantity of withered branches on the hearth,
and two doors without any fastening, opposite to each other, both
opening on the black night and wild country, and so contrived that

10 one of them always blew the other open; a novelty in domestic
architecture, which I do not remember to have seen before, and
which I was somewhat disconcerted to have forced on my attention
after getting into bed, as I had a considerable sum of gold for our
travelling expenses. Some of the luggage, however piled against
the panels, soon settled this difficulty.

CHARLES DICKENS, *American Notes*

8. We decided to send to our Ambassador in Berlin instructions
which he was to hand at nine o'clock this morning to the German
Foreign Secretary, and which read as follows:

SIR,

5   In the communication which I had the honour to make to you
on 1st September, I informed you, on the instructions of His
Majesty's Principal Secretary of State for Foreign Affairs, that
unless the German Government were prepared to give His
Majesty's Government in the United Kingdom satisfactory assur-
10   ances that the German Government had suspended all aggressive
action against Poland and were prepared promptly to withdraw
their forces from Polish territory, His Majesty's Government in
the United Kingdom would, without hesitation, fulfil their
obligations to Poland.
15   Although this communication was made more than 24 hours
ago, no reply has been received, but German attacks upon Poland
have been continued and intensified. I have, accordingly, the
honour to inform you that unless not later than 11 a.m., British
Summer Time, to-day, September 3rd, satisfactory assurances to
20   the above effect have been given by the German Government and
have reached His Majesty's Government in London, a state of
war will exist between the two countries as from that hour.

NEVILLE CHAMBERLAIN (*September* 3, 1939)

[Comprehension questions in Chapter VI, Exercise *B*, 3.]

9. It is the mark of the adult male that he likes to travel light;
and however much the ladies of his household will curb the tendency
when they take him on a trip to the briny, for fifty-odd weeks of the
year he is able to have his way. He may carry a load of troubles.
5 His cares may weigh him down; but to all outward appearances his
accoutrements will be limited to a brief case or a carrier bag.
   A man's own disregard of luggage, however, does not rob him
of sympathy for those who are more encumbered. Most people will
stand aside for a fellow passenger who is trying to jockey a mastiff
10 on to the Tube. Few will insist on pushing in front of a charmer

carrying his snakes; and any musician who climbs into a crowded carriage with his double bass can rely, English reticence notwithstanding, on a dozen voices to guide his steps. There should then be some support for the cleaners of school windows at Birkenhead who have asked for travelling expenses. Anyone whom dint of circumstances has forced to carry an aspidistra or a hat stand through the streets will know that the operation can be fraught with considerable embarrassment. A bundle of pea-sticks on the bus can bring some icy stares; but all that is nothing to the difficulties of the man who must travel with a ladder and a bucket of water. 20

The Times Educational Supplement

[Your summary should indicate the spirit in which the above passage is written.]

[Comprehension questions in Chapter VI, Exercise *B*, 4.]

MORE ADVANCED PRÉCIS

PROCEDURE

1. *Read the passage through* two or three times to see what it is about. Write down the main theme. (This will be useful when you come to consider the giving of a title.)

2. *Select the main points.* Most passages can be divided into three or four broad sections each of which marks a stage in the development of the author's theme. Sometimes, though not necessarily, these sections are indicated by paragraphs. They need not be of uniform length.

Give each of these sections a definite heading. These headings will form the skeleton of your précis.

3. *Examine each section*, picking out those points which are essential to the theme, and putting aside (or crossing out) details which are not thus essential. Illustrative examples, repetitions, and figurative expressions can be cut out (for the purposes of précis) or reduced to simple terms. Write down, so far as possible in your own words, the chief points which must be included.

About one-third of your time should be spent on these preliminaries.

4. *Write a rough draft* of your précis, using only the notes you have made. This draft should be written as far as possible in your own language, though essential words or phrases in the original may be retained if they are necessary for exactness or conciseness.

Note the following points:

(i) You are required to bring out the author's meaning: do not express your own ideas.

(ii) It may be necessary, however, to indicate the tone of the original passage. If the author's arguments are light-hearted, for instance, it would be wrong merely to summarize them soberly as if they had been seriously advanced. Similarly, irony must not be interpreted literally. Such a comment as "The author light-heartedly (or ironically) suggests" may be used.

(iii) Generally you will keep the author's points in the original order; but you may rearrange them if this helps the smooth reading of your précis.

(iv) Such interpolations as "The author added" and "He then went on to say" (which do not help to indicate the tone of the passage) are only occasionally necessary. Avoid them if possible; they are clumsy unless they serve a very definite purpose.

(v) Usually a précis should be written in a single paragraph, but if there is a distinct break in the thought of the original passage it may be better to take a new paragraph in your précis.

(vi) If you have neglected to provide an adequate skeleton précis (see 2) you may get a disjointed and ill-proportioned summary.

5. *Compare your draft with the original passage* to make sure that you have not omitted any essential points. Count the number of words you have used. If you have exceeded the number allowed, go through your draft to see what can be eliminated or expressed more briefly. If your summary is

too short you have probably omitted some points which should be included. (It is *possible* to write a précis of any length; if you are invited to write one of, say, about 120 words, do not write one of 80 words.)

6. *Polish up your draft*, with the following points in mind:

(i) Make any necessary alterations arising from 5.

(ii) See that your style is adequate. Avoid jerky, disconnected sentences; each sentence should lead naturally to the next. Never use 'telegraphese' (omitting the definite article, etc.).

(iii) Your summary should be a readable piece of English prose, intelligible to a reader who has not seen the original passage.

7. *Write out your final version* from your rough draft. In the main this will be merely copying, though you should be on the watch to effect any last-minute improvements. Read your summary through carefully when you have finished.

Example of Advanced Précis

A sort of doubt has always hung around the character of Tolstoy, as round the character of Gandhi. He was not a vulgar hypocrite, as some people declared him to be, and he would probably have imposed even greater sacrifices on himself than he did, if he had not been interfered with at every step by the people surrounding him,   5
especially his wife. But on the other hand it is dangerous to take such men as Tolstoy at their disciples' valuation. There is always the possibility—the probability, indeed—that they have done no more than exchange one form of egoism for another. Tolstoy renounced wealth, fame, and privilege; he abjured violence in all   10
its forms and was ready to suffer for doing so; but it is not easy to believe that he abjured the principle of coercion, or at least the *desire* to coerce others. There are families in which the father will say to his child, "You'll get a thick ear if you do that again," while the mother, her eyes brimming over with tears, will take the child   15
in her arms and murmur lovingly, "Now, darling, *is* it kind to Mummy to do that?" And who would maintain that the second method is less tyrannous than the first? The distinction that really matters is not between violence and non-violence, but between

20 having and not having the appetite for power. There are people
    who are convinced of the wickedness both of armies and of police
    forces, but who are nevertheless much more intolerant and inquisi-
    torial in outlook than the normal person who believes that it is
    necessary to use violence in certain circumstances. They will not
25 say to somebody else, "Do this, that or the other or you will go to
    prison," but they will, if they can, get inside his brain and dictate
    his thoughts for him in the minutest particulars. Creeds like paci-
    ficism and anarchism, which seem on the surface to imply a complete
    renunciation of power, rather encourage this habit of mind. For
30 if you have embraced a creed which appears to be free from the
    ordinary dirtiness of politics—a creed from which you yourself
    cannot expect to draw any material advantage—surely that proves
    that you are in the right? And the more you are in the right, the
    more natural that everyone else should be bullied into thinking
35 likewise.[1] [398 *words*]

Write a summary of this passage in about a third of its
present length, giving a precise title.

1. First we read the passage through. We discover that it
is partly about Tolstoy and partly about pacifism and
anarchism. But neither of these topics can be said to be
the main theme. We read the passage through once or twice
more, and the author's main point begins to emerge. The
key to the passage really lies in the sentence in the middle:

> The distinction that really matters is not between violence and
> non-violence, but between having and not having the appetite for
> power.

There is more than one type of coercion; and Tolstoy
represents the non-violent type. This, then, is the main
theme of the passage. For the **title** we might express the
theme as follows: "Tolstoy as typical of the non-violent
idealist who does not abjure coercion."

2. The passage falls into three main sections:

(*a*) Contradictory aspects of Tolstoy's character. (From
    the beginning to "coerce others.")

[1] George Orwell in the essay "Lear, Tolstoy, and the Fool," in *Shooting
an Elephant*.

(b) Two types of coercion. ("There are families" to "minutest particulars.")

(c) Creeds which breed mental coercion. ("Creeds like" to the end.)

3. *Chief points of Section (a):*

Tolstoy's character uncertain—not hypocritical in renunciation of wealth, privilege—ready for even further sacrifices—wife and others prevented. But probably egoistic in another way—opposed to violence but not unwilling to coerce.

[*Note.* Gandhi (line 2) is not referred to again, and has no direct bearing on the rest of the passage.

The reference to wealth and privilege is brought forward from line 10 in order to explain "sacrifices" in line 4.]

Chief points of Section (b):

Coercion shown not only by threat of violence but also by peaceful persuasion. Real point is not violence but desire for power. Some people opposed to use of force by military and police—but even more intolerant—desire to direct thoughts of others.

[*Note.* The reference to the father's and the mother's methods is merely an illustration of two different types of coercion: the point must be expressed in simple terms.

"Do this or you will go to prison" is a repetition of the idea already expressed in the reference to "armies and police forces" in line 21.]

Chief points of Section (c):

Such intolerance encouraged, despite surface appearances, by pacifism, anarchism, etc. Convinced of rectitude—purity of motive, freedom from selfishness—determined other people should accept point of view.

[*Note.* "A creed which appears to be free from the ordinary dirtiness of politics" implies purity of motive.]

4. From the above notes we now make a rough draft:

1   Tolstoy's character was hard to determine. Though not hypo-
2 critical in his sacrificing of wealth and privilege, and though ready
  for even further sacrifices if his wife, among other people, had not
3 prevented this, he was perhaps egoistic in another way. Although
4 opposed to violence, he was not averse to coercion. Coercion may
  be shown not only by threats of violence, but also by peaceful
5 persuasion. The real distinction is not between violence and its
  opposite, but between the desire for power and the freedom from
6 this desire. Some people who are opposed to force in military and
  civil affairs are none the less more intolerant than those who accept
7 the need for force in certain circumstances. They possess the desire
8 to direct the thoughts of others. This intolerance is encouraged,
  despite surface appearances, by creeds like pacifism and anarchism.
9 Persons convinced of the rightness of their cause by its purity of
  motive, and by their own freedom from selfishness, are apt to be
  the more determined that other people should accept their point
  of view

5. We count up the number of words and find that we have used 175. As a third of the original passage would be 132 words we have to reduce our draft by just over 40 words. We examine it sentence by sentence, comparing our draft with the original passage to see that we have interpreted it correctly, and to see where we can cut out a few words here and there without misinterpreting the original:

Sentence 1. This rather suggests that the passage is going to be about Tolstoy's character as a whole. It can be omitted.

Sentence 2. It does not really matter *who* prevented the further sacrifices, so the reference to his wife can go. On re-reading the original passage we wonder if we ought to have retained the point that some people have declared him to be a hypocrite; the words "as sometimes supposed" can be put in brackets after "hypocritical."

Sentence 3. The similarity in construction between the opening of this and the opening of the previous sentence is clumsy. The two sentences can be combined. The clause "he was not averse to coercion" is perhaps more emphatic than is warranted by the words "it is not easy to believe that he abjured the principle of coercion" in the original: "hardly implied a dislike" is nearer the mark.

Sentence 4. May be left as it is.

Sentence 5. This is to some extent a repetition of the previous sentence. The essential point is the reference to the desire for power, and this could be linked to the previous sentence by the expression "if this (peaceful persuasion) is accompanied by the desire for power."

Sentence 6. Comparison with the original shows that the idea contained in the phrase "normal person" has not been brought out. The words "those who accept the need for force in certain circumstances" might be covered by the term "normal non-pacifists," which also covers the previous point.

Sentence 7. May be left as it is.

Sentence 8. May be left as it is. Need we retain the specific mention of "pacifism and anarchism"? Yes; to say merely "certain creeds" would be vague and misleading.

Sentence 9. "By its purity of motive" could be expressed by the keyword "purity" and placed with the parallel word "rightness"; "point of view" is equivalent to the single word "viewpoint."

6. With the above points in mind we rewrite our draft as follows:

Though not hypocritical (as sometimes supposed) in his sacrificing of wealth and privilege, and though he would have made, if not prevented, even further sacrifices, Tolstoy was egoistic in that his opposition to violence hardly implied a dislike of coercion. Coercion may be shown not only by threats of violence but also by peaceful persuasion, if this is accompanied by the desire for power. Some people who are opposed to force in military and civil affairs are yet more intolerant than normal non-pacifists. They possess the desire to direct the thoughts of others. This intolerance is encouraged, despite surface appearances, by creeds like pacifism and anarchism, for persons convinced of the rightness and purity of their cause are apt to be the more determined that others should accept their viewpoint.

This gives us 130 words, which is just about right.

The above example illustrates the way in which a précis
should be tackled. It is not suggested, however, that the
final version is perfect, and a teacher and class may be able
to go through the drafts and suggest further improvements.

EXERCISES ON LONGER PASSAGES (C)

1. Read the following passage carefully:

Even in the days of Nelson, when its heroic exploits were world-
famous, the British Navy was recruited mainly through the activities
of the press-gang. It was a chaotic and atrocious system. Some
form of compulsion was required to man the fighting ships when
5   they were made ready for active service, for conditions of life in the
Royal Navy were too bad to attract the required number of volun-
teers. But the method by which compulsion was applied was the
worst possible. A register of seamen from whom conscripts might
be taken in a just and orderly manner had been proposed some
10   eighty years previously, but nothing had been done. Official incompetence, characteristic of the eighteenth century, was evident in this
as in other activities of the Government. Thus it was that even in
the heroic age of the Navy, the press-gang was the terror of life along
the coasts and in the harbours of England. Bands armed with
15   cutlasses were led by the King's Officers to press into service by force
or fraud mariners and landsmen from ships in harbour or at sea,
from ale-houses and streets. They even interrupted weddings, and
carried off the bridegroom and all the men in the congregation.
Widespread injustice and misery were caused; families were ruined
20   or broken up; and often most unsuitable recruits were obtained.

Once on board the King's ship, the pressed man had too much
reason to bemoan his fate. The food provided by swindling con-
tractors was often disgusting and the pay doled out by a penurious
government was always insufficient. Improvement in these respects
25   followed only as a consequence of the dangerous mutinies of 1797.
Thereafter the sailor's hardships were gradually mitigated, on lines
that had been advocated by the best naval officers for generations
in their struggles with the authorities at home. Nevertheless, it must
stand on record that many of the common sailors who saved Britain
30   in her long struggle with Napoleon were often mutinous, and the
contrast between their grievances and insubordination on the one
hand and their splendid spirit in action on the other may seem
unaccountable.

But there was an explanation. In those days Britain was in mortal
35   danger; her armies had failed; her allies had deserted; and invasion

from the Continent was nearer than it had been for more than seven hundred years. It was only the ceaseless vigilance of the Royal Navy that kept her shores inviolate. The men before the mast knew that in spite of their ill-treatment, which was a disgrace to the humanity and to the gratitude of English public men, the nation as a whole 40 regarded them as its bulwark and its glory and that at the sight of one of Nelson's men with his tarry pigtail the landsman's eye kindled with affection and pride. The country that used them so ill looked confidently to them to protect her, and they knew it.

Make a summary of the *first two paragraphs* [350 words] ("Even in the days of Nelson . . . may seem unaccountable") in *not more than 120 words*, taking care to give a continuous connexion of ideas, and using your own words as far as possible. Failure to keep within the limit of 120 words will be penalized.

(Cambridge)

[Comprehension and Vocabulary exercises on this passage will be found in Chapter VI, Exercise C, 1, and Chapter VII, Exercise B, 3.]

2. The existence of "wild, hairy men" who live high in the snow-fields is widely accepted in parts of Tibet, Sikkim, and Nepal, where they are variously known as *Metohkangmi, Mirka, Mi-Go,* or *Yeti.* About their appearance, as over nomenclature, there are differences —some are black or brown and hairy, others are naked and white- 5 skinned, with long hair on the shoulders and arms. By nature both varieties are uniformly fierce: the smaller ones prey on human beings, the larger on yaks; and the female is only less formidable than the male in that her pendulous breasts impede her running or walking. In common with other spirits of the East, the knee and elbow joints 10 are reversed and the toes point backwards. Either by reason of their savage temperament or on account of some supernatural power, an encounter with one generally means death.

The tracks of these creatures were seen at 20,000 ft. by Colonel Howard Bury's reconnaissance expedition in 1921, and often since 15 then by other explorers. In 1937 a report from Mr Ronald Kaulbeck published in *The Times* revived speculation on the subject; but the question was generally taken to be settled when Mr F. S. Smythe returned from the Garwhal Himalayas with photographs of a set of tracks which were identified by zoologists as those of *Ursus arctos* 20 *isabellinus*—the red mountain bear. The tracks seen and photo-graphed this year by Mr Shipton, however, are pronounced by the authorities of the Natural History Museum definitely not to be those of a bear, but more probably the langur monkey *Presbytis* 25 *entellus achilles*. In support of this theory an interesting exhibit has

been arranged in the central hall of the museum, and is now on view
to the public.
The Times. "The Mount Everest Reconnaissance Expedition, 1951"

Write a summary of this passage, which deals with the so-called
"Abominable Snowmen," in not more than 100 words.

[Comprehension and Vocabulary exercises in Chapter VI, Exercise
D, 1, and Chapter VII, Exercise *B*, 4.]

3. If they have a bull which is the terror of the parish they send
for Ted Allen. For half a sovereign he will round up the bull and
pen him in a yard. For a sovereign he will get him into the bull-cart.

Once, ten years ago, when I first held that enchanted marsh, a
5 bull came suddenly over the sea-wall, trotting towards me. He was
heavy in the shoulders, fleet in the legs, with an eye like a balefire.
He came across the marsh, head up, tail straight as a poker with
the kink in it which means mischief. I cocked my gun.

"Hold you tight," said Ted quietly beside me. "Take me bag and
10 me owd[1] gun. I'll give him a taste of me cosh. Stand you still."

He took an ash cudgel out of his great, blood-stained, feather-
littered, canvas-side bag. He walked towards the bull. The bull
stopped, stared. Allen walked steadily on. Down went the bull on
his knees, horning the earth, tossing tussocks of grass into the air.
15 He moaned and he groaned, that blood-curdling rumble which is
the warning of a charge.

Down flopped Allen on hands and knees. He too bellowed and
grumbled. He grabbed handfuls of earth and grass, flung them high
into the air, and, still muttering, waddled on hands and knees like
20 a fantastic guinea-pig towards the bull.

The bull, unaccustomed to such unwonted acrobatics, rose from
his knees, stared uncertainly at the advancing human quadruped,
lashed a nonplussed tail. Allen still advanced. He crawled to within
two yards of that puzzled bull. Then, springing to his feet, he fetched
25 it a mighty clout on its snout with his ash cosh and, as it wheeled
about, seized it by the tail and galloped after it, belabouring its
buttocks.

"I larnt that little owd[1] trick when I was a titty-totty owd boy no
more'n ten. I was on this here marsh with me catapult, stalkin' a
30 lot of larks on me hands and knees when a herd o' cattle cum
latherin' round me. I worn't no bigger'n tuppence, so I makes a
run at 'em on me hands and knees, and off they goes. All 'cept one.
He was an owd bull. He stood and groaned. So, thinks I, if I can
make the cows run I can make the master too   I hulls up a lot of
35 grass and lets out a horrible row and makes a run at the guv'nor on

[1] Old.

me hands and knees. Blast! he went off like a train! You can allus scare a bull if you do something he can't make out."

J. WENTWORTH-DAY, *Farming Adventure*

Write a summary of the above passage in Reported Speech, using not more than 120 words. Give a title to your summary.
[Comprehension exercise in Chapter VI, Exercise *D*, 2.]

4. In November, 1951, at a specially convened meeting of its members the M.C.C. voted £15,000 to inaugurate and to finance for at least a period of years the M.C.C. Youth Cricket Association. The function of this body is to advise, assist, and co-ordinate the work of the Area Youth Councils or kindred bodies which will tackle 5 by counties the two primary problems of "facilities" and coaching.

Upon the first, the provision of more and better grounds and pitches, neither the M.C.C. nor the counties can of their own resources make any great impact. Something can be, and is being, done to persuade clubs to take local schools under their wing and 10 to put match and practice facilities at their disposal on certain evenings or on Saturday mornings; the Youth Council of our smallest county, Rutland, has already by private subscription improved the playing conditions at some of its schools; a joint committee of the M.C.C. and the National Playing Fields Association 15 is studying alternative types of artificial pitch, has already issued a report on them and is continuing its researches, while the latter body has accepted in principle the policy of contributing to the cost of laying down such wickets. But the real solution of this problem can be reached only by the educational and civic authorities, and it will 20 be one of the most important duties of area councils to impress upon these bodies the lack of cricket facilities for boys in their area and the urgent need to remedy it. It is unfortunate that this task should coincide with a general drive for public economies, but cricket should surely not be regarded as an educational luxury. 25

In its approach to the problem of coaching, the association has rejected the quick and superficially attractive dividend open to it if it concentrated on the naturally gifted minority. Its aim is to provide at least some basic coaching for every boy who wants to play the game, and by doing so to sustain the enthusiasm with which 30 the great majority of small boys begin to play it but which, for lack of such help, tends to evaporate, with the result that they are lost to the game.

H. S. ALTHAM, in *The Times Educational Supplement*

Write a summary of the above passage in not more than 120 words, giving a precise title.

[Comprehension and Vocabulary exercises in Chapter VI, Exercise *D*, 3, and Chapter VII, Exercise *B*, 5.]

5. I shall always be ready to join in the common opinion that our public schools, which have produced so many eminent characters, are the best adapted to the genius and constitution of the English people. A boy of spirit may acquire a previous and practical experi-
5   ence of the world; and his play-fellows may be the future friends of his heart or his interest. In a free intercourse with his equals, the habits of truth, fortitude, and prudence will insensibly be matured. Birth and riches are measured by the standard of personal merit; and the mimic scene of a rebellion has displayed in their true
10   colours the ministers and patriots of a rising generation. Our seminaries of learning do not exactly correspond with the precepts of a Spartan king, 'that the child should be instructed in the arts which will be useful to the man'; since a finished scholar may emerge from the head of Westminster or Eton, in total ignorance of the
15   business and conversation of English gentlemen in the latter end of the eighteenth century. But these schools may assume the merit of teaching all that they pretend to teach, the Latin and Greek languages: they deposit in the hands of a disciple the keys of two valuable chests; nor can he complain, if they are afterwards lost or
20   neglected by his own fault. The necessity of leading in equal ranks so many unequal powers of capacity and application will prolong to eight or ten years the juvenile studies, which might be dispatched in half that time by the skilful master of a single pupil. Yet even the repetition of exercise and discipline contributes to fix in a vacant
25   mind the verbal science of grammar and prosody. For myself, I must be content with a very small share of the civil and literary fruits of a public school. In the space of two years (1749, 1750), interrupted by danger and debility, I painfully climbed into the third form; and my riper age was left to acquire the beauties of the Latin, and the
30   rudiments of the Greek tongue. Instead of audaciously mingling in the sports, the quarrels, and the connexions of our little world, I was still cherished at home under the maternal wing of my aunt; and my removal from Westminster long preceded the approach of manhood.   EDWARD GIBBON, *Autobiography*

Write a summary of the above passage in Reported Speech, using not more than 110 words.

[Comprehension exercise in Chapter VI, Exercise *D*, 7.]

6. MR EDELMAN (Coventry, North) asked the Home Secretary whether he had considered the resolution passed by the Coventry

Federation of Parent-Teacher Associations on June 13, expressing concern at the circulation of sensational American-style comics 5 among British school children, and urging the Government to follow the example of Canada and Sweden in prohibiting their sale and distribution; and what action he proposed to take.

SIR HUGH LUCAS TOOTH, the Under-Secretary, replied that the considered view of the Minister of Education and the Home Secretary was that the best hope for a solution to this problem was for 10 parents and teachers to discourage children from reading these magazines and to direct their attention to more suitable reading matter. The Home Secretary was not satisfied that any action by the Government would be effective short of censorship, which would be unacceptable to public opinion in this country. 15

MR EDELMAN said that this type of reading matter, stimulating the appetite for undesirable violence, had proved to be the favourite reading matter of many juvenile delinquents who had been guilty of crimes of violence, and—while opposing any forms of literary censorship—should not children at least be protected? 20

SIR HUGH LUCAS TOOTH said that all would agree in deploring this type of literature, but it was fair to say that there was no evidence to show that the reading of these publications helped to cause juvenile delinquency one way or another. (Cries of "Oh!")

MR ANTHONY GREENWOOD (Rossendale) said that if the Under- 25 Secretary discussed this problem with any juvenile court magistrate he would find that he was extremely wide of the fact. Would he consider prohibiting the importation of these comics? (Cheers.)

SIR HUGH LUCAS TOOTH said he had no evidence of the fact, but if anyone had any evidence he would be glad to see it and consider it. 30

MRS MANN (Coatbridge and Airdrie) asked if it cost us dollars to import them.

SIR HUGH LUCAS TOOTH said that it did not. There was no question of dollar expenditure for bulk imports from the United States. Nearly all the examples which had come here had been printed 35 either in this country or in other European countries from American material. Since March 11, bulk imports from European countries had not been allowed either.

MR EDELMAN said that reading matter of this kind, printed in America and exported to this country, was on sale in the London 40 shops. He had comics of this kind in his possession (cries of "Oh!" and laughter) which he bought specifically to establish the facts which he indicated in his question. In the circumstances, would the Under-Secretary consult with the Home Secretary, the Board of Trade, and the Chancellor of the Exchequer with a view to restricting 45 importation of them?

SIR HUGH LUCAS TOOTH said he could not guarantee that individual publications of this sort were not brought into the country. If Mr Edelman had any evidence to show there had been bulk imports 50 from America, he would be glad to have it.

The Times Educational Supplement (July 25, 1952)

Reduce the above passage to about 160 words, using Reported Speech. Give your summary a suitable title.

[Comprehension and Vocabulary exercises in Chapter VI, Exercise *D*, 4, and Chapter VII, Exercise *B*, 6.]

7.   (i)

EXAMINERS PLOUGHED

To the Editor of "The Daily Telegraph"

Sir—Your report of the General Certificate examination contained an item of special interest to those who have regard for the niceties of the Queen's English.

Candidates who sat for English Language had the opportunity of writing a composition on "the wisdom or otherwise of not presenting a candidate under 16 to sit for the General Certificate of Education." One would expect a candidate who sat for English Language, no matter what his age, to know that an adverb cannot supply the parallel to a noun.

It ought not to be beyond the wit of an examining body to frame a simple question in an English Language paper without doing violence to the principles of English grammar.

Yours faithfully,

NORMAN COPELAND

(ii)

EXAMINER-BAITING

To the Editor of "The Daily Telegraph"

Sir—When engaging in the pleasant and profitable sport of examiner-baiting, it is well to be sure of one's stance. Otherwise a fall may result.

On the ground that "otherwise" is an adverb, Mr Norman Copeland objects to the phrase "the wisdom or otherwise" in an English Language paper set at an examination for the General Certificate of Education.

He has raised his objection about three-and-a-half centuries too late. Although originally an adverb only, "otherwise" has since the end of the Middle Ages been used substantivally (that is, as a substitute for a noun or adjective of significant content) by authors respectable and otherwise.

Yours faithfully

J. H. JAGGER

(iii)

In *Yesterday he was our hero, but to-day he is otherwise, otherwise* is parallel not to an adverb, but to the noun *hero*; nevertheless grammar is not offended, because the complement of *to be* can be noun, adjective, or adverb, indifferently: *He is a hero, He is dead, He is abroad.* That is why *Governor Sulzer is the hero (or otherwise) of a quaint election story* is excusable; though not itself legitimate, it is a slight and natural extension of something that is legitimate; yet it remains true that *or villain* (or other opposite of hero according to the sense desired) would be better.

H. W. FOWLER, *Modern English Usage*

Give a summary of the above passages in a continuous summary of about 130 words, using Reported Speech. Provide a suitable title.

8. The situation that faces the author, the publisher, and the bookseller is that of sharply rising costs against a background of stationary, if not falling, demand. . . . There may be a long-term trend towards more book-buying, as a result of the spread of education, but it is not a strong force in the short run.   5

In this situation the publishers must either find means of cutting other production costs to balance those which must rise, or they must raise their prices. But neither course will solve all the problems. The possibilities of economies in production are very limited: paper covers instead of cloth boards, for example, would save about $7\frac{1}{2}$p   10 per copy. The public is prepared to accept an inferior presentation —poorer paper, narrower margins, and so on—only if the difference in price is considerable; or if, as in wartime, there is no choice in the matter. In normal times it relates the price of a book to its appearance and, indeed, to its weight. It may ungrudgingly pay the   15 price of a full-length novel for a short book printed on thick paper with wide margins, although the same work produced as a "slender volume" would be thought too dear. There is a danger that any practicable savings along these lines would defeat their own object.

Would it, then, be possible to make inroads into the margins?   20 The usual arrangement for novels is that the author gets between 10 and 20 per cent. of the retail price in royalties; the bookseller's discount is $33\frac{1}{3}$ per cent.; and the publisher gets what remains after

25 paying for printing and overheads. On a book selling at 75p the author will make between 7½p and 15p compared with 25p gross earned by the bookseller. Yet few booksellers make fortunes; like every one else in the trade, they now bemoan their difficulties, as wages, carriage costs, and other overheads rise. Like the publishers, they need more capital for the same volume of business, and expect
30 a return on that capital. More and more they turn to stationery and fancy goods to supplement their earnings. Some publishers are critical of their lack of enterprise and describe them as "book middlemen" rather than booksellers; but they play an indispensable part in the trade and cannot be made to accept a lower discount.

The Economist

Summarize the above passage in about 140 words, giving a short but precise title.

[Vocabulary exercise in Chapter VII, Exercise *B*, 9.]

9. Summarize, *in your own words* as far as possible, the argument of the following passage (which contains about 500 words), reducing it to about 170 words, and assign a short appropriate title. At the end of your précis state the *exact* number of words you have used.

Many critics of our Public Schools consider that far more stress is placed upon achievements in athletics than in the academic sphere, and, in particular, complain against games being compulsory. We are told that it is tyranny to compel boys with no athletic bent to
5 spend hours of misery on a cricket or football field, when, if left to themselves, they would occupy their time far more usefully and enjoyably in some profitable hobby. The drawback to this argument lies in the facile assumption that every non-athlete has some profitable hobby. This is not true; and even if it were, model engineering
10 or stamp-collecting is no substitute for being out in the fresh air, exercising the muscles and having contact with other human beings.
    Yet the youthful idolizing of athletes, which tends to upset a boy's sense of values and may do actual harm to the objects of this hero-worship, is a very different matter. The schoolboy athlete may suffer
15 enormously through being adorned at an early age with a spurious halo of artificial light. From Preparatory School to University his career is a triumphal procession. Then he becomes a legend for the future, one of the greatest products of the school that is proud to call him her son, although she may have taught him nothing except
20 to play football—which he could do already. Not until he hangs up his football boots for the last time and takes his stock out into the open market of the world does he realize his true value—or the lack of it. It would be better for everybody if this tinsel pageantry

were stripped from games at an early stage. The boy who is good at games is entitled to the admiration of his fellows; they will 25 certainly never put the scholar on the pedestal which the athlete now occupies, but the community must lay emphasis on the essential triviality of talents that are merely physical, unless we are willing that our ideals should be those of the jungle.

But there are still those devotees of sport who support the em- 30 phasis laid on school games for much deeper reasons, and for whom sport is a kind of religion. To them the sporting spirit is the finest attitude with which to face life, since its possessor is very conscious of his obligations to the community. Yet the truth about the religion of sport is that it does not deliver the goods; it fails to produce 35 sportsmen. In actual fact, games have practically no effect on character, for a selfish man will play his games selfishly in spite of all that has been talked about the team-spirit, while a chivalrous man will be chivalrous in his games. Games afford an opportunity for showing the spirit within; they are a vehicle for virtue or for vice; 40 and it is for this that we should value them, not as some miraculous process for making a bad man good or a crooked man straight. If we support the system of compulsory games, let it be for the right reasons.

(*London.*)

[Comprehension and Vocabulary exercises in Chapter VI, Exercise *D*, 5, and Chapter VII, Exercise *B*, 8.]

10. If legend be correct, the championships at Wimbledon take place because 75 years ago the pony roller at the All-England club was in grievous need of repair. Most British institutions had obscure beginnings and contained the seeds of their own growth. Lawn tennis came to the All-England Croquet Club as an afterthought, 5 an innovation due to an empty treasury.

It is reputed—the actual figures are no longer extant—that the first Wimbledon Championship of 1877 made a profit of £10. Thus encouraged, with the roller again in good order and the croquet hoops glistening in fresh paint, the committee decided to keep on a 10 good thing. And a very good thing it has proved. Not only the Wimbledon Championships, with their world-wide interest and an aggregate attendance of over a quarter of a million, but the game of lawn tennis grew from that opening meeting in July three-quarters of a century ago. In that first year, 1877, play was suspended for 15 the duration of the Eton and Harrow cricket match at Lord's, and the winner, Spencer W. Gore, served underhand because neither he nor the 21 other competitors had thought of doing otherwise.

Lawn tennis owes much to the first championship committee. Thanks to Julian Marshall, Henry Jones, C. G. Heathcote, and 20

J. H. Walsh, the game took the right road, avoiding the pitfalls of
extravagance as a new-fangled stunt. The rules they adopted have
remained the bedrock of the game. They decreed the size and shape
of the court, that one service fault should be permitted, and that
25 scoring should follow the venerable practice of royal tennis.

The pressure of finance has always remained. Were it not for
Wimbledon the present administration of the British game could
hardly continue. It is no longer a matter of a few pounds to repair
a damaged roller, but of thousands to run coaching schemes, to send
30 teams abroad, to make loans to clubs. From Wimbledon the Lawn
Tennis Association—a body younger than the All-England Club—
received £22,294 in 1950, £26,022 in 1949. Its estimated share of
the 1951 profits was £29,000 No doubt the Club, with heavy
commitments to debenture holders who financed the building of
35 the present ground, opened in 1922, received as much.

Championship meetings of Victorian days had the air of a garden
party. Modern Wimbledon, progressive in that it looks to the
future, but with an eye cast back always on its traditions, has never
lost the atmosphere. More perhaps than some of the players, the
40 institution has retained an amateur spirit. In the course of years
Wimbledon has become something more than a lawn tennis tourna-
ment, though as such, of course, it is the most important in the
world. It has become an occasion, a part of British life, a social
phenomenon that will doubtless puzzle the historian of the future.[1]

The Daily Telegraph

Summarize the above passage in about one-third of its present length
(about 475 words). Give your summary a title.

[Comprehension exercises in Chapter VI, Exercise D 6.]

11. Every one will admit that of all the disgusting labours of life,
the labour of lexicon and dictionary is the most intolerable. Nor is
there a greater object of compassion than a fine boy, full of animal
spirits, set down on a bright sunny day, with a heap of unknown
5 words before him, to be turned into English, before supper, by the
help of a ponderous dictionary alone. The object in looking into
a dictionary can only be to exchange an unknown sound for one
that is known. Now, it seems indisputable that the sooner this
exchange is made the better. The greater the number of such
10 exchanges which can be made in a given time, the greater is the
progress. Would it not be of advantage if the dictionary at once
opened at the required page, and if a self-moving index at once
pointed to the requisite word? Is any advantage gained to the world

[1] The first sentence in the above passage has been slightly altered in
order to avoid a purely topical reference.

by the time employed first in finding the letter P, and then in finding
the three guiding letters PRI? This appears to us to be pure loss 15
of time, justifiable only if it be inevitable. And even after this is
done, what an infinite multitude of difficulties are heaped at once
upon the wretched beginner! Instead of being reserved for his
greater skill and maturity in the language, he must employ himself
in discovering in which of many senses which his dictionary presents 20
the word is to be used; in considering the case of the substantive,
and the syntactical arrangement in which it is to be placed, and the
relation it bears to other words. The loss of time in the merely
mechanical part of the old plan is immense. We doubt very much if
an average boy, between ten and fourteen, will look out or find 25
more than sixty words in an hour; we say nothing at present of the
time employed in thinking of the meaning of each word when he
has found it, but of the mere naked discovery of the word in lexicon
or dictionary. It must be remembered, we say an *average* boy—not
what Master Evans, the show boy, can do, nor what Master 30
Macarthy, the boy who is whipped every day, can do, but some boy
between Macarthy and Evans; and not what this medium boy can
do while his superior is frowning over him; but what he actually
does when left in the midst of noisy boys, and with a recollection
that by sending to the neighbouring shop, he can obtain any quantity 35
of unripe gooseberries upon credit. Now if this statement be true,
and if there are 10,000 words in the Gospel of St John, here are
160 hours employed in the mere digital process of turning over
leaves! But in much less time than this, any boy of average quickness
might learn, by the Hamiltonian method, to construe the whole four 40
Gospels, with the greatest accuracy, and the most scrupulous correct-
ness. The interlineal translation of course spares the trouble and
time of this mehanical labour. Immediately under the Italian word
is placed the English word. The unknown sound therefore is
instantly exchanged for one that is known. The labour here spared 45
is of the most irksome nature; and it is spared at a time of life the
most averse to such labour; and so painful is this labour to many
boys, that it forms an insuperable obstacle to their progress. They
prefer to be flogged or to be sent to sea. It is useless to say of any
medicine that it is valuable, if it be so nauseous that the patient 50
flings it away. You must give me, not the best medicine you have
in your shop, but the best you can get me to take.
    SYDNEY SMITH, in the *Edinburgh Review*, 1826

Write a summary, in continuous prose, of the above passage, using
not more than 170 words. Give your summary a title.
[Vocabulary exercise in Chapter VII, Exercise *B*, 10.]

F

12. There is a tendency to-day to regard pupils as falling into two distinct categories. One is the 'bookish' group: these may be given their books and left to pore over them. The other, much larger, is the 'non-academic' group: these must be protected from the tyranny of book-learning, and nourished instead with films, film-strips, charts, pictures, models, comic strips, radio lessons, television, visits, and endless 'activities.' Nothing must be done to make the child who finds reading less easy than watching films or making models feel that he is in any way at a disadvantage compared with those of his companions who have mastered the intricacies of print, and who find the school library (if there is one) as interesting as the workshop. If a boy cannot read the plays of Shakespeare, then let him be assured that it is just as good to make a model of the Globe Theatre. If he finds any difficulty in reading *Treasure Island*, let him draw a map of the island instead and be told that he is not really missing anything. He that cannot write, let him draw, as his caveman ancestors did; and let no teacher dare suggest that he is one whit inferior to his more literate fellows.

This is hardly an unfair summary of the attitude of those modern educationists who regard the essentials of schooling as being activity methods and visual aids. The term 'bookish' has come to be used in educational circles in a derogatory sense, or at least with a depreciatory implication. The "bookish minority"—a favourite phrase in official reports—is commonly referred to as though it comprised a queer collection of eccentrics who persist in clinging to an outmoded convention. The teacher who is a book-lover is made to feel guilty of a secret vice. The author of a well-known and widely-read book on the New Teaching, for instance, reminds teachers that they "were brought up in an academic tradition, and may find that for their part they prefer to read rather than to look." They must not, it is implied, allow this old-fashioned reading habit to influence their teaching of the modern child who cannot be bothered with print and who prefers to lounge in the plush seats of the local cinema.

It would be foolish to condemn the use of films, models, and manual activities in modern education. They have a place, and a useful one—for 'bookish' children as well as for the others. But these things are not substitutes for books, and there is no need to advocate them by playing down the value of book-learning. There are no very apparent signs that we are in danger of becoming a nation of bookworms. Why, then, is it considered necessary to boost Plasticine by belittling print?

Books are not a feeble substitute for life: at their highest they are one of its noblest manifestations. They are the life-blood of civilization. There can be no education worthy the name which does

not have its roots in literature. Most of us, it is true, have met
bookish men and women who were not educated, and unlettered
countryfolk who had a wisdom gained from the land and not from
the library; but these anomalies do not invalidate the general truth
that without books and without literature civilized society could not
exist. Without books we should know almost nothing of man's
attempts to solve the mysteries of the universe; almost nothing of
the story of man's discovery of his own globe and of himself; almost
nothing of the progress of science and medicine. Through books
most of our traditional standards of thought and moral feeling have
been transmitted from one era to another. Our spiritual values as
well as our intellectual discoveries owe their permanence largely to
manuscripts and printed books.

From "Books and Education," an article in *Books*

Write a summary of the above passage in not more than 180 words.

13. LADY TEAZLE. Sir Peter, I hope you haven't been quarrelling
with Maria. It is not using me well to be ill-humoured when I am
not by.

SIR PETER. Ah, Lady Teazle, you might have the power to make
me good-humoured at all times.

LADY TEAZLE. I am sure I wish I had; for I want you to be in a
charming sweet temper at this moment. Do be good-humoured
now, and let me have two hundred pounds, will you?

SIR PETER. Two hundred pounds; what, an't I to be in a good
humour without paying for it! But speak to me thus, and i' faith
there's nothing I could refuse you. You shall have it; but seal me
a bond for the repayment.

LADY TEAZLE. Oh, no—there—my note of hand will do as well.
[*Offering her hand.*

SIR PETER. And you shall no longer reproach me with not giving
you an independent settlement. I mean shortly to surprise you; but
shall we always live thus, hey?

LADY TEAZLE. If you please. I'm sure I don't care how soon we
leave off quarrelling, provided you'll own you were tired first.

SIR PETER. Well—then let our future contest be, who shall be
most obliging.

LADY TEAZLE. I assure you, Sir Peter, good nature becomes you.
You look now as you did before we were married, when you used
to walk with me under the elms, and tell me stories of what a gallant
you were in your youth, and chuck me under the chin, you would;
and ask me if I thought I could love an old fellow, who would deny
me nothing—didn't you?

SIR PETER. Yes, yes, and you were as kind and attentive——

LADY TEAZLE. Ay, so I was, and would always take your part, when my acquaintance used to abuse you, and turn you into ridicule.

SIR PETER. Indeed!

LADY TEAZLE. Ay, and when my cousin Sophy has called you a stiff, peevish old bachelor, and laughed at me for thinking of marrying one who might be my father, I have always defended you. and said, I didn't think you so ugly by any means.

SIR PETER. Thank you.

LADY TEAZLE. And I dared say you'd make a very good sort of husband.

SIR PETER. And you prophesied right; and we shall now be the happiest couple——

LADY TEAZLE. And never differ again?

SIR PETER. No, never . . . though at the same time, my dear Lady Teazle, you must watch your temper very seriously; for in all our little quarrels, my dear, if you recollect, my love, you always began first.

LADY TEAZLE. I beg your pardon, my dear Sir Peter: ndeed, *you* always gave the provocation.

SIR PETER. Now, see, my angel! take care—contradicting isn't the way to keep friends.

LADY TEAZLE. Then, don't you begin it, my love!

SIR PETER. There, now! you—you are going on. You don't perceive, my life, that you are just doing the very thing which you know always makes me angry.

LADY TEAZLE. Nay, you know if you will be angry without any reason, my dear——

SIR PETER. There! Now you want to quarrel again.

LADY TEAZLE. No, I'm sure I don't; but if you will be so peevish——

SIR PETER. There, now! Who begins first?

LADY TEAZLE. Why you to be sure. I said nothing—but there's no bearing your temper.

SIR PETER. No, no, madam, the fault's in your own temper.

LADY TEAZLE. Ay, you are just what my cousin Sophy said you would be.

SIR PETER. Your cousin Sophy is a forward impertinent gipsy.

LADY TEAZLE. You are a great bear I am sure, to abuse my relations.

SIR PETER. Now may all the plagues of marriage be doubled on me, if ever I try to be friends with you any more!

LADY TEAZLE. So much the better!

SIR PETER. No, no, madam; 'tis evident you never cared a pin for me, and I was a madman to marry you—a pert, rural coquette, that had refused half the honest squires in the neighbourhood!

LADY TEAZLE. And I am sure I was a fool to marry you—an old dangling bachelor, who was single at fifty only because he never could meet with anyone who would have him.

R. B. SHERIDAN, *The School for Scandal*

Write a summary in continuous prose of the above extract, using Reported Speech. Your summary should be in your own words, and should not exceed 150 words.

14. The scientific synthesis of new compounds, and the recovery of valuable materials from the by-products and waste products of industrial processes, are the main basis on which the substitution of home-produced raw materials for imports will have to rest. In many of its branches, however, the synthesis of new materials starts from a coal product, and any study of the problem brings out once more the imperative need for a higher output from the pits. This is a fundamental condition of lasting economic recovery, and there is no way round it.

Familiar examples of synthetic products are rayon, derived from wood-pulp; nylon, derived from coal; and plastics, derived chiefly from coal and oil. Since wood-pulp and oil are imports, rayon and plastics may not sound like useful import-savers, but they are. With rayon, the point is that, at current prices, a given value of imported wood-pulp yields exports of a much higher value than can be got from the same amount of imported cotton or wool. As regards plastics, we have anyway to import oil as a source of fuel, and we are starting now to import much more of it in the crude form and to refine it here. The by-products of refining are thus becoming available to feed our plastics industry—for instance, in providing substitutes for lead in piping systems and the sheathing of electric cables, and in replacing leather with much longer-lasting compounds in the soles of boots and shoes.

There is still a popular habit of looking down on synthetic substitutes and making fun of *Ersatz*. This is not only antiquated and stupid; it is in our position positively suicidal. It amounts to a Luddite refusal to recognize the second industrial revolution, which is now achieving in the raw-material field what the first industrial revolution achieved in the field of manufacture.

As an example of the recovery of valuable materials from waste, who would have thought ten years ago that ordinary flue-sweepings could become the source of a most important raw material? Yet now germanium, which promises to revolutionize the amplifying valves used in radio and other electronic instruments, need no longer be expensively imported, for it is actually being won from the soot in our industrial chimneys.

These examples are not freakish—similar discoveries have been coming thick and fast during the last decade and others appear to be just round the corner—nor are they windfalls which the community need passively wait for. Modern science is in itself a major industry. It demands heavy capital and complex organization for its research and experimental work; on the other hand, it will generally, within reasonable limits, produce what is asked of it if the necessary talent and capital are assembled for a specific purpose. The organization of science for the production of synthetic materials and the treatment of by-products is a key operation in Britain's struggle to reduce her dependence on imported raw materials—a struggle on which her future solvency may largely depend.

The Observer

Write a summary of the above passage in about 160 words, supplying a suitable title.

Other passages suitable for précis will be found on pp. 32–33, 35–39, 52–54, 58–59, and in *Précis and Comprehension for General Certificate*, by Lamb and FitzHugh (Harrap).

CHAPTER VI

COMPREHENSION AND STYLE

EVERY time you summarize a passage you must also perform an exercise in comprehension: for if you do not comprehend what the author has written you cannot summarize it. You probably also show some appreciation of literary style, for unless you can appreciate the author's attitude of mind, as revealed by his style, your summary can hardly convey his meaning.

None the less, comprehension and the appreciation of literary style do not necessarily involve précis-writing; and many examining bodies test these separately.

COMPREHENSION TESTS

A comprehension test of some kind often forms part of an English Language paper. Sometimes the questions are based on the passage set for précis. Whether or not you are working for an examination, you will find it a valuable exercise in intelligent reading to examine in detail sections of a passage in order to make sure that you have fully grasped the author's meaning and intention, and a useful exercise in expression to explain these points in your own words. Précis, valuable though it is as an exercise in grasping the main essentials, does not require quite the same analytical study.

Answers to comprehension questions should be full enough to offer an adequate explanation of the point raised in the question, but they should be strictly relevant and should never be long-winded. As a rule the answer should be as far as possible in your own words, and should consist of a complete sentence or complete sentences. You should not introduce into your answer any material that is not in

the original passage, unless the question specifically invites
you to do so. Some examining bodies restrict the answer to
thirty words or two or three lines. In any case it should
rarely exceed four or five lines.

Examples of Comprehension Answers

[These questions are based on the passage on p. 149.]

(i) "Tolstoy was not a vulgar hypocrite." Why, is it implied,
have some people supposed him to be one?

ANSWER

The implication in lines 3 and 4 is that Tolstoy's failure to make
greater personal sacrifices has led some people to assume that his
professed unselfishness was hypocritical.

(ii) On what grounds does the author refute the charge of hy-
pocrisy?

ANSWER

The author maintains that the probable reason for Tolstoy's
failure to make greater sacrifices was the interference of his companions, especially his wife.

(iii) On what grounds does the author suggest that Tolstoy was
none the less selfish?

ANSWER

The author suggests that Tolstoy replaced the egoistic desire for
wealth, fame, and privilege by the desire to coerce others to think
as he did.

(iv) What is the point of the sentence *There are families   . . do
that?*" on lines 13–17?

ANSWER

This sentence illustrates the author's point that there is more than
one method of coercion—the oblique as well as the direct—and that
both are equally "tyrannous".

EXERCISES (*A*)

Answer concisely the following questions after reading carefully the
passage concerned:

1. Read the passage in Exercise I, p. 133.

(i) What objection did Johnson offer to living in the country?

(ii) On what condition did he consider living in the country preferable to living in the town?

(iii) Express in your own words what is liable to happen when a man "walks out in London".

(iv) What is the point of the quotation from Pope?

(v) Do you think that Boswell contradicts himself in his comment?

2. Read the passage in Exercise 4, p. 134.

(i) What does Lamb mean by "Turks and Tartars"?

(ii) Is there any indication that the term "bookseller" has a meaning rather different from its modern meaning?

(iii) What advice did Lamb give to Barton? Give the answer in your own words.

(iv) What evidence did Lamb bring forward to support his advice?

(v) In what respect, according to Lamb, did Southey differ from other authors, and in what respect did he resemble them?

(vi) In what circumstances did Lamb consider authorship tolerable?

3. Read the passage in Exercise 5 on p. 134.

(i) From the evidence of the passage, what appears to have been the cause of Nicholas's rueful expression (line 1)?

(ii) What impression is given of Mr Crummles's attitude to his profession?

(iii) What proposal does he make to Nicholas?

(iv) Why does he make it?

EXERCISES (B)

The following questions relate to certain passages in the short passages for précis on pp. 143 to 147. Answer them as far as possible in complete statements in your own words.

1. Read the passage in Exercise 1.

(i) In what respect are feature programmes for schools similar to those for adults?

(ii) Name four respects in which school feature programmes differ from adult feature programmes.

(iii) State the chief gain and the chief loss arising from these differences (from the point of view of the school programme).

(iv) What has particularly enabled the feature programme for schools to develop its own characteristics?

(v) Explain what is meant by "streamlined" in lines 15 and 16.

2. Read the passage in Exercise 5.

(i) Why was there no intention that Shipton's party should attempt the conquest of Everest in 1951?

(ii) To what is Everest likened? In what respect is the comparison particularly apt?

(iii) In what particular respect is it implied (though not actually stated) that the expedition· under consideration differs completely from previous expeditions?

(iv) What connexion is there between politics and Everest expeditions?

3. Read the passage in Exercise 8.

(i) By what means did Neville Chamberlain's letter reach the German Government?

(ii) What conditions were required of the German Government?

(iii) What evidence is there that the German Government was likely to disregard the letter?

(iv) How long was the German Government given to make a final communication with the British Government?

(v) Name one expression (dictated by the conventions of such formal communications) which seems quite out of keeping with the tone of the letter.

4. Read the passage in Exercise 9.

(i) What difference is suggested between the male and female members of a family?

(ii) What difference is it suggested may exist between a man's internal and external self?

(iii) Name the first three examples of encumbered passengers. How can you tell whether or not they are intended to be taken seriously?

(iv) Illustrate the author's use of climax in the passage.

(v) In what spirit is the passage written? How do you know this?

EXERCISES (C)

1. Read the précis passage on p. 154, Exercise 1. Then answer concisely, and as far as possible in your own words, the following questions. Each answer should consist of a complete sentence or complete sentences, and must not exceed *thirty* words. You must not introduce into your answers any material which is not contained in the passage.

(i) Why did the writer describe the press-gang as atrocious and chaotic?

(ii) What contributed to bring about a gradual improvement in the lot of the common sailor at sea?

(iii) What compensations had the common sailor of Nelson's time to offset against the unsatisfactory conditions of his service?

(iv) How did the attitude of the people of England at large towards the seamen of the Royal Navy differ from that of the Government and public men? *(Cambridge)*

2. The endeavour to maintain proper standards of fairness in journalism must be pursued. It is fatally easy for the journalist to deviate from the straight path. There is his natural desire to "make a story," and the insidious temptation to twist facts to square with his paper's policy. Both are as indefensible as the framing of mis- 5 leading headlines for the sake of effect. The conscientious journalist must check any tendency to bías, and guard against the dangers inherent in personal antipathies or friendships, and in traditional opposition between rival schools of thought. When a political opponent, whose stupidity provokes attack, makes an effective 10 speech, honesty requires that he be given credit for it. Where personal relationships might make it easier and more congenial to keep silent than to criticize, the journalist must never forget his duty to the public and the supreme importance of recording the truth.

Answer concisely, and as far as possible in your own words, the following questions, in accordance with the directions given in Exercise *C*, 1, above:

(i) What problems, arising from his profession, may the journalist encounter in trying to maintain proper standards of fairness in journalism?

(ii) What other considerations may make it hard for a journalist to be impartial?

(iii) When may a journalist have to act against his own inclinations? *(Cambridge)*

3. Read the following passage carefully and then answer the questions on it:

There exists in many minds an obscure prejudice against the choice of books as presents. It is an unfortunate reluctance, for the giver of a well-chosen book is blessed in this, as in no other, gift. He may carry it home with him and may himself enjoy it before bidding it farewell; he may write in it his own as well as his friend's 5 name, thus perpetuating his good wishes and earning for himself remembrance on many an evening far away. A fly-leaf inscription,

re-discovered long after the writer of it is forgotten, proves again
and again to be the kindliest of epitaphs. And if the buyer of a book
10 be of a practical mind and little careful for his own epitaph, he may
yet be pleased after his own manner. He may wrap up his gift with
less labour of brown paper than is required by any other offering,
for none is more conveniently shaped; and he may be glad in the
thought that his few shillings have helped the art of letters to its not
15 too frequent reward. How much more amusing to send on its
adventures some essay in immortality, however imperfect, than to
lavish upon a well-fed acquaintance goods which are by name
"perishable" and which he may have weighed out to him, in return
for his own shillings, from any tradesman's pan!
20   But could he not equally have bought our volume over any
bookseller's counter? Indeed he could not. He could have bought
the same cigars, the same chocolates; but our own personality
dwells in the choice of the book we send, and that is a jewel not to
be had for all the shillings in the world. With works of art—and
25 none is more accessible than a book—we may send a part of ourselves. Therein lies the peculiarity and the danger of the gift;
therein lies also the pleasure of the giving.

(a) Summarize, in about 60 of your own words, all the advantages,
according to the passage, of choosing a book as a present.

(b) Explain the meaning in the passage of the following expressions:

   (i) "unfortunate reluctance" (line 2).
   (ii) "perpetuating his good wishes" (line 6).
   (iii) "little careful for his own epitaph" (line 10).

(c) What do you think is meant by (i) "he may yet be pleased after
his own manner" (lines 10–11); (ii) "therein lies . . the danger of
the gift" (line 26)?

(d) What do you think the writer implies by the use of the word
"adventures" in line 16?

(e) How far do you think that "jewel" (line 23) is an apt metaphor?

(f) For each of the following words, as used in the passage, give
one word or phrase with the same meaning: "obscure" (line 1),
(ii) "prejudice" (line 1), (iii) "lavish" (line 17), (iv) "accessible" (line
25).

                              (Northern Universities General Certificate.)

EXERCISES (D)

The following questions relate to the précis passages on pp. 154 to
170. Answer them in complete statements and as far as possible in
your own words.

1. Read the passage in Exercise 2.

(i) Why do you suppose the words "wild, hairy men" (line 1) are put in inverted commas?

(ii) In what respects are these creatures said to differ, and in what respects are they said to be alike?

(iii) "An encounter with one generally means death" (line 13). Does this mean that the writer believes this to be a fact? Explain how you arrive at your answer.

(iv) What theories have been put forward to explain the tracks of these creatures?

(v) In what way have explorers endeavoured to provide evidence about the creatures?

2. Read the passage in Exercise 3.

(i) What particular aspects of the approaching bull first suggested to the author that the animal was dangerous?

(ii) What particular adjective is Allen rather fond of using? Mention one place where he uses it in a way that would be quite out of place in ordinary English.

(iii) Explain Allen's method of getting close to the bull.

(iv) Express in your own words the principle behind Allen's curious actions.

(v) Comment on Allen's simile concerning his youthful size (line 31).

3. Read the passage in Exercise 4.

(i) How is the M.C.C. proposing to help young cricketers?

(ii) What other bodies is it suggested must play their part?

(iii) What special and immediate difficulty does the author perceive, and how does he attempt to dispose of it?

(iv) What two policies are open to the Youth Cricket Association with regard to coaching, and which one does it propose to follow?

4. Read the passage in Exercise 6.

(i) What objections to American-style comics were raised during the discussion?

(ii) What evidence, if any, of the bad influence of these comics was actually brought forward during the discussion, and what was the attitude of the Under-Secretary on this matter?

(iii) What solutions to the problem did the Under-Secretary put forward, and on whose behalf?

(iv) State three ways, mentioned in the discussion, in which the comics might appear in this country.

(v) Explain "(cries of 'Oh!' and laughter)" in lines 41 and 42.

5. Read the passage in Exercise 9.

(i) Why does the writer consider even a "profitable hobby" no substitute for games?

(ii) Explain what the author means by "a spurious halo of artificial light" (lines 15 and 16), bringing out the significance of *spurious* and *artificial*.

(iii) What, in the author's opinion, are "the ideals of the jungle" (line 29)?

(iv) State, with a reason, whether you agree or disagree with the statement: "they will certainly never put the scholar on the pedestal which the athlete now occupies" (lines 25–27).

(v) What do you understand by "Obligations to the community" (line 34)? Give *two* examples of such obligations, not necessarily from the passage.

(*London*)

6. Read the passage in Exercise 10.

(i) In what respect is it true that damage to a roller at a croquet club has brought about the present Wimbledon tennis championships?

(ii) What does lawn tennis owe to the first championship committee?

(iii) Explain the significance of the words "the British game" (line 27).

(iv) Why could the present administration of the game hardly continue if it were not for Wimbledon?

(v) From the evidence of the passage, what connexions has the present game of lawn tennis with the Victorian game?

7. Read the passage in Exercise 5.

(i) What does Gibbon mean by the expression "the future friends . . of his interest" (lines 5 and 6)?

(ii) In what sense is the word "insensibly" (line 7) used?

(iii) Suggest one word for what Gibbon means by "seminaries of learning" (line 11).

(iv) What is meant by "a finished scholar" (line 13)?

(v) What things of value, according to Gibbon, are locked up in 'two valuable chests" (lines 18 and 19)?

(vi) Say very briefly in your own words how Gibbon suggests that a foolish or idle boy be taught grammar.

(vii) What does "debility" (line 28) mean?

(viii) What expression does Gibbon use to refer to the period of his manhood?

(*Oxford*)

[The passage set for précis in Exercise 5 is slightly longer than the passage set for comprehension in the Oxford examination.]

LITERARY STYLE

Do not imagine that style is an ornament that literary people attach to their writing. All writing has some kind of style, and it is good or bad according to whether or not it is suitable to its purpose; though it remains true that some authors are so gifted in the handling of words that whatever they write is delightful to read. Such authors are sometimes, though misleadingly, known as 'stylists'.

The well-known saying "The style is the man himself" is basically true; but it must not be taken as meaning that every author has certain peculiarities of expression that he always uses, or that every author has a single, unvarying style. Johnson was not always solemnly rhetorical, nor was Charles Lamb always quaint and whimsical. A good author will have many styles, though his own personality will reveal itself in each. Style is the way an author expresses himself on a given occasion. It is something inherent in his way of communicating his ideas; it is not a kind of literary garment that he puts on for formal occasions.

It is unwise to try to apply a label to every style (*e.g.*, the graceful style, the plain style, the whimsical style, the forceful style, etc.). Good writing cannot be so simplified, for it is the expression of that highly complex thing, a human personality.

In examining an author's style, as revealed in a given passage, there are three essential questions to be put:

(1) What has the author tried to achieve?
(2) How has he tried to achieve it?
(3) How far has he succeeded?

It needs to be added that to answer these questions fully will require a wisdom at least as great as the author's; but that need not deter us from doing the best we can. If we follow the plan of seeking the author's intention we shall at least avoid the kind of false criticism which (for example) compares a passage from Milton's *Paradise Lost* with a lyric by Carew or Donne and arrives at the conclusion that Milton's writing is 'good' because it is 'sincere' and 'sublime,' and that the writing of Carew or Donne is 'bad' because it is 'insincere'.

Other points which may be considered in estimating the 'style' of a given passage are: vividness, aptness in choice of words and images, simplicity, euphony, sincerity, authority, fluency, crispness, wit, pungency. We must always remember that we cannot adequately gauge an author's quality from a short passage: it may need a long and thoughtful study of a whole book, or of several books, before we can properly appreciate his worth. Some authors, moreover, are more easily enjoyed than others. Dickens, for example, offers little difficulty; but few readers can appreciate the excellence of Charles Lamb or Samuel Johnson on a first acquaintance.

For brief examples of comments on the style of a given passage see pp. 57–58 and p. 63, Example 3.

EXERCISES

1. Consider the following passages from the point of view of literary style, and write a short comment on each:

    (a) A Summer's Day on the Farm, p. 32.
    (b) Description of the Isle of Wight, pp. 58–59.
    (c) The Electric Bell, p. 68.
    (d) Chapter V, Exercise B, 6, p. 145.
    (e) Chapter V, Exercise B, 9, p. 146.
    (f) Example of précis passage, p. 149.
    (g) Chapter V, Exercise C, 1, p. 154.
    (h) Chapter V, Exercise C, 3, p. 156.
    (i) Chapter V, Exercise C, 5, p. 158.
    (j) Chapter V, Exercise C, 9, p. 162.
    (k) Chapter V, Exercise C, 11, p. 164.
    (l) Chapter V, Exercise C, 12, p. 166.

2. Rewrite the following passage, correcting errors of grammar, spelling, and style. Give concise reasons, where possible, for your corrections:

    The Bard of Avon found a sympathetic caste in the rendering of his immortal *Macbeth* at the X Theatre yesterday evening. Mr A.B.

showed his ability both as a producer as well as in the interpretive sphere. As for the rest of the caste space does not permit us to more than say that every one was excellent in their own particular part. Adaptations from Elizabethan music were played between the acts, the first part being conducted by Dr W—— while the second was under the baton of Mr Y.Z. The performance was very different and far superior to that of last year.

(*London*)

3. Rewrite the following in simple English:

(*a*) The inebriated man was conveyed to his residence with celerity and dispatch.

(*b*) The bride entered the sacred edifice on the arm of an avuncular relative.

(*c*) The choice of Hutton as England's skipper is a consummation devoutly to be wished.

(*d*) He received an intimation that his services were superfluous.

(*e*) The adverse climatic conditions necessitated the cessation of the game.

(*Oxford and Cambridge*)

4. Replace each italicized word in the following passage by a word of one syllable (you need not write out the whole passage):

From the *summit* of the *eminence* a beautiful *prospect* of the river can be *observed* as it *meanders* through the *verdant pastures*.

(*Oxford and Cambridge*)

CHAPTER VII

VOCABULARY

THE MEANING OF WORDS
Definitions

WE all have at least two kinds of vocabulary—a reading vocabulary and a writing vocabulary. Our first experience with a word new to us usually comes from seeing it in print, guessing at its meaning from the context, and perhaps looking it up in the dictionary to make sure—sometimes finding to our surprise that it did not mean quite what we had supposed. Every time we come across that word again in print we grow a little more familiar with it, seeing it in a fresh context; and we may gradually learn to appreciate the precise shades of meaning that it bears. At length we may come to be so familiar with it that we use it naturally in our own writing; it has become a part of our writing vocabulary.[1]

A familiar exercise in many examinations is to ask the candidate to define a given word and to use it in a sentence of his own in such a way as to show that he fully understands its meaning.

The exercise should be tackled carefully, your aim being to convince the examiner that you really understand the exact sense in which the word should be used.

Let us suppose that you have been asked to define the word *dissect* and use it in a sentence so as to illustrate its meaning. A student's definition might be 'to cut up,' and his illustrative sentence might run: "The doctor began to dissect the body."

Now, this student might have quite a correct idea of the meaning and use of the word, but it is unlikely that he

---

[1] It may also, of course, become part of our speaking vocabulary.

would score many marks for such an answer. 'Cut up' is too imprecise as a definition. You can cut up paper, or cut up an old dress to make a new hat, or cut up the turf when you are playing golf. Moreover, the sentence is not a satisfactory one, though the given word is correctly used. No clear indication is given of the *precise* use of 'dissect': there is nothing to show that it does not mean (for example) 'examine', or 'weigh', or 'insert an injection into'.

A more exact *definition* would be:

(a) to cut up and divide a dead body or a plant for the purpose of studying its structure.

The *illustrative sentence* might run as follows:

(b) The anatomist began to dissect the body, showing the assembled students the various organs and muscles that lay beneath the flesh.

Here the specific meaning of the given word is plainly indicated, though the sentence is not a mere repetition of the definition. The student could, if he wished, add to his definition a note on the secondary meaning of *dissect* ('analyse critically a piece of writing or other creative work'), and construct his sentence to illustrate this meaning of the word:

(c) It was this critic's practice to dissect a book given to him to review, laying bare any weaknesses of structure and style that a careful reading revealed.

It is by no means easy to construct a good illustrative sentence. You should work your sentence out in rough first of all, and test it to make sure that it really does indicate the exact meaning and specific use of the given word, without becoming just a definition.

EXERCISES (A)

1. Criticize the following illustrative sentences. In each case suggest a better sentence:

(a) *garrulous*. He was a very garrulous person.

(b) *vocation.* Teaching was obviously her vocation, for she really enjoyed it.

(c) *ovation.* The actor received a remarkable ovation.

(d) *onerous.* This was an onerous burden.

(e) *apathy.* She listened with apathy to his account of his misfortunes.

2. In the following groups define each of the words, as for a dictionary, and then use *five* of them in sentences so as to show their correct use:

(a) archaic; impending; diagnosis; banal; exponent; ingredient; elicit; obliterate; primary; centenary.

(b) precocious; preoccupation; inevitable; integrity; notorious; erudite; category; eccentric; derogatory; heinous.

(c) bravado; extempore; corroborate; innovation; discern; unanimous; supersede; pseudonym; amenity; dilettante.

3. Use *ten* of the following words in sentences so as to illustrate the meaning of each word:

migration; feasible; analogy; unobtrusive; exuberant; exportation; eulogy; alienate; recumbent; exemplify; instigation; dilemma; ameliorate; retaliation; desiccated.

Words in their Contexts

A word can vary in its meaning according to its use in a particular context. Thus the word *dissect*, as we have already noted, can be used in connexion either with a body or with a book. A useful exercise, found in a good many examinations, is to choose words from a given passage (often a passage for précis) and ask students to explain each word *in its context.* Here a simple dictionary definition will not necessarily do. If the word *dissect*, for instance, were used in its secondary sense, as in example (c) on p. 183, the dictionary definition given in example (a) would hardly meet the case.

EXAMPLES

Among the distinguished scientists who have attempted, on relatively scanty data, theoretically to outline geographically the extended land areas of the Antarctic regions, Sir John Murray, of the *Challenger* expedition, was the most advanced and definite.

Basing his theory on a study of sediments from the southern seas, he outlined a southern continent, which he christened Antarctica. Although some scientists believe that the continent is divided into two great ice-capped lands, most attentive and authoritative students accept Murray's conclusion.

(a) Explain the meaning, in its context, of the word *data* (line 2).

One dictionary defines *data* as "a collection of facts." That may be good enough as a rough-and-ready impression, but it is not sufficiently exact to form an explanation. An article in a magazine or in an encyclopedia may be a collection of facts. A better dictionary offers the definition: "Things certainly known, forming the basis of an argument, or from which inferences can be drawn." This brings out more effectively the special significance of the word *data* (note that the word is plural), but for our particular purpose our explanation should be more precisely related to the context.

ANSWER. "Data" here means those scientific facts already known about Antarctic conditions, from which inferences can be drawn concerning the geographical formation of Antarctica.

(b) Explain concisely the meaning of the phrase *authoritative students* in lines 8 and 9.

It would be quite wrong to offer separate definitions of *authoritative* and *students*. The two words must be taken together. *Authoritative* in its context here does not mean, as it often does when used of persons, "accustomed to command," but has the meaning (more usually applied to a statement than to persons), "entitled to credit because it proceeds from an established authority." The word *student*, in the present case, clearly does not bear its usual meaning, "a person engaged in a course of study at a college," but refers to an expert engaged in advanced investigation in some special branch of knowledge. Our answer, therefore, might run:

ANSWER. "Authoritative students" in the given context refers to persons who have engaged in expert research upon a subject (in this case Antarctic conditions), and who are therefore entitled to be regarded as authorities upon the matter.

EXERCISES (B)

1 (p. 144, Exercise 5). Explain carefully but concisely the meaning of the following words and phrases in their contexts:

system of fortifications (line 4); embattled (line 5); strategic elaboration (line 8); dispositions (line 10); thrown back from the grim battlements (line 14).

2 (p. 145, Exercise 6). Explain the meaning of the following words and phrases as used in the given passage:

shrine (line 5); vouchsafe (line 6); manifestations (line 6); latent energies (line 6); scalded gullet (line 14).

3 (p. 154, Exercise 1). Both parts of the question to be answered.
(i) Choose *seven* of the following words, which are taken from the passage, and give for each another word, or a phrase, of similar meaning, which might be used to replace the word in the passage:

chaotic (line 3); conscripts (line 8); incompetence (lines 10 and 11); penurious (line 23); advocated (line 27); insubordination (line 31); inviolate (line 38); bulwark (line 41).

(ii) Choose *four* of the following phrases, which are taken from the passage, and explain *concisely* the meaning of each:

heroic exploits (line 1); by force or fraud (lines 15 and 16); to bemoan his fate (line 22); stand on record (line 29); ceaseless vigilance (line 37); kindled with affection (lines 42 and 43).

(*Cambridge*)

4 (p. 155, Exercise 2). Explain the meanings, in their contexts, of *five* of the following words or phrases in the passage.

widely accepted (line 2); nomenclature (line 4); uniformly fierce (line 7); pendulous (line 9); supernatural power (line 12); reconnaissance expedition (line 15); revived speculation (line 17); pronounced by the authorities of the Natural History Museum (lines 22 and 23).

5 (p. 157, Exercise 4). Answer parts (i) and (ii).
(i) Choose *seven* of the following words, and give for each another word, or a phrase, of similar meaning, which might be used to replace the word in the passage:

convened (line 1); inaugurate (line 2); co-ordinate (line 4); facilities (line 11); researches (line 17); principle (line 18); superficially (line 27); dividend (line 27); sustain (line 30).

(ii) Choose *five* of the following phrases and explain concisely the meaning of each:

kindred bodies (line 5); primary problems (line 6); of their own resources (lines 8 and 9); by private subscription (line 13); artificial pitch (line 16); civic authorities (line 20); a general drive (line 24)

6 (p. 158, Exercise 6). Explain carefully but concisely the meaning of the following words and phrases as used in the passage:

resolution (line 2); expressing concern (line 4); prohibiting their sale and distribution (lines 6 and 7); short of censorship (line 14); juvenile delinquents (line 18); wide of the fact (line 27); specifically (line 42); restricting importation (lines 45 and 46).

7 (p. 175, Exercise C, 2). Answer both parts.
(i) Choose *five* of the following words, and give for each another word, or phrase, which might be used to replace the word in the passage:

insidious (line 4); indefensible (line 5); conscientious (line 6); inherent (line 8); antipathies (line 8); effective (line 10); congenial (line 12).

(ii) Choose *four* of the following phrases, and explain concisely the meaning of each.

to deviate from the straight path (line 3); to square with his paper's policy (lines 4 and 5); any tendency to bias (line 7); traditional opposition (lines 8 and 9); rival schools of thought (line 9).
(*Cambridge*)

8 (p. 162, Exercise 9). Explain the meanings, in their contexts, of *five* of the following words or phrases:

the academic sphere (line 2); athletic bent (line 4); facile assumption (line 8); sense of values (line 13); tinsel pageantry (line 23); devotees (line 30); a vehicle for virtue or for vice (line 40).
(*London*)

9 (p. 161, Exercise 8). Explain the meanings, in their contexts, of *eight* of the following words and phrases:

long-term trend (lines 3 and 4); make inroads (line 20); margins (line 20); retail price (line 22); overheads (line 24); gross (line 25); carriage costs (line 28); return on that capital (line 30); "book middlemen" (lines 32 and 33); discount (line 34).

10 (p. 164, Exercise 11).
(i) Give another word or phrase for *six* of the following, bearing in mind the context:

intolerable (line 2); requisite (line 13); inevitable (line 16); construe (line 40); scrupulous (line 41); irksome (line 46); insuperable (line 48); nauseous (line 50).

(ii) Explain the meaning, in their contexts, of *four* of the following phrases:

object of compassion (line 3); self-moving index (line 12); syntactical arrangement (line 22); the show boy (line 30); upon credit (line 36); mere digital process (line 38).

Prefixes and Suffixes

There are some words in our language which are directly derived from simple root words in Old English, or in Latin, Greek, French, or some other foreign language (e.g., *like*, *stand*, *forest*). Many words, however, are built up by the addition of an affix to a simple root. An affix placed at the *beginning* of a word is known as a **prefix** (e.g., *un*like, *with*stand). An affix placed at the *end* of a word is known as a **suffix** (*e.g.*, like*ly*, forest*er*).

Some words are constructed with both a prefix and a suffix (e.g., *un*like*ly*, *in*cite*ment*), or even with more than one prefix or suffix (e.g., *not*/*with*stand*ing*, purpose*ful*/*ness*).

SOME PREFIXES

Prefixes Indicating Negation

un- (Old Eng.) .	.	.	.	*un*happy, *un*willing
dis- (Latin)	.	.	.	*dis*appear, *dis*advantage
in- (Latin)	.	.	.	*in*capable, *im*possible
non- (Latin)	.	.	.	*non*sense, *non*-fiction

Note 1. The last consonant of a prefix (here *-n*) is sometimes assimilated into the first consonant of the root word (*il*literate = *in*literate; *ir*regular = *in*regular), or is otherwise affected by this consonant, as in *im*possible.

Note 2. The prefixes *dis-* and *in-* do not necessarily indicate negation (e.g., *dis*syllable, *dis*locate, *in*vade).

Prefixes Indicating Opposition

with- (Old Eng.), 'against' .	.	*with*stand, *with*hold
a-, *ab-* (Latin), 'away from'	.	*a*vert, *ab*normal, *ab*scond
contra- (Latin), 'against' .	.	*contra*dict, *contra*band
retro- (Latin), 'back' .	.	*retro*grade, *retro*action
anti- (Greek), 'against' .	.	*anti*dote, *Ant*arctic

Prefixes Indicating Connexion

con- (Latin), 'with'	.	.	.	*con*nect, *col*lect,* *cor*respond*
ad- (Latin), 'to'	.	.	*ad*join, *ac*count,* *at*tract*
homo- (Greek), 'same'	.	.	*homo*phone, *homo*geneous
syn- (Greek), 'with'	.	.	*syn*onym, *sym*pathy*

[* See *Note* 1 above.]

Some Other Common Prefixes

ante- (Latin), 'before'	.	.	*ante*cedent, *ante*-room
bene- (Latin), 'well'	.	.	*bene*fit, *bene*volent
circum- (Latin), 'around'	.	.	*circum*ference, *circum*navigate
male- (Latin), 'evil'	.	.	*male*factor, *male*volent
post- (Latin), 'after'	.	.	*post*pone, *post*-war
re- (Latin), 'again'	.	.	*re*turn, *re*vise, *re*peat
trans- (Latin), 'across'	.	.	*trans*fer, *trans*atlantic
ultra- (Latin), 'beyond'	.	.	*ultra*-fashionable
vice- (Latin), 'in place of'	.	.	*vice*-captain, *Vice*-Admiral
arch- (Greek), 'chief'.	.	.	*arch*bishop, *arch*-criminal
auto- (Greek), 'self'	.	.	*auto*graph, *auto*biography
mono- (Greek), 'single'	.	.	*mono*poly, *mono*tone
poly- (Greek), 'many'	.	.	*poly*gon, *poly*gamy
tele- (Greek), 'from afar'	.	.	*tele*phone, *tele*gram

Explain the meaning of each word in the column of examples, using a dictionary if necessary, and show how the prefix affects the meaning. (E.g., *with*stand = to stand up *against* an opponent; *re*vise = to look at *again*.)

SOME SUFFIXES

Noun Suffixes Denoting the Performer (Agent)

-er (Old Eng.)	.	.	teach*er*, read*er*, employ*er*
-or (Latin)	.	.	auth*or*, act*or*
-ant, -ent (Latin)	.	.	merch*ant*, stud*ent*
-ist (Greek)	.	.	art*ist*, motor*ist*, loyal*ist*

Noun Suffix Denoting the Receiver

-ee (Latin)	.	.	employ*ee*, trust*ee*

NOUN SUFFIX DENOTING QUALITY, STATE, OR CONDITION

-hood (Old Eng.)	.	.	child*hood*, parent*hood*
-dom (Old Eng.)	.	.	wis*dom*, free*dom*
-ness (Old Eng.)	.	.	kind*ness*, good*ness*
-ship (Old Eng.)	.	.	hard*ship*, friend*ship*
-ance, *-ence* (Latin)	.	.	abund*ance*, prud*ence*
-tude (Latin)	.	.	atti*tude*, forti*tude*
-ty (Latin)	.	.	cruel*ty*, safe*ty*
-ation (Latin)	.	.	centraliz*ation*, coron*ation*
-ment (Latin)	.	.	amaze*ment*, arrange*ment*
-ism (Greek)	.	.	patriot*ism*, social*ism*

NOUN SUFFIXES DENOTING SMALLNESS (DIMINUTIVES)

-ling (Old Eng.)	.	.	duck*ling*, under*ling*
-let (Latin)	.	.	stream*let*, rivu*let*

ADJECTIVE SUFFIXES

-ful (Old Eng.)	.	.	beauti*ful*, grace*ful*
-less (Old Eng.)	.	.	sense*less*, care*less*
-y (Old Eng.)	.	.	dirt*y*, pluck*y*
-able (Latin)	.	.	port*able*, miser*able*
-ous (Latin)	.	.	barbar*ous*, religi*ous*
-ive (Latin)	.	.	act*ive*, competit*ive*
-al (Latin)	.	.	princip*al*, exception*al*

VERB SUFFIXES DENOTING 'TO MAKE' OR 'BECOME'

-en (Old Eng.)	.	.	dark*en*, strength*en*
-fy (Latin)	.	.	modi*fy*, sancti*fy*

VERB SUFFIX DENOTING 'TO TREAT IN A CERTAIN WAY'

-ize (Greek) .		minim*ize*, equal*ize*

[*Note.* On the spelling of words in *-ize* and *-ise* see the end of this chapter, p. 209.]

EXERCISE (*C*)

1. Referring if necessary to a suitable dictionary, give another example for each of the *prefixes* given on pp. 188–189.

2. In the same way give another example for each of the *suffixes* given on pp. 189–190.

3. State the prefix and indicate its force (*i.e.*, effect) in each of the following words:

   anticlimax, automatic, renew, accumulate, correct, polysyllable, contravene, abstain, disrepute, antediluvian.

4. State the suffix and indicate its force in each of the following words:

   quicken, chemist, pensive, agent, wisdom, courageous, deify, manageable, eminence, darling.

5. Give the force of the affix in each of the following:

   *tele*gram, *con*nect, sail*or*, *post*pone, art*ist*, *un*fasten, *ultra*-modern, fashion*able*, free*dom*, *bi*ped, *circum*stances, fraudul*ent*, *sub*marine, *ir*regular, love*ly*, muck*y*, *contra*vene, *trans*port, engin*eer*, black*en*.

Use a dictionary where necessary.

Words from Various Sources

LATIN AND GREEK ROOTS

A very large number of our words are taken, directly or indirectly, from Latin (especially) and Greek sources. A few of these have already been indicated in the lists of prefixes and suffixes. A knowledge of some of the commoner Latin and Greek words which have played a part in the formation of our vocabulary is a great help towards both the understanding and the spelling of many English words. Thus if we know that *ped-* is the stem[1] of the Latin word *pes*, 'a foot,' we at once add several words to our English vocabulary: for example, *pedal* (relating to, or pushed with, the foot), *pedestal* (the foot of a column), *pedestrian* (a foot-passenger), *pedometer* (an instrument for recording distances covered on foot), *expedition* (originally, a setting-out on foot), *biped* (creature with two feet), *quadruped* (creature with four feet).

Here is a list of a few of the Latin and Greek words which have similarly influenced our vocabulary. The words in

---

[1] That part of a word to which endings and prefixes are added (known also as the *root*).

brackets are the genitives (of nouns) and past participles (of verbs), as these parts best indicate the stem of certain words.

Latin

Some Derivatives

æquus, 'equal'	. .	equality, equivalent
aqua, 'water'	. .	aquatic, aquarium, aqueduct, aqueous
annus, 'a year'	. .	annual, annuity, anniversary
caput (*capitis*), 'head'	.	capital, captain, cap
corpus (*corporis*), 'body'	.	corporal, corpulent, corpse
dico (*dictum*), 'I say'	.	dictate, diction, predict
duco (*ductum*), 'I lead'	.	educate, conduct, introduce
erro (*erratum*), 'I wander'	.	error, erratic, err
finis, 'an end'	. .	finish, infinite, confine
jungo (*junctum*), 'I join'	.	conjunction, joint
latus (*lateris*). 'a side'	.	lateral, equilateral
liber, 'free'	. .	liberal, liberty, liberate
loquor, 'I speak'	. .	eloquent, loquacious, soliloquy, colloquial
magnus, 'great'	. .	magnanimous, magnitude
mitto (*missum*), 'I send'	.	transmit, missile, mission
novus, 'new'	. .	novel, novice, innovate, renovate
porto, 'I carry'	. .	porter, transport, export, deportment, portfolio
scando, 'I climb'	.	ascend, transcend, descend
scribo (*scriptum*), 'I write'	.	scribe, inscribe, scribble, manuscript, Scripture
solvo (*solutum*), 'I loosen'	.	absolve, dissolve, solution, dissolute
tango (*tactum*), 'I touch'	.	tangible, tangent, contact
unus, 'one'	. .	unit, uniform, unanimous

Greek

anthropos, 'a man'	. .	anthropology, philanthropist, misanthrope
demos, 'people'	. .	democracy, democrat
grapho, 'I write'	. .	autograph, biography, orthography, telegraph, graphite
khronos, 'time'	. .	chronicle, chronological, synchronize, chronic
ops, 'an eye'	. .	optical, optician
phonē. 'voice,' 'speech'	.	telephone, gramophone, phonetic, euphony
theos, 'god'	. .	theology, atheist, pantheism

Give the literal meaning of each of the above words, so as to show how the present meaning has been derived from the Latin or Greek root. (E.g., *equivalent* = equal in value, worth.)

WORDS FROM OTHER LANGUAGES

Many of our words derive from French and Scandinavian sources, and a comparatively small number of words have been introduced into our language from other nations, as a result either of foreigners coming to England or of English travellers and merchants going abroad. Among these words (sometimes called *loan-words* or *borrowings*) are the following:

French: garage, menu, rendezvous, café, souvenir
Danish: sky, harbour, leg, fellow, call, take, them
Dutch: yacht, skipper, trek, waggon
Italian: piano, opera, duet
Spanish: cigar, cargo, galleon
Arabic: alcohol, coffee, algebra
Persian: chess, bazaar
Chinese: china, tea

WORDS FORMED FROM PROPER NAMES

A few words have come into the language either from the names of places with which they are connected or from the names of persons, real or fictitious. Here are some examples:

bayonet (from Bayonne in France, where the weapon was said to have been first made).
canter (from the pace at which the Canterbury pilgrims are supposed to have travelled).
copper (from Cyprus, the chief source of copper in ancient times)
currant (short for 'raisins of Corinth').
lumber (a variant of Lombard, probably because many emigrants from Lombardy were pawnbrokers and moneylenders, and accumulated an assortment of articles in their shops. Lombard Street, in the City of London, is still a great banking centre).
meander (from the river Meander, a slow, winding river in Asia Minor).

muslin (from Mosul [Mussolo], a town in Iraq, where the material was originally made).

port (a strong, sweet red wine of Portugal, shipped from Oporto, the centre of the Portuguese wine trade).

solecism (an error in grammar or behaviour, especially the sort of blunder regarded as vulgar or provincial, from the town of Soloi, in Cilicia, whose inhabitants, colonized by the Greeks, spoke a corrupt form of the language).

boycott (from Captain Boycott, an Irish land agent, who was ostracized by tenants).

derrick (a type of movable crane, from Derrick, an early seventeenth-century hangman, the crane being regarded as suggesting the appearance and performance of a gallows).

galvanize (from Galvani, an Italian scientist, who in 1792 discovered the process of galvanism).

jeremiad (a tale of woe, from the Scriptural Lamentations of Jeremiah).

jovial (from Jove [Jupiter], the Roman deity, to be born under whose planet was believed to produce a cheerful temperament).

nicotine (from Jean Nicot who introduced tobacco into France in 1560).

panic (from Pan, the Greek god of the woods and fields, who was supposed to cause wild, unreasoning fear among shepherds).

sandwich (from the fourth Earl of Sandwich, who in the eighteenth century started the habit of eating thin slices of meat between two slices of buttered toast, in order to continue gambling without having to stop for meals).

tantalize (from Tantalus, in classical mythology, who was compelled to stand up to his chin in water, with fruit dangling above his head, both food and drink receding whenever he tried to reach them).

EXERCISES (*D*)

A good dictionary should be used in working each of the following exercises.

1. Give at least one additional example of words formed from each of the following Latin or Greek words:

dico, magnus unus, grapho. scribo, corpus, latus. phonē, annus. æquus.

2. Find at least two English words formed from each of the following Latin or Greek words:

animus, 'mind'; *brevis*, 'short'; *fortis*, 'strong'; *rex* (*regis*), 'a king'; *bios*, 'life'; *terminus*, 'end'; *logos*, 'word,' 'speech'; *octo*, 'eight'; *sequor (secutus)*, 'I follow'; *polis*, 'city.'

3. From which Latin or Greek words are the following words derived?
topography, fallacy, hospital, local, melody, revive, nominate, sympathy, civilian, decimal.

4. Explain the derivation of the following words:
cake, biscuit, horde, admiral, damson, shrapnel, saxophone, sardine, milliner, July.

5. Explain the meaning of each of the following idiomatic expressions, and suggest briefly how it has come to have that meaning:
to let a person have his head; robbing Peter to pay Paul; to serve before the mast; once in a blue moon; a good Samaritan; to cross the Rubicon; a Job's comforter; cut the ground from under his feet; a bone of contention; to burn one's boats.

6. Choose *six* of the following expressions, and in regard to each of the six that you choose give in plain language its meaning, and suggest *briefly* why it has that meaning:
(*a*) to be taken aback. (*b*) a fair-weather friend.
(*c*) to take the plunge. (*d*) to ape another person's behaviour.
(*e*) to pay the piper. (*f*) to sail close to the wind.
(*g*) to play second fiddle to someone. (*h*) a Satanic invention.
(*i*) a Gilbertian situation. (*j*) to set the Thames on fire.

(*Oxford*)

7. Give *briefly* the meaning of any *six* of the following metaphorical expressions:
(Example: *to leave a person in the lurch*—to desert a person when he is in difficulties.)
to burn the candle at both ends; to keep the wolf from the door; to be born with a silver spoon in one's mouth; to put the cart before the horse; to be in a person's good books; to bury the hatchet; to cry over spilt milk; to build castles in the air; to show the white feather. (*Associated Examining Board*)

THE CHOICE OF WORDS

Synonyms and Antonyms

If you think that the old gentleman living next door to you is bad-tempered there are a good many other adjectives of similar meaning at your disposal. You might call him 'ill-natured,' 'grumpy,' 'irritable,' 'surly,' 'morose,' 'churlish,' 'crusty,' 'cross-grained,' 'malevolent,' 'vicious'.

Words having a similar meaning are known as **synonyms.**
A fluent writer is able to draw on a wide range of synonyms,
choosing the particular word which best suits his shade of
meaning.

Although the English language is rich in synonyms, and
many words have at least one parallel, synonyms cannot be
used mechanically as substitutes for each other. Each word
possesses, or has tended to develop, a special significance
which makes it the right word in some contexts, but the
wrong word in others. If you were offering, for instance, a
vague general criticism of your elderly neighbour's disposition, then most of the words suggested in the first paragraph would probably meet the case well enough. But
special occasions would considerably restrict the number of
appropriate synonyms. Thus if the old man's nature was
such that he was prepared to hit you over the head with the
garden fork if he found you leaning over his wall to pick
an apple it would be an understatement to describe him as
'grumpy.' This word carries an insinuation that his bark
is perhaps worse than his bite. (One of the dwarfs in Walt
Disney's *Snow-white* was aptly named Grumpy.) 'Vicious'
would perhaps be the most suitable of our synonyms.

Each word has its own characteristics. 'Irritable,' for
example, implies a bad temper which is apt to show itself in
impatient outbursts, often over trifles; 'churlish' contains a
hint that a person's bad temper is particularly shown in his
response to other people's sociability (you wish him 'good
morning,' and he responds with a snarl); 'surly' and 'morose'
indicate a more settled disposition than 'irritable,' which
might apply to a passing mood; moreover, surly and morose
people tend to express their ill-temper by moody silence,
whereas an irritable person is likely to reveal his mood by
sharp language; a 'cross-grained' person will probably add
perverse action to sharp speech.

These are merely indications of the kind of differences
which may exist in synonyms. If you want to avoid repeating

a word (though repetition is not necessarily a fault) it is unwise to refer to a dictionary of synonyms and choose at random one of the alternatives offered.

This is not to say that a list of synonyms has no value. Sometimes a writer knows that the first word that comes to mind is not just the word he wants, and a thesaurus or dictionary of synonyms may remind him of a word that will more exactly convey his shade of meaning. But it cannot teach him the meaning and use of a word that he does not already know. Only a good dictionary can do that. (The smaller dictionaries, unfortunately, tend to 'explain' a word by merely giving an approximate synonym.)

A word of opposite meaning is known as an **antonym.** There may be more than one antonym to a word, according to the sense in which it is used. Thus the antonym to *clear* might be *opaque* (of glass), *overcast* (of the sky), *obscured* (of a view), *muddled*, *obscure* (of reasoning), *thick* (of soup).

EXERCISES (E)

1. Choose the most suitable of the given synonyms for each of the blanks in the following sentences, using a dictionary if necessary:

(i) (*a*) She liked her generosity to be noticed, and I saw her —— drop half a crown into the church alms plate as it was passed along the aisle.

(*b*) The mayor was very conscious of his dignity, and —— gave me a mere nod at the reception.

(boastfully, pretentiously, ostentatiously, vainly, conceitedly, pompously, proudly, noticeably)

(ii) (*a*) A spirit of —— characterizes the Youth Hostel movement, and members of the association feel a certain kinship with each other.

(*b*) Those interested in a certain type of art seem to have established a little —— of their own, from which other painters are excluded.

(sympathy, brotherhood, class, gang, company, society, clan, clannishness, fraternity, coterie)

(iii) Talking of white ants, the author says that they all but ——

G

the town of Darwin in five years, and —— the pioneers' houses to shells of masticated pulp.

(reduced, overthrew, ruined, broke up, spoilt, extinguished, demolished, eradicated)

(iv) Many people are sent to prison every year without the —— of a fine.

(preference, choice, option, selection)

(v) (a) A dog that has shown its —— by biting a human being must be kept under proper control.

(b) The criminal gave a cry of —— when he found that he had been outwitted.

(fierceness, wildness, cruelty, fury, rapacity, inhumanity, ferocity, violence)

(vi) You did not take the trouble to shut the gate after you, and owing to your —— the cows strayed into the adjacent cornfield.

(neglect, slackness, negligence, indifference, inattention, failure, laziness)

2. Each of the following sentences contains a word or words (italicized) not quite appropriate to the occasion. Using, if necessary, a list of synonyms and a good dictionary, choose a more suitable word of somewhat similar meaning.

(i) We all admired the girl's *lean* figure as she waltzed round the ballroom.

(ii) He is very *idle* in his movements, and cannot be induced to run briskly to meet the ball.

(iii) The rabbit sat gazing helplessly at the snake, *enchanted* by the reptile's beady eyes.

(iv) Now that I have bought an *aged* seventeenth-century cottage in the country I am going to settle down *mirthfully*.

(v) I have done all the work, but I expect the head of the department will take all the *repute*.

(vi) The old gentleman is very *scrupulous* over little points of etiquette.

(vii) After snatching a case of jewels from the *broken* window the thief drove off at a *sprightly* pace.

(viii) To leave litter in the corridors is a *crime* against school rules.

3. Suggest differences in the use of the following synonyms, using a dictionary if necessary:

(a) advance (verb), promote, progress (verb), exalt.

(b) collusion, co-operation, connivance.

(c) eternal, incessant, continual.

(d) benevolent, unselfish, charitable.
(e) diffident, modest, bashful.

4. Write sentences to illustrate differences in the use of the following synonyms:

(a) harmless, innocuous.
(b) onerous, oppressive.
(c) elicit, discover.
(d) anxiety, solicitude.
(e) poverty, penury.
(f) fatigued, exhausted.
(g) misfortune, calamity.
(h) firm, peremptory.

(i) noted, notorious.
(j) recover, recuperate.
(k) fictitious, spurious.
(l) ignorant, illiterate.
(m) cajole, persuade.
(n) exigency, necessity.
(o) disconsolate, desolate.

5. (a) Write down FOUR verbs that express approximately the same notion as *dislike*.

(b) Write down FOUR adjectives that express approximately the same notion as the word *proud*.

(If, for example, the word given were *mourn* your answer could consist of the words *fret*, *bewail*, *lament*, and *grieve*.)

(c) Choose TWO words from your answer to (a) and TWO from your answer to (b). Write FOUR sentences, one for each of these words, to illustrate its use and meaning clearly.   (*Oxford*)

6. Give *antonyms* for the italicized words in the following:

a *voluntary* payment to club funds; *insolent* behaviour; *lasting* happiness; *entirely* my own work; *vulnerable* to attack; to *obscure* the main point of the argument; *enthusiasm for* a cause; *barbarous* custom; to *limit* the amount of homework; *adverse* fortune.

7. Give two words that express an opposite notion to each of the following:

freeze; simple; solid; audible; failure; dilatory; erroneous; previous; deceitful; raise.

Choose FIVE of the above words, and compose sentences to illustrate the use of each of the antonyms you have given (ten sentences in all).

8. (a) Give the abstract nouns formed from the following adjectives: plain, worthless, constant, culpable, long.

(b) By adding the suffix *-able* (or *-ible*) to the following words, and making any necessary changes in spelling, form adjectives from: notice, pity, response, excite, discern.

(c) Using the correct prefix, give opposites of: orderly, ambitious, legible, cautious, reverent.   (*Oxford and Cambridge*)

Similarities between Words

Confusion sometimes exists, in the minds of students and others, between two or more words which are rather similar in form, but have different meanings. The best way of avoiding the confusion is to look up in a good dictionary the exact meaning of each word concerned, and note down examples of its use as you come across them.

Here are some examples of words commonly confused:

PRINCIPAL, PRINCIPLE

Principal is primarily an adjective meaning 'chief,' though it can be used as a noun in a closely associated sense: the Principal of a college is the chief of the lecturers or teachers.

Principle is a noun, and means a basic scientific truth, or a basis of moral behaviour.

The Prime Minister is the head of the British Government and the *principal* adviser of the sovereign.

I will endeavour to explain the *principle* on which the internal combustion engine works.

AFFLICT, INFLICT

To *afflict* is to torment or grieve a PERSON *with* some kind of suffering.

To *inflict* is to thrust some kind of SUFFERING *upon* a person.

Thus the object of *afflict* is always a creature, whereas the object of *inflict* is always a type of suffering.

The headmaster's reference to the cane in his study *afflicted* the boy with much mental uneasiness.

The headmaster decided to *inflict* a severe punishment upon the boy who deliberately smashed the hall window.

CONTINUAL, CONTINUOUS

Continual means going on and on, though not necessarily without interruption.

Continuous means going on and on without interruption.

We may think of the *dripping* of water from a tap as representing *continual* and the *flow* of water from a tap as representing *continuous*.

> The dog's *continual* barking got on my nerves, for we had only brief interludes of peace throughout the day.
>
> After the afternoon performance at a theatre, there is an opportunity for the auditorium to be cleaned, but this is not so at a cinema, for the performance is *continuous*.

Among other words of similar form which are sometimes confused, the following may be noted:

> human, humane; hypercritical, hypocritical; momentary, momentous; verbal, verbose; epigram, epitaph; summon, summons; stationary, stationery (goods bought from a station*er*); deprecate, depreciate; ingenious, ingenuous; luxurious, luxuriant; temporary, temporal; veracity, voracity; perspicacity, perspicuity; appreciative, appreciable; contemptuous, contemptible.

[See Exercise *F*, 1.]

Words which have the same sound but differ in spelling and meaning are known as **homophones** (*homo-* = same):

> practice, practise; their, there; course, coarse; guilt, gilt; flower, flour; compliment, complement.

Words which differ in meaning but are similar in form are known as **homonyms**:

> fair (= market), fair (= just and reasonable).
> pole (= stick), Pole (*e.g.*, North Pole).
> mine (= belonging to me), mine (*e.g.*, coal-mine).

When a word is wrongly used in place of another word somewhat similar in form, the error is sometimes known as **a malapropism.** This term derives from the famous character Mrs Malaprop in Sheridan's play *The Rivals*, a lady who has a habit of using wrong words (*mal* = bad, *apropos* = to the point).

> Then, sir, she [a young girl] should have a *supercilious* knowledge in accounts; and as she grew up I would have her instructed in *geometry*, that she might know something of the *contagious* countries.

EXERCISES (*F*)

1. In place of the words in italics in each of the following sentences insert a word chosen from the list of pairs given on p. 201:

(*a*) She was a fine tennis-player herself, and adopted a very *scornful* attitude towards my feeble efforts to hit the ball.

(*b*) I foolishly crossed the road close to the *motionless* car, and was knocked down by a bicycle.

(*c*) His manner was so *artless* that I felt sure he could not be guilty of listening at the keyhole.

(*d*) When I insinuated that I did not believe that he had broken the record for the long jump he angrily demanded whether I questioned his *truthfulness*.

(*e*) The members of the team seemed to take it for granted that they were going to lose, but the captain strongly *disapproved of* this attitude.

(*f*) I do not like books which give long, *wordy* descriptions of characters and scenes.

(*g*) I do not know much about philosophy, but the *clearness* of Bertrand Russell's exposition enabled me to follow his talk without difficulty.

(*h*) One ribbon was supposed to be 'sky blue' and the other 'pale blue,' but I could see no *easily noticeable* difference between the colours.

(*i*) After all the rain we have had this summer the plants in my garden are as *fertile* as the vegetation in the tropical jungle.

(*j*) So many new houses are now being built that house property is tending to *decline in value*.

2. Explain the differences in meaning in each of the following pairs of words:

(*a*) precipitous, precipitate; social, sociable; stimulus, stimulant; honorary, honourable; venal, venial.

(*b*) descent, dissent; envelop, envelope; illicit, elicit; masterful, masterly; septic, sceptic.

3. Write sentences which will illustrate the difference in meaning between each of the two words in the following pairs:

(*a*) urbane, urban; intelligent, intellectual; averse, adverse; sensible, sensitive; judicious, judicial.

(*b*) credulous, credible; illusion, delusion; infer, imply; imaginary, imaginative; official, officious.

4. Distinguish between the meanings of the two words in each of the following pairs, and construct sentences which illustrate their use:

(*a*) ceremonial, ceremonious; affect, effect; punctual, punctilious; benevolent, beneficent; fortunate, fortuitous.

(*b*) salubrious, salutary; opposite, apposite; pertinent, pertinacious; exceedingly, excessively; expedient, expeditious.

5. Give five examples of homophones other than those on p. 201, and write sentences illustrating the correct use of each word.

6. Give five examples of homonyms other than those on p. 201, and write sentences illustrating the correct use of each word.

7. (*a*) Give the abstract nouns corresponding to the following verbs or adjectives (*e.g.*, verb, *depart*; abstract noun, *departure*):

(i) resolve (ii) notorious, (iii) redeem, (iv) choose, (v) cynical, (vi) strive, (vii) extend, (viii) retain, (ix) prevail, (x) high, (xi) expel, (xii) mimic, (xiii) collide.

(*b*) Use each of the following words or phrases in a sentence (two separate sentences for each pair) so as to bring out the difference in meaning between the first and the second word or phrase in each pair:

(i) altogether, all together; (ii) inflame, in flame; (iii) sometimes, some times; (iv) everyone, every one; (v) recover, re-cover; (vi) spoonful, spoon full.   (*Northern Universities*)

8. (*a*) Choose any four of the following pairs of words. Explain clearly the difference in meaning between the words in each pair.

(i) a lecture, a discussion; (ii) a wallet, a purse; (iii) a sketch, a photograph; (iv) a dictionary, an encyclopedia; (v) a friend, a companion; (vi) a tour, an excursion.

(*b*) Choose any THREE of the following words. Compose two sentences for each word to show that it can be used as (i) a noun, (ii) a verb:

spur, bore, toll, contract, sentence.

       (*Associated Examining Board*)

SPELLING

There is no merit in being unable to spell correctly. Some people of ability, it is true, seem to take almost a pride in admitting that they are bad spellers; but their self-satisfaction is misguided. Bad spelling is merely a form of mental laziness; and it is a weakness which most employers are inclined to associate with other forms of laziness. Whether you are writing for an examination, or to a prospective employer, or to a business firm, or to an editor, or to a friend, bad spelling gives an impression of incompetence. It is almost as serious a limitation in a writer as the inability to use a plane or chisel correctly is a weakness in a wood-worker.

The difficulties of English spelling are often exaggerated. Correct spelling is largely a matter of careful observation, a knowledge of a few simple rules, common sense, and a willingness to take a little trouble.

Many apparent illogicalities in spelling are explained if the student takes the word to pieces and examines its construction. Take the notorious teaser *yacht*, the spelling of which appears, at a glance, to be designed especially to baffle pupils and logicians. Actually the spelling is perfectly logical, and easily remembered by anyone who takes the trouble to look in a dictionary. The word derives from the Dutch as follows:

Dutch: j a ch t

Modern English: y a ch t

The *ch* represents the Dutch guttural sound (as in the Scottish word lo*ch*), though we no longer pronounce it. Once this point has been noted, there is no excuse for getting the *c* or the *h* misplaced.

Some Spelling Rules [1]

(i) Where the final syllable of a word (*a*) is stressed, *and* (*b*) has a single vowel before a single consonant (e.g., b*at*,

---

[1] It is suggested that to avoid confusion not more than one or two of these rules should be studied in a single lesson. Exercise (*G*), 1, should not be attempted until all rules have been covered, but the rest of the spelling section can be dealt with side by side with a study of the rules.

regr*et*), that consonant is doubled before a suffix beginning
with a vowel (e.g., -*ed*, -*ing*):

bát	batted	batting	
plán	planned	planner	planning
regrét	regretted	regretting	
refér	referred	referring	
appál	appalled	appalling	
begín	beginning	beginner	

Note 1. Where the last syllable contains two vowels (*e.g.*,
app*ea*r, b*oa*t) or two end consonants (attra*ct*, pa*rt*), then
the final consonant is NOT doubled:

appeal	appealed	appealing	
appear	appeared	appearing	appearance
boat	boated	boating	boater
attract	attracted	attracting	attraction
part	parted	parting	
boil	boiled	boiling	boiler

Note 2. Where the stress is NOT on the last syllable the
final consonant is NOT doubled:

límit	limited	limiting	
fócus	focused	focusing	focuses
cómmon	commoner	commonest	
bías	biased	biasing	
óffer	offered	offering	

Note 3. With a word ending in *l* the last consonant is
doubled even if the syllable is not stressed:

travel	travelled	travelling	traveller
imperil	imperilled	imperilling	
revel	revelled	revelling	reveller
cruel	crueller	cruellest	
jewel	jewelled	jewellery	

Exception: (un)paralleled

The *l* is not doubled, however, if the last syllable contains
two vowels forming a single vowel sound, when the usual rule
is followed. (See Note 1: *boil, appeal.*)

(ii) Words ending in *n* retain this letter when the suffix *-ness* is added:

keen	keenness
plain	plainness

(iii) Words ending in a single mute *e* after a consonant (e.g., *come*) drop the *e* before adding a suffix beginning with a *vowel* (*-ed*, *-ing*, *-er*, *-able*, etc.):

fate	fated	file	filed	wire	wired
come	coming	file	filing	wire	wiring
mine	miner	take	taker	move	movable
excite	excitable				

Note 1. *Singeing* (= burning) retains the *e* to distinguish it from *singing*. *Dyeing* (= colouring) retains the *e* to distinguish it from *dying*.

Note 2. *Noticeable*, *peaceable*, *changeable*, etc., retain the *e* in order to keep the *c* or *g* soft (contrast with *applicable*, *singable*).

(iv) A mute *e* is retained before a suffix beginning with a *consonant* (*-ly*, *-ty*, *-ment*, etc.):

ove	lovely	fine	finely	fineness	safe safely safety
extreme	extremely	immediate	immediately	excite excitement	

Note. In *judgement*, *acknowledgement* the *e* is sometimes dropped as an alternative spelling (*judgment*, *acknowledgment*).

(v) When the suffix *-ly* is added to a word ending in either *-l* or *-ll* the result is always *-lly*:

beautiful	beautifully	especial	especially
dull	dully	full	fully

(vi) When the suffix *-full* is added to a word it drops its final *l*:

wonder	wonderful	play playful

Note. A word ending in *-ll* also drops its final *l* before adding *-ful*:

skill	skilful	will wilful

And -*till* follows the same practice as -*full*:

till   until

(vii) Words of more than one syllable ending in -*y* change the *y* to *i* before adding any suffix except (for obvious reasons) -*ing*, -*ish*:

busy	business	
lovely	lovelier	loveliness
happy	happier	happiness
fancy	fancier	fanciful (*but* fancying)
beauty	beautiful	

Exception: babyhood, *as well as* babyish

Most single-syllabled words ending in *y* follow this rule:

try	tries	tried	trier (*but* trying)
dry	dries	dried	drier drily (*Exception:* dryness)
sky	skies	skied	skier [cricket] (*but* skying)

But the adjectives *shy*, *sly*, and *wry* usually retain the *y*.

Note. The above rule does not usually apply where a vowel immediately precedes the -*y*: chimneys, buyer, employed, sprayed. But note *gaily* and *paid*.

(viii) When the vowels *i* and *e* combine to form the sound *ee* the *i* comes before the *e* except immediately after *c*:

	believe	retrieve	achieve	siege	field
but	receive	deceive	conceit	ceiling	

Note. Seize, counterfeit, weir(d) are exceptions.

(ix) Where the vowels *e* and *i* combine to form the sounds *ay* or *ĕ* (as in *pet*), the *e* comes before the *i*:

neighbour	weight	vein	rein	reign	heinous
leisure	heir	heifer	(*Exception:* friend)		

(x) Several nouns ending in -*ce* (-*cy*) have a verb ending in -*se* (-*sy*), as *advice* and *advise*:

advice	licence	practice	device	prophecy	(*nouns*)
advise	license	practise	devise	prophesy	(*verbs*)

(xi) Most common nouns ending in *-o* form their plural in *-oes*:

Negro   Negroes   hero   heroes   potato   potatoes

But a few words (often foreign words connected with music, and engineering abbreviations) form their plural without the *e*:

solo   solos   piano   pianos   dynamo   dynamos
magneto   magnetos

(xii) Our tendency towards blurred pronunciation causes a good many spelling difficulties, particularly in words ending in *-able* and *-ible*. No precise rules exist, but the following points may be helpful:

(*a*) Where a word ends in mute *e*, the *e* is normally dropped and the suffix is *-able*:

advisable	arguable	believable	debatable
forgivable	(in)dispensable	lovable	lik(e)able
movable	notable	unmistakable	sal(e)able

(*Exceptions:* collapsible, reducible, forcible)

See Rule (iii), Note 2, for words ending in *-ce*, *-ge*.

(*b*) After *s* or *ss* the ending is generally *-ible*:

accessible	admissible	comprehensible
divisible	inexpressible	indefensible
ostensible	plausible	repressible responsible

(*Exception:* passable)

(xiii) There is some confusion about the use of the endings *-ise* and *-ize*. Not only do writers and even printers differ in practice, but, worse still, grammarians tend to give contradictory advice. The difficulty arises from the fact that some words derive direct from the Greek (*-izo*), and others derive from the French (*-ise*). As few people can be expected to know which are which, confusion reigns. Probably the best plan for the ordinary person is to get to know those words in which *-ise* is undoubtedly correct, and to use *-ize* (which is favoured by most of the leading printers and publishers, and which represents the pronunciation as well as the correct etymology) for the others.

Common words which require -ise:

advise	advertise	comprise	compromise
despise	devise	enterprise	excise
exercise	improvise	supervise	surmise
surprise	disguise	franchise	merchandise

(xiv) The modern tendency is to avoid ligatures (*i.e.*, æ, œ) where possible; they serve no useful purpose. The following spellings, for example, are to be preferred:

medieval   manoeuvre   encyclopedia   Caesar   Aeneas

Taking Difficult Words to Pieces

The following examples will show how words which present spelling difficulties can be taken to pieces and examined:

accommodate   ac-commo-date. (Latin *commodare* = 'to fit.') Note *cc mm o*. Also commodity. (*ac = ad* = 'to.')

acquaintance   ac-quaint-ance. Note that in English *q* is always followed by *u*. (*ac = ad*.)

battalion   batt-a-lion Compare ba*tt*le.

committee   com-mitt-ee. Note three double letters—*mm tt ee*.

dissatisfied   dis-satis-fied. (Latin *satis* = 'enough.') Note double *s* because *satisfy* begins with *s* (contrast *disappear*).

embarrass   em-barr-ass. Note double letters *rr* and *ss* (emba*rr*assed by a ba*rr*ier).

harass   har-ass. One *r* (ha*r*assed by a ha*r*e).

isosceles   iso-sceles. (Greek *iso* = 'equal,' *scelos* = 'leg.')

paraffin   par-affin. *Par* = 'little.' The word means 'having little affinity with other substances.'

separate   se-par-ate. (Latin *se* = 'apart,' *parare* = 'to prepare.')

science   sci-ence. (Latin *scio* = 'I know.') Also *scientific*, *conscience*.

tobacco   to-bacc-o. Compare the colloquial *baccy*.

Go through these (and any other words which give difficulty) *regularly* until the correct spelling sticks in your mind.

EXERCISES (*G*)

1. Refer to the rules which govern or suggest the spelling of each of the following words:

(*a*) allo*tt*ing, annu*ll*ed, benefi*t*ing, unbe*lieva*ble, carg*oes*, cata-log*u*ing, chang*e*able, commi*tt*ed, de*cei*ve, envelo*p*ed.

(*b*) especia*ll*y, fi*r*ing, licen*c*e, loa*d*ing, ne*tt*ing, peda*ll*ed, refe*rr*ing, reprehen*s*ible, spoonfu*l*, trac*e*able.

(*c*) carpe*t*ed, chimn*eys*, chor*us*es, dete*rr*ed, develo*p*ing, ech*oes*, enamel*l*ed. enro*l*. eve*nn*ess. inesca*p*able.

2. Prepare for a spelling test by taking to pieces any of the following words which may give difficulty, and analysing the difficulty in the way indicated on p. 209 above. Use a dictionary where it would be helpful.

(*a*) accelerator, aeroplane, Antarctic, asphalt, bicycle, carburettor, colossal, correspondent, corroborate, diphthong.

(*b*) disagreeable, encyclopedia, erroneous, exaggerate, honorary, humorist, indefatigable, independence, laboratory, manoeuvred.

(*c*) miscellaneous, mortgage, necessarily, omission, oscillate, parallel, possesses, propaganda, reconnaissance, science.

(*d*) tobacco, conscience, umbrella, underrate, whereas, woollen, grammar, heighten, hereditary, heredity.

(*e*) aggressor, analysis, anonymous, apparent, assassin, author, Britain, bygone, carcass, catarrh.

(*f*) chauffeur, chrysalis, chrysanthemum, college, conjurer, corol-lary, courageous, disappoint, dissipate, ecclesiastical.

(*g*) ecstasy, etymology, exceed, exercise, exonerate, extraordinary, ghastly, gramophone, guarantee, honourable.

(*h*) hundredth, hypothesis, imminent, immensely, immovable, impromptu, incessant, indefensible, indelible, indefinitely.

(*i*) humorous, indictment, initialled, innocuous, instalment, inventor, irresistible, labyrinth, lassoed, liaison.

(*j*) livelihood, Magna Carta, mahogany, malleable, medicine, Mediterranean, mementoes, Mississippi, misspelt, unmistakable.

(*k*) mosquitoes, murmured, negligible, observatory, occurrence, omniscient, perpendicular, personnel, phenomenon, physicist.

(*l*) predecessor, procedure, professor, proletariat, propeller pseudonym, psychology, psychiatrist, Pyrenees, quarrelling.

(*m*) recognizable, reminiscences, renaissance, resurrection, rhodo-dendron, rhubarb, ricochetting, silhouetted, somersault, stereotyped.

(*n*) strychnine, subsistence, subterranean, superintendent, super-sede, surreptitious, syllabuses, synopsis, syringeing, teaspoonfuls.

(*o*) teetotaller, temperance, Tennessee, tobogganing, tomatoes, tonsilitis. torpedoes, trousseau, Westmorland, zigzagging.

CHAPTER VIII

ESSENTIALS OF GRAMMAR

PARTS OF SPEECH

Verbs

FINITE AND INFINITE

A *Finite* Verb is one which has a Subject and is thus 'limited' to a definite person and number by that Subject:

The sun *shines*. The stars *shine*. He *is running*. The players *are running*. You *have been scoring* freely.

The parts of a verb which are *Infinite* are infinitives, participles, and gerunds, which are not 'limited' as they have no Subject (though they may possess an Object):

I want *to play* tennis. He went out, *slamming* the door. *Dancing* is a healthy exercise.

Note that a participle may combine with an auxiliary to form a finite verb (*e.g.*, is *running*), though by itself it is infinite.

TRANSITIVE AND INTRANSITIVE

A verb is said to be *Transitive* when it has an Object to complete the sense:

He kicked *the ball* (OBJECT).

A verb is said to be *Intransitive* when its sense is complete without an Object:

Everybody cheered.

Some verbs are always either the one or the other; but many can be used both transitively and intransitively.

Select examples of transitive and intransitive verbs from any reading-book or from any extract in this book.

INCOMPLETE PREDICATION

A verb which requires a word or phrase (other than an Object) to complete the sense is known as a Verb of Incomplete Predication, and the words which complete the sense are known as the *Complement*:

I am *utterly miserable*. (ADJECTIVE COMPLEMENT.)

He became *a sailor*. (NOUN COMPLEMENT.)

Be careful to distinguish between a Noun Complement (which refers to the same person or thing as the Subject) and an Object (He MET *a sailor*). Note that the verbs *to be*, *to become*, always take a Complement and never an Object.

ACTIVE AND PASSIVE VOICE

When the person or thing denoted by the Subject *performs* the action of the verb, the verb is said to be in the *Active* Voice:

The magician swallowed a large sword.

When the person or thing denoted by the Subject *is affected by* the action of the verb, the verb is said to be in the *Passive* Voice:

A large sword was swallowed by the magician.

THE SUBJUNCTIVE MOOD

In modern English the *Subjunctive* is used only in expressing a wish, condition, or assumption *which is unlikely to be fulfilled*. It rarely appears except in the form *were* of the verb *to be*:

I wish I *were* a millionaire. (Not *was*.)
If he *were* interested in that book he would not be looking out of the window. (*Unlikely assumption*.) BUT If he *was* interested in that book I will lend him another by the same author.

THE INFINITIVE

The Infinitive expresses a verbal notion without reference to any Subject. The simple infinitive often has a *noun* function, and may act as Subject, Object, or Complement:

To cross the road carelessly is foolish. (*To cross* is the Subject of the verb *is*.)

I wanted *to win*. (*To win* is the Object of the verb *wanted*.)

My chief delight was *to sit* in the sun. (*To sit* is the Complement of the verb *was*.)

The infinitive may at the same time have a *verb* function: thus in the sentence above, 'to cross' has its own Object ('road') and is modified by an adverb ('carelessly').

The infinitive may have an adjectival function ("This is a good book *to read*"—adjective qualifying *book*), and occasionally an adverbial function ("I went *to see* the match"—Adverb of Purpose, modifying *went*).

After certain verbs (*e.g.*, can, must, will, dare, make) the infinitive is often used without the word 'to,' to make up compound tenses, or as Object:

I can (= am able to) *play* hockey to-morrow.

I must (= have got to) *listen* to the radio play to-night.

He will (= is going to) *feel* better in the morning.

I dare (to) *do* all that may become a man.

My dog made me (to) *run* all the way home.

I heard him (to) *sing* in his bath.

Give similar examples of the use of the infinitive without 'to,' and of the use of the infinitive as Subject, Object, and Complement.

THE GERUND

Like the infinitive, the *Gerund* (sometimes known as a verbal noun) is a verb with a noun function and may also have verbal characteristics:

Writing stories is not so easy as it may seem. (*Writing* is the Subject of *is*, and also has its own Object, *stories*.)

I enjoy *writing* stories. (Object of *enjoy*, and having *stories* as its own Object.)

In such compounds as 'dining-table,' 'walking-stick,' the first half of the word is a gerund, not an adjective: the expressions mean 'a table for dining,' 'a stick for walking.'

THE PARTICIPLE

The *Present Participle* (ending in -*ing*) and the *Past Participle* (usually ending in -*ed*, -*d*, -*t*, or -*n*) have an adjectival function, and (like the infinitive and the gerund) may also have a verbal function:

> A *jumping* cracker. A *fallen* idol.
> I hear the lark *singing*. I saw the boxer *beaten*.
> *Opening* his purse, he drew out a shilling. (*Opening* is an adjective qualifying *he*, and also a verb with *purse* as its Object.)

Give similar examples of the use of participles.

Do not confuse the present participle with the gerund, which is similar in form; the participle *qualifies* a noun or pronoun, whereas the gerund *acts as* a noun (Subject, Object, or Complement of a verb, or Object of a preposition).

The present participle is used to complete the tense in Continuous Tenses (I am *going*, I was *going*, I shall be *going*), and the past participle to complete the tense in Perfect Tenses (I have *gone*, I had *gone*, I shall have *gone*).

SEQUENCE OF TENSES

As a general rule, if the main clause of a sentence is in a Past Tense a subordinate clause must also be in a Past Tense (unless the subordinate clause expresses a universal or habitual fact):

> We *did* not play cricket, because John *would* not let us have the bat.
> BUT We *explained* to them that the English *do* not play cricket in the winter. (*Habitual fact*.)

A main clause in the Present or Future Tense may be followed by a subordinate clause in any tense, according to the time that the writer wishes to express:

> I *like* tennis because it *is* such a vigorous game.
>   „   „   „   „   I *have played* it since I was quite young.

I *shall explain* that I *am* feeling too ill to work.
„ „   „   „   I *was* suddenly taken ill last night.

In a conditional sentence *should* or *would* in the one clause should be followed by *should* or *would* in the other:

I *should* be glad if you *would* get off my foot. BUT I *shall* be glad if you *will* get off my foot.

Nouns

A noun may have *Number* (Singular or Plural), *Gender*, and *Case*. Distinctions of *Kind* (Concrete, Abstract, Common, Proper) have no grammatical significance. In modern English, distinctions of gender and case are of little importance, for we now rarely inflect nouns, except in the possessive case. One or two French words, such as *fiancé* (masculine), *fiancée* (feminine) are inflected.

A few words still have a feminine form (*e.g.*, tigress, actress).

Collective nouns, denoting a collection or group of things or persons (*e.g.*, crowd, team, committee) may be regarded as singular if the group is considered as a single unit, and as plural if the members forming the group are considered as individuals:

The school team *is* playing away to-morrow. BUT The school team *have* been told to stay in *their* form rooms until after lunch.

Suggest similar examples for *crowd* and *committee*.

Pronouns

Pronouns may be *Personal* (*e.g.*, I, he, you, they); *Demonstrative* (*e.g.*, this, those); *Interrogative* (*e.g.*, who? what?); *Relative* (*e.g.*, who, which, that).

I am going to give you *this*.
What would you like?
Let me carry that bag, *which* is too heavy for you.

Reflexive (*e.g.*, myself, himself, yourselves); *Distributive* (*e.g.*, each, either, neither); *Indefinite* (*e.g.*, some, anything, none, anyone, somebody); *Possessive* (*e.g.*, mine, yours, hers, his).

> I could kick *myself*.
> I really wanted the new ball, not the old one, but *either* will do.
> Has *anyone* got a pound note? Yes, but it's not *yours*.

Note the difference between the *reflexive* pronoun, which is the Object of a verb whose Subject and Object refer to the same person or thing (*e.g.*, I could kick *myself*), and an *emphasizing* pronoun, which always stands in apposition to a noun or pronoun (*e.g.*, I *myself* am the best judge).

Indefinite pronouns do not stand for a particular noun in a given context, but *personal* and *relative pronouns* normally have a noun (known as the *antecedent* or *principal*) to which they relate. The writer should be particularly careful to see that the pronoun *it* has an antecedent: beware of falling into the error of assuming that this antecedent noun has been expressed, when in fact it has only been implied:

> He has resigned from the team, but the captain will not accept *it*.
> COMMENT. The pronoun *it* assumes that there is an antecedent, *resignation*, whereas the noun is only implied in the verb *resigned*. This is slovenly writing.
> CORRECT. He has resigned from the team, but the captain will not accept his resignation.

A pronoun should be as near as possible to the antecedent which it represents, and there should be no doubt which noun the pronoun represents. If there is any doubt, then the noun should be repeated.

Adjectives

Any word which qualifies a noun or noun-equivalent is adjectival in function. Adjectives may be classified as Qualitative, Quantitative, Demonstrative, Relative, Possessive, Interrogative, and Distributive; but all these classes have the same function, and the classification is of little real significance.

When an adjective stands with its noun (usually in front of the noun) it is known as Attributive. (The *good* earth.)

When an adjective forms the complement of a verb it is known as Predicative. (His bowling was *good*.)

Select from any reading-book some further examples of attributive and predicative adjectives.

Some pronouns and adjectives are similar in form, but they can easily be distinguished by the difference in function. The pronoun stands *in place of* the noun; the adjective *qualifies* the noun:

> *What* is the matter? (Pronoun)
> *What* book are you reading? (Adjective, qualifying 'book')
> I will not tolerate *this*. (Pronoun, standing for an *unexpressed noun, e.g.*, 'behaviour')
> Have you seen *this* play? (Adjective, qualifying 'play')
> This is *his* racket (Adjective), not *hers*. (Pronoun)

Suggest some further examples.

The definite and the indefinite article are really adjectives (*the, a*, and *an*) and should be classified as such.

The demonstrative adjectives (*this, these, that, those*) agree in number with the nouns they qualify:

> *This sort* of person (singular); *these sorts* of people (plural). (*NOT* These sort of people.)
> BUT it would be better to write: People of this sort.

Adverbs

Adverbs may qualify (i) verbs (They shouted *loudly*), (ii) adjectives (I am *so* sorry), (iii) adverbs (We ran *very* quickly), and occasionally even prepositions and conjunctions. They never qualify nouns or pronouns.

Adverbs may indicate Manner (e.g., *loudly*), Degree (e.g., *so, very*), Time (e.g., *again*), Place (e.g., *here*).

Give some further examples of each of the uses (i), (ii), and (iii).

Prepositions

The preposition governs a noun or pronoun, usually indicating a relationship in time or place to some other word in the sentence. Adverbial and adjectival phrases are commonly introduced by a preposition (e.g., *in* the night, *during* the day, *along* the ground, *over* the wicket).

The same word may often be used either as a preposition or as an adverb. The function and meaning of the word will indicate which part of speech it is: a preposition normally governs a noun or pronoun; an adverb usually adds the notion of time, place, or manner to the verb:

> He is hiding *behind* the desk. (Preposition)
> I went first, and he followed *behind*. (Adverb—Place)
> I have never seen him *since* that day. (Preposition)
> I have never seen him *since*. (Adverb—Time)

The so-called 'rule' that we must not end a sentence with a preposition cannot be justified in English, and is not observed by any good writer. (See Fowler's *Modern English Usage*.)

The preposition governs its object in the accusative (objective) case. This does not matter in English as regards nouns, which are not inflected, but it must be remembered with pronouns which change their form to indicate case:

> Give one to *him* and one to *her*. (*NOT* one to *he* and one to *she*.)
> Between you and *me*. (*NOT* Between you and *I*.)

The preposition 'between' refers to *two* things or persons. In referring to *more than two* we must use the preposition 'among':

> The legacy was divided *between* the two sons. BUT The fortune was divided *among* the various members of the family.

As *between* refers to *two* things, we must not use it with the distributives *each* and *every* (which indicate *one* thing at a time) followed by a single noun. If we say, for example, "There is a space of ten metres between each house," we imply a structural disaster. We must say:

> There is a space of ten metres between each house and the one beside it (*or* between the houses).

After the words *differ* and *different* it is better to use the preposition *from* than the preposition *to* (though *different to* is defended by some grammarians). But although we differ *from* our neighbour, we have a difference of opinion *with* him. We are always *in*different *to* pain or people.

The use of the right preposition after certain verbs often gives difficulty, and is largely a matter of idiom. It is too complicated to be fully dealt with here; but a few examples are given:

> to *agree with* a person, to *agree to* a suggestion.
> The performance *ended with* a full chorus.
> The quarrel *ended in* her returning to her mother.
> I *prefer* cricket *to* baseball.
> You *instil* hope *into* me. You *inspire* me *with* hope.
> to be *oblivious of* (= *forgetful of*) one's surroundings.
> to *protest against* one's treatment.

When the same preposition governs two nouns separately it should be repeated:

> This is not *for* Harry but *for* Hilda.

Conjunctions

Co-ordinating conjunctions join words, phrases, or clauses of *equal* grammatical importance. The most common are: and, but, yet, still, or.

> William *and* Mary reigned.
> Look under the table *or* in the cupboard.
> I told him what I thought of him, *and* I threw a book at his head.

Subordinating conjunctions join subordinate clauses to main clauses. Among the most common are: that, when, after, as, if, because, than, unless.

EXERCISE (*A*)

1. Use each of the following verbs in sentences, (*a*) transitively, (*b*) intransitively:

> serve, dance, grow, flourish, contribute.

2. Turn the transitive sentences in Exercise 1 from the Active into the Passive.

3. Fill in the appropriate part of the verb *to be* in the following:

    (*a*) If I (to be) you, I should confess the truth.

    (*b*) If I (to be) not mistaken, that is the Prime Minister.

    (*c*) I wish I (to be) good enough to play for England.

    (*d*) If that (to be) Smith who called, it proves he has recovered from his illness.

    (*e*) If it (to be) Smith who took the money, the police would have arrested him.

4. Explain the function of the infinitive in the following, and state whether the noun infinitive is Subject, Object, or Complement:

    (*a*) You must remember to watch the ball.

    (*b*) He is a man to remember.

    (*c*) To know all is to forgive all.

    (*d*) I come to bury Caesar, not to praise him.

    (*e*) Now is the time to speak, and I want to say this.

    (*f*) To play the fool is not the way to impress me.

5. Distinguish between gerunds and present participles in the following:

    (*a*) *Flying* to New York, she arrived in time to take the *leading* part in Mr Coward's play.

    (*b*) I dislike *flying*; but I must pay a *flying* visit to my cousin. who has no objection to *flying*.

    (*c*) At the *opening* function we all sat round a huge *dining*-table.

    (*d*) I am *studying* French, but I find *learning* languages a *trying* occupation.

6. In the following passage select the nouns or noun-equivalents (words or phrases acting as nouns) and say whether their function is that of Subject, Complement, Object, or Object of a preposition:

    Four officers who took part in a recent expedition to Greenland described how over a hundred tonnes of stores were flown by Sunderland flying-boats to a camp which was 1,400 kilometres from the North Pole. Their task was to take stores and twenty-five members of the expedition to the base, but flying was difficult in the prevailing conditions. However, after some delays the plane succeeded in its attempt.

7. Select the pronouns in the following, and describe their kind and function (*e.g.*, possessive, standing for the noun ——, and Object of the preposition ——):

Do you belong to your local public library? I belong to mine, and anyone who does not use his library facilitites is very unwise. Every ratepayer is entitled to a general ticket, and this is usually supplemented by a non-fiction ticket. His family, too, are entitled to theirs. Libraries often contain thousands of books, each being borrowable free of charge. Who would not wish to enjoy advantages like these?

8. Distinguish between adjectives and pronouns in the following. State whether the adjectives are attributive or predicative, and explain the kind and function of each pronoun:

In the book I am reading the husband puts poison in his wife's tea, but, instead of drinking it, she accidentally drinks his. Not realizing that his wife is drinking his tea, he himself proceeds to drink hers. He gives a fearful scream, and then collapses, gasping that he has been murdered. The wife is naturally apprehensive when a detective calls. He asks her to tell him exactly what has happened, and what money her husband had in the bank, each question clearly indicating his unjust suspicions. At this she is so overcome that she faints in his arms—an action that is quite unexpected, and which rather embarrasses this honest policeman.

9. Distinguish between adverbs and prepositions in the following, in each case indicating the function of the word:

I opened the door and went in. To my amazement my friend was standing on the table, his back towards me. In his hand he held a rapier, with which he was very vigorously attacking an imaginary person in the corner beyond. Fearing for his sanity, I was thinking of creeping quietly out again, when he heard me and turned round. An explanation was obviously called for. Rather sheepishly he climbed down, putting his rapier beyond my reach on the mantel-shelf behind him. Then he explained that he was practising fencing. Owing to lack of space he carried out his exercises above the floor, for during previous practices he had almost ruined the arm-chairs.

10. A number of words in English are normally followed by certain prepositions. Construct sentences to show what prepositions are used after *eight* of the following: *preferable; reconciled; familiar; compatible; impatient; indignant; composed; subordinate; acquainted; contemptuous; inexperienced.* For example, if the word had been *susceptible*, your sentence might have been: "Englishmen who have lived in the East often remain susceptible to attacks of fever after their return to England."   (*Oxford*)

PHRASES AND CLAUSES

A **phrase** is a combination of words not containing a finite verb. It makes sense, but not complete sense on its own, as its meaning partly depends on its relation to some other part of the sentence in which it stands:

In the early morning	the way to win the match
of the chief examining bodies	rushing to the cliff's edge

A **clause** is a combination of words containing a finite verb and having its own Subject and Predicate. A *Main Clause* may make sense by itself, but a *Subordinate Clause* depends for its meaning on some other part of the sentence:

I get up in the morning (Main) when I hear the alarm clock (Subordinate) which stands on my dressing-table (Subordinate).

State the Subject and the finite verb in each clause.

Co-ordinate Clauses are clauses of equal grammatical rank, joined by a co-ordinating conjunction (usually *and* or *but*) or by a semi-colon:

I go to bed late/*but* I get up early.

Sentences which contain two or more co-ordinate clauses are known as **Compound** Sentences; they may be either *Double* or *Multiple*:

Good nature will always supply the absence of beauty, /but beauty cannot long supply the absence of good nature. ADDISON. (Double.)

The village takes its place in the scheme of things;/it is the work of generations of living, labouring men. IVOR BROWN. (Double.)

Soon the whole world will know the truth,/ and wise men will praise us for our conduct;/but you still remain blind to the realities. (Multiple.)

If more than one clause has the same Subject it is often left to be understood in the second or later clauses:

I retired to my room, and (I) remained there for two hours. (Double sentence with Subject understood in second clause.)

State the finite verbs in each of the above examples.

ANALYSIS OF SENTENCES

Simple Analysis

IN analysing a sentence we examine its construction. A **Simple Sentence** is one that contains only one Subject and Predicate. The *Subject* states the person(s) or thing(s) about which something is said. The *Predicate* expresses (*i.e.*, predicates) something about the Subject, either in the form of a statement, a question, a command, or an exclamation:

Too many COOKS spoil the broth. (Statement.)
Will MEMBERS *of the audience* kindly remove their hats? (Question.)
Do not (YOU) leave litter about. (Command.)
How beaut.fully *the school* ORCHESTRA played Schubert's "Ave Maria"! (Exclamation.)
TO LIVE *as long as possible* is the wish of almost every one. (Statement.)

Note 1. The Subject of each of the above sentences is in italics, the chief Subject-word being printed in small capitals.

Note 2. Questions should be turned into statements before being analysed. (*E.g.*, "Members of the audience will kindly remove their hats.")

Note 3. In commands the Subject (usually the 2nd person pronoun) is often unexpressed; but it should be explicitly stated in an Analysis exercise.

There are at least three ways of setting out an exercise in Simple Analysis. The different parts of the sentence may be shown (*a*) in columns, (*b*) by graphic diagram, or (*c*) line by line. Each teacher has his own preference. In the examples below, the line-by-line method is used.

EXAMPLES

In a very short time a modern railway will link Baghdad with Europe. (Simple sentence.)

Subject-word: railway
Enlargement of S.: a modern
Verb: will link

Extension of V.: In a very short time, with Europe
Object: Baghdad

Give me the smooth turf of the Sussex Downs to walk on, and I am completely happy. (Compound sentence.)

Subject-word: (You)
Verb: give
Extension of V.: to walk on
Object-word: turf
Enlargement of O.: the smooth, of the Sussex Downs
Indirect Object: me
Connective. and
Subject: I
Verb: am
Complement: completely happy

EXERCISES (*B*)

1. In the following sentences, (*a*) state the Subject and the Predicate of each clause, underlining the Subject-word; (*b*) say whether the sentence is a statement, question, command, or exclamation; and (*c*) say whether it is a Simple or Compound sentence:

(i) Every bullet has its billet.
(ii) The unkindness of this last remark deeply affected him, and made him turn away.
(iii) Why do unhappy people so often delight in giving pain?
(iv) To tell the bitter truth is not always wise or kind.
(v) Make up your mind never to say an unkind word.
(vi) The bowler walked slowly back, turned and began his run up to the wicket, and at length released the ball with the speed of an express train.
(vii) How beautifully those two new actresses speak!
(viii) Nobody contradicts me now, and the salt has gone out of my life.—QUEEN VICTORIA (after the death of Prince Albert).
(ix) Let sleeping dogs lie.
(x) What has happened to my old school friends, and where are they now?

2. Analyse the sentences in Exercise 1.

Analysis into Clauses

A sentence consisting of a main clause together with one or more subordinate clauses is known as a **Complex**

Sentence. A subordinate clause may do the work of a noun (*noun clause*), an adjective (*adjective clause*), or an adverb (*adverb clause*). It cannot stand by itself, but is dependent on another clause, and is usually introduced by a subordinating conjunction (see p. 219).

ADJECTIVE CLAUSES

An adjective clause invariably qualifies a noun or pronoun, and is commonly introduced by a relative pronoun (who, which, that, whose, whom):

> Happy is the man *who has never known fame.*
> It is you *to whom I am referring.*
> Happy are the people *whose annals are blank in history-books.*—
> CARLYLE.
> Yet oblivion is a fate *from which we all shrink.*
> A poor player, *that struts and frets his hour upon the stage.*—
> SHAKESPEARE, *Macbeth.*

The relative pronoun is sometimes omitted:

> That is the desk (that) *I bought yesterday.*

State the nouns or pronouns which are qualified in the above examples, and suggest other adjective clauses which might be substituted for those given.

An adjective clause is occasionally introduced not by a relative pronoun, but by another part of speech acting as a relative (known as *relative adverb* or *relative conjunction*):

> This is the ground *where I scored my century* (qualifying 'ground').
> I have moments of happiness *when I am glad to be living in this age* (qualifying 'moments').
> [*where* = on which; *when* = in which.]

NOUN CLAUSES

A noun clause performs exactly the same function as a noun:

> *What cannot be cured* must be endured. (Subject.)
> He said *that he would come to the match.* (Object.)
> This is *what I believe.* (Complement.)

Note that the noun clauses in the above sentences perform exactly the same function as the simple nouns or pronouns in:

> *This* must be endured. (Subject.)
> He said *something*. (Object.)
> This is *my belief*. (Complement.)

Although noun clauses are often introduced by the conjunction *that* or by the relative *what* (= *that which*), they are sometimes introduced by other conjunctions, especially in dependent questions:

> He asked *whether I had done my homework*. (Object of 'asked.')
> I explained *how I had lost it*. (Object of 'explained.')

A noun clause, like a noun, may be the object of a preposition or participle, or be in apposition to a noun:

> Let us not talk rashly of *what we do not understand*. (Object of preposition 'of.')
> Thinking *that this was the king*, I bowed low. (Object of present participle 'thinking.')
> My spirit was sustained by the conviction *that I was going to win*. (In apposition to 'conviction.')

Note the construction in which the pronoun 'it' is used as a *Provisional Subject* before the verb, the real subject being a noun clause which follows the verb:

> *It* is remarkable *that he escaped with his life*.
> [The sentence means: "That he escaped with his life is remarkable."]

The conjunction 'that' is sometimes omitted in noun clauses:

> I believe (that) this is my train.

Avoiding Confusion

Care should be taken to distinguish an adjective clause, which *describes* the noun, from a noun clause in apposition, which *refers to the same thing* as the noun. In an adjective clause 'which' and 'that' are often interchangeable, but in a noun clause 'which' cannot be substituted for 'that'.

At length he told me the truth *that was so hard to tell.* (Adjective clause *describing* 'truth.')

At length he told me the truth *that I had failed in my examination.* (Noun clause in apposition to 'truth'; it does not describe 'truth,' but states what the truth *is.* 'Which' could not be substituted for 'that' without destroying the sense of the sentence.)

EXERCISE (C)

Give the noun clauses and adjective clauses in the following sentences, stating the function of each clause:

(*a*) Virtue best loves those children that she beats.

(*b*) The player who can field well at cover-point will prove that he is worth his place in any side.

(*c*) What I cannot understand is how a person who has never played the game before can hope to beat an experienced player.

(*d*) Asking whether I was brave enough to follow, he plunged into the river and swam to the other side, where bushes were growing near the bank.

(*e*) The certainty that I would follow made him scale the bank without once looking back to see if I was behind him.

(*f*) I do not know whether we are certain to win the match, for a belief that has not been tested is not really a certainty.

(*g*) I remember the house where I was born, but I cannot tell you where it is.

(*h*) It is not surprising that she has been asked to take the leading part in the school play, for she is a girl who has shown great promise in the plays that have been presented during the last two years.

(*i*) I hope I am not exaggerating when I say that the boy who takes the leading male part is the best actor the school has had for some years.

ADVERB CLAUSES

Time. (Introduced by *when, before, after, while, till, as, since, as soon as*):

When the cat's away the mice will play.
The winning hit was made *as the clock struck six.*

Place. (Introduced by *where*):

Where the offence is let the great axe fall.
I found my book *where I had left it.*

Cause (*Reason*). (Introduced by *because, since, as*):

I got out of my chair quickly *because there was a drawing-pin on the seat.*

As you forgot the tickets you had better go home and fetch them.

Purpose. (Introduced by *that, so that* [= in order that], *lest* [negative]):

They cut notches in the trees *so that they could find their way back.*

Result. (Introduced by *so . . . that* [as a result]):

The room was so quiet *that you could hear his watch ticking.*

Condition. (Introduced by *if, unless* [negative], *provided that*, or by conditional construction with Inverted Subjunctive):

If you have tears, prepare to shed them now.

We shall finish the match *unless it starts to rain* (= *if* it does *not* start . . .).

Should he follow you again, I should inform the police. (Inverted Subjunctive = 'If he should follow . . .')

Concession. (Introduced by *though, although, even if*):

Though this be madness, yet there's method in it.—SHAKESPEARE, *Hamlet.*

We shall continue the game *even if it starts to rain* (= even *though* it may start . . .).

Comparison. (i) MANNER. (Introduced by *as, as if, as though*):

He ran *as if a tiger were at his heels*

(ii) DEGREE. (Introduced by *as, than*):

He is working harder *than I expected.* (Modifying 'harder.')
Smith is as lazy *as he can be.* (Modifying 'lazy.')

EXERCISE (*D*)

Pick out the adverb clauses in the following, and state their kind (Time, Place, etc.) and function (modifying the verb ——, etc.):

(*a*) When the troops reached the top of the hill they saw the enemy's tents far below them in the valley.

(*b*) George Eliot had a face like a horse, and if you will imagine a very sad horse you will get her expression correctly.

(c) I was surprised to see him at school to-day, because he was obviously unwell yesterday.

(d) A tennis-court was made where the ground was fairly level, although there was not much grass there.

(e) Although she would have liked another helping of apple tart, she was afraid to ask for it, because she had been told not to be greedy.

(f) The football pitch was so slippery that the players could hardly keep their feet.

(g) I am asking Jones to open the discussion, as he has had a good deal of experience in public speaking.

(h) He looked as though he was about to burst into tears when she asked him to dance with her.

(i) Had I known the bus service was so bad, I would have walked home.

(j) She left the office early so that she could go to the dance in the evening.

(k) The policeman could run faster than the two boys had imagined, as he was an experienced athlete.

(l) I have not been able to play tennis since the season started, as I sprained my ankle early in May.

(m) I was naturally beaten in the singles, since my opponent was the best player in the club.

(n) He looked at me as if I were an unpleasant kind of insect when I asked him to join me in a game.

(o) He agreed to join the party provided that they did not object to his dog, an animal as fierce as if it had just been let out of a cage.

Analysis of Complex Sentences

1. In analysing a complex sentence the first step is to find and underline the *finite verbs*, ignoring infinitives and simple participles. This gives us the number of clauses in the sentence.

2. The next step is to find the *main clause*, since this is the pivot on which the whole sentence hangs. Unlike the subordinate clauses, it will not normally be introduced by a conjunction or relative word. (There may, however, be two or more co-ordinate main clauses, and the second and subsequent clauses may be introduced by *and*, *but*, or some other co-ordinating conjunction.)

H

3. Next we should determine the *function* of each subordinate clause. Sometimes the introductory word helps us; but we have to remember that words such as *that* and *as*, for example, may introduce more than one type of clause. The work that the clause is doing is the important thing. We must bear in mind that relatives, conjunctions, and Subjects are sometimes omitted.

4. Finally we write out each clause, and put beside it the kind of clause and its function.

EXAMPLE 1

Since you live close to me I hope you will find time to call on me when an opportunity offers itself in the spring. which will soon be here.

(Finite verbs are: *live, hope, will find, offers, will be.*)

Special points: 'to call' is an infinitive, and must not be included among the finite verbs. 'Since,' 'when,' and 'which' obviously introduce subordinate clauses. The word 'that' must be understood before 'you will find.' 'I hope,' then, remains as the main clause.

(i) I hope	*Main clause.*
(ii) Since you live close to me	*Adverb clause of cause, modifying 'hope' in (i).*
(iii) you will find time to call on me	*Noun clause, Object of 'hope' in (i).*
(iv) when an opportunity offers itself in the spring	*Adverb clause of time, modifying 'to call' in (iii).*
(v) which will soon be here	*Adjective clause. qualifying 'spring' in (iv).*

EXAMPLE 2

Every one takes for granted that in his childhood, as later when he made his great marches, he was muscular and strongly built. This was so far from being the case that there were many anxious consultations over him, and the local doctor said he could not become a sailor as he could never hope to obtain the necessary number of inches round the chest.

SIR JAMES BARRIE (*on* Captain Scott)

(Finite verbs are: *takes, made, was, was, were, said, could become, could hope.*)

Special points: There are two separate sentences in this passage, and they must be analysed separately. 'Takes for granted' is a single notion, equivalent to 'assumes,' and may be regarded as a verb.

Sentence 1

(i) Every one takes for granted	*Main clause.*
(ii) that in his childhood, as later, he was muscular and strongly built	*Noun clause, object of 'takes (for granted).'*
(iii) when he made his great marches	*Adverb clause of time, in apposition to 'later' in* (ii), *modifying 'was' in* (ii).

Sentence 2

(iv) This was so far from being the case	*Main clause.*
(v) that there were many anxious consultations over him	*Adverb clause of result, modifying 'so far' in* (iv).
(vi) and [connective] the local doctor said	*Main clause, co-ordinate with* (iv).
(vii) (that) he could not become a sailor	*Noun clause, object of 'said' in* (vi).
(viii) as he could never hope to obtain the necessary number of inches round the chest	*Adverb clause of cause, modifying 'could not become' in* (vii).

EXAMPLE 3

If the bad cricketer says, "I remember when I took a century in forty minutes off Lockwood and Richardson," he is nothing but a liar.   A. A. MILNE

(Finite verbs are: *says, remember, took, is.*)

(i) He is nothing but a liar	*Main clause.*
(ii) If the bad cricketer says	*Adverb clause of condition, modifying 'is' in* (i).

Quoted sentence (Object of 'says' in (ii))

(iii) I remember	*Main clause.*
(iv) when I took a century in forty minutes off Lockwood and Richardson	*Noun clause, Object of 're-member' in* (iii).

EXERCISES (*E*)

Analyse the following passages into clauses, stating the kind and function of each clause, showing its relationship to the rest of the sentence in which it stands. State the grammatical function of each of the words in italics.

1. As the skater was *performing* a graceful figure-of-eight he tripped over a glove that *some one* had carelessly dropped, and sat down on the ice *most* ungracefully.

2. It sometimes seems *that* those who live in towns are more devoted to the country than [are] countryfolk *themselves*, who are too busy *to observe* its delights.

MARY CROSBIE

3. *Writing* a novel is more difficult than it seems. If this *were* not so, the number of books which masquerade under the title would be appreciably fewer, just as violinists are *scarcer* than [are] persons who can, in an emergency, *beat* upon a drum.

MORCHARD BISHOP

4. *Had* we lived, I should have had a tale *to tell* of the hardihood, endurance, and courage of *my* companions which would have stirred the heart of every Englishman. These rough notes and our dead bodies must *tell* the tale.

CAPTAIN SCOTT

5. There is a well-known story of a *university* don who, having been engaged all the week in setting examination papers, was heard to murmur, as he listened *to* the Ten Commandments in church, "Not more than five should be *attempted.*"

Birmingham Post

6. I confess that I have known *so* many instances of boys going *through* Eton without learning anything that I should not *like* to send one without a private tutor who should force him to learn something.

DUKE OF WELLINGTON

7. *Ulysses* preferred his old woman to immortality, and this absence of *mine* has led me *to see* that he was *as* wise in this *as* [he was] in other things.

T. H. HUXLEY (to his wife)

8. *If* I ask myself why I prefer the poetry of Dante to that of Shakespeare, I should have *to say*, because it seems *to me* to illustrate a saner attitude towards the mystery of life.

T. S. ELIOT

9. The fruit *which* decorates churches and chapels at the Harvest Thanksgiving services is *usually* distributed later to the sick or infirm people of the area. It happened recently that an invalid in a West Riding village received *these* gifts from both church and chapel on the *same* day. When the vicar called shortly afterwards his parishioner thanked him heartily, and added the tribute: "An' t'Church were a banana up on t'Chapel."

Yorkshire Post

10. Analyse into clauses the sentence given below, writing out each clause in full. Give the grammatical description of each clause and state its grammatical function in the sentence.

As I stood on the terrace, which gave a commanding view of the whole valley, I saw in the distance what I took to be a collection of military vehicles, moving slowly along the opposite ridge, where they caught the light of the morning sun.   (*London*)

11. In that year (1851), when the Great Exhibition spread its hospitable glass roof high over the elms of Hyde Park, and all the world came *to admire* England's wealth, progress, and enlightenment, there might *profitably* have been another 'exhibition' to show how our poor were housed and to teach the admiring foreign visitor *some* of the dangers *that* beset the path of the vaunted new era.

(*a*) Give the grammatical description of the clauses and show their connexion with each other.

(*b*) State the grammatical functions of the words italicized.

(*London*)

12. Analyse into clauses the passage quoted below, and state the relation of each subordinate clause to the rest of the sentence:

The probability is that the barber-surgeon left the house at the Schlamm with the child on the coach beside him. There were times in his life when he took a spasmodic interest in the members of his family. In a heart that had known little tenderness and much severity there were moments of human understanding, which came at intervals like the glow of a short burst of sunshine over ice.

(*Oxford*)

13. Re-write each of the following sentences, replacing the underlined phrase by a dependent clause that does not alter the meaning. Write a full description of each clause you have introduced.

Example. The flood waters having receded, they decided to attempt to cross the river.

Answer. As the flood waters had receded, they decided to attempt to cross the river. Adverbial clause of reason.

(i) The idea *of my flying to the moon* is preposterous.

(ii) He is a man *to be avoided.*

(iii) *Having read the letter*, he immediately wrote a reply.

(iv) The lawyer demanded *the release of the younger prisoner.*

(v) *Weather permitting*, we shall go for a picnic tomorrow.

(vi) *Without careful preparation of your plans*, you cannot hope to succeed.   (*Cambridge*)

14. State the kind and function of the italicized dependent clauses in the following:

(*a*) I have always thought that *what was strange about those fairs* was the sense of lawlessness, and yet the good behaviour of most of the people.

(*b*) Those who could not keep silence had voices so broken *that they no longer sounded human.*

(*c*) I have wondered, indeed, *if Bunyan did not take old Lilmouth for a model of his fair,/ for we were in actual fact of a "blood red colour".*

(*d*) These voices belonged to the world of the great fair where anything was possible and *everything was strange.*

(*Southern Universities*—adapted)

15. From Wakeham was taken the stone of the new Midland Bank in Manchester, which is *using altogether* four thousand tons. Mr Vincent Harris's Manchester Library comes from another quarry in *that* neighbourhood, so *that* the stone of these two buildings lay in the Dorsetshire ground at much the same distance from each other as the buildings stand from one another in Manchester.

JAMES BONE

16. Analyse the following passage into clauses, showing their kind and, where necessary, dependence or relation:

When I visited the old town, the house in which my father was born was still standing, but it seemed very shabby. It was evident, however, that the occupant enjoyed sunning himself in that quiet garden.

(*Northern Universities*)

17. Give from the passage in (16) above *one* example of each of the following, writing each answer on a separate line: (i) a reflexive pronoun, (ii) a relative pronoun, (iii) a co-ordinating conjunction, (iv) a subordinating conjunction, (v) a possessive adjective, (vi) a present participle, (vii) a past participle, (viii) an auxiliary verb, (ix) a preposition, (x) an adverb of degree, (xi) an adverb of time, (xii) an adjective used predicatively (*i.e.*, as complement).

(*Northern Universities*)

SYNTHESIS

Hilaire Belloc begins an essay on cats with the words:

(i) I do not like Them. It is no good asking me why, though I have plenty of reasons.

He did *NOT* begin in either of the following ways:

(ii) I do not like Them. It is no good asking me why. I have plenty of reasons.

(iii) I do not like Them, but it is no good asking me why, though I have plenty of reasons.

The disconnected sentences in (ii) would have been clumsy and confusing. The stringing together of clauses in (iii) would have been weak and ineffective. It was clear to the author that the first idea needed to be expressed in a short, pungent sentence, and that the next two ideas needed to be connected together.

The ability to join together different ideas in various ways is an important element in easy, flexible writing. The decision when and how to join ideas is made instinctively by good writers, but there is no reason why we should not practise the art deliberately. This joining is known as **Synthesis** (a 'putting together'); it is the opposite process to Analysis, which is a 'taking apart.'

EXAMPLE 1. WAYS OF JOINING IDEAS

    I climbed the hill. I sat down for a rest.

  (i) *Using a connective:*

    I climbed the hill *and* sat down for a rest.

  (ii) *Expressing one idea as a phrase:*

    After climbing the hill I sat down for a rest.

  (iii) *Expressing one idea as a subordinate clause:*

    I sat down for a rest *when I had climbed the hill.*

EXAMPLE 2. ALTERING THE STRESS

    The dawn broke. We saw the desert before us. It stretched away to the horizon.

    (i) When the dawn broke we saw the desert before us stretching away to the *horizon.*

      [This is a natural order which lays a slight stress upon the last word *horizon.*]

    (ii) The *desert* lay before us, stretching away in the light of the dawn to the horizon.

      [A stronger stress is laid upon *desert* by bringing it to the beginning of the sentence and making it the Subject of the main verb.]

    (iii) The desert, stretching away before us to the horizon, was not revealed until the *dawn* broke.

      [The form of the sentence throws the stress upon the subordinate clause at the end, and thus upon the breaking of *dawn.*]

EXAMPLE 3. COMPRESSION OF IDEAS

Some lending libraries are busy. The books get out of order on the shelves. They have to be checked. They also have to be rearranged. This happens every day.

In some busy lending libraries the books get out of order on the shelves, and have to be checked and rearranged every day.

EXERCISE (F)

1. Join each of the following statements in three different ways. You may make any necessary alterations in the wording, but you must not alter or omit any of the facts.

(a) Suddenly I saw the lion. He was about to spring on me.

(b) Miss Nightingale's position was an official one. It was hardly the easier for that.

(c) The first attempt to cross the Atlantic was made in 1873. Three Americans started off in a balloon.

(d) One of the party had fallen sick. He was saved by a daring descent of the mountain. They had only a candle in a lantern to light the way.

(e) I opened the trap-door. I dropped a flag. This was over the calculated position of the South Pole.

2. Combine the following ideas into a single sentence:

(a) I lost my way. It happened when I was on a walking tour. I was in the New Forest.

(b) The old man carried a viper with him. This was his general practice. He had made it quite tame. He had extracted the fangs from it. These were poisonous.

(c) Magnolia loved the pilot-house. She loved this best of all. It was bright and gay. It stood high above the rest of the boat. It was reached by a flight of stairs. The stairs were narrow.

(d) All the travellers went into the kitchen. There were four of them. Each had a glass. He carried this in his hand. Sam Weller headed the procession. This was to show them the way.

(e) A flight was made. It lasted 59 seconds. This was at the fourth trial. In this time the machine flew more than half a kilometre. This was the distance flown through the air. Over the ground the distance was 256 metres.

3. To the following main clauses add the clauses indicated in brackets. Clauses should be added in the order given, but the main clause need not come first.

(a) We gazed at the great cathedral. (Adverb Clause of Time—Adjective Clause.)

(*b*) The crowd filled the ground. (Co-ordinate Main Clause—Adverb Clause of Place—Adverb Clause of Result.)

(*c*) The player should watch the ball. (Adverb Clause of Condition—Adverb Clause of Manner—Adjective Clause.)

(*d*) At school they used to tell us. (Noun Clause—Adjective Clause—Adverb Clause of Cause.)

4. Use each of the following subordinate clauses in the ways indicated, by supplying suitable main clauses:

(*a*) when we get to the top of the hill.
   (i) as Adverb Clause, (ii) as Adjective Clause, (iii) as Noun Clause.

(*b*) who won the Open Golf Championship.
   (i) as Noun Clause, (ii) as Adjective Clause.

(*c*) where there is an opening in the hedge.
   (i) as Adverb Clause, (ii) as Noun Clause, (iii) as Adjective Clause.

5. Combine each of the following groups of four simple sentences into a complex sentence, thus making a continuous passage from (i), (ii), and (iii). The order of sentences in each group need not be kept.

(i) Another collection of short plays has been published.
   The B.B.C. has helped to popularize such plays.
   Many people will welcome this collection.
   The publishers believe that.

(ii) Drama has been loved for many centuries in England.
   It is loved intelligently and enthusiastically to-day.
   It has never been so popular.
   Amateur dramatic societies may be counted in thousands.

(iii) The new volume is intended to provide pleasant reading.
   It offers material for acting to amateurs.
   Their needs have been considered.
   No elaborate production is necessary.

(*Northern Universities General Certificate.*)

CHAPTER IX

ERRORS TO AVOID

ERRORS IN THE USE OF WORDS

Words Wrongly Used

Alright—there is no such word. The correct form is *all right*, and its opposite is *all wrong*. In other combinations with *all*, however, the two separate words have become one, with a consequent dropping of the final *l* of *all* (e.g., *almost*, *already*, *although*). In these the force of the word *all* is less clearly felt; *all ready* has quite a different meaning from *already*.

Aggravate. This is not a synonym for *irritate*. To *aggravate* is to make heavier, metaphorically, and the word is applied to an offence, a disagreement, or an affliction, in the sense of to increase the seriousness (or gravity) of these things. It is wrong to apply the word to a person; a person can be irritating or exasperating, but not aggravating.

Less does not mean *not so many*. The word applies to degree or extent, not to number. "There are *fewer* (not *less*) pupils in the class this year, but they are *less* intelligent." As an epithet with *number*, the correct word is *small* (e.g., *a small number*, *a smaller number*).

Literally is sometimes wrongly used in the exact opposite of its true sense. A person who says "You could *literally* have knocked me down with a feather" really means "You could *figuratively* (or *metaphorically*) have . . . feather"— unless he is abnormally light and the feather abnormally powerful! *Literally* means "according to the exact sense of the word, without metaphor".

Infer (= to come to a conclusion) and *imply* (= to make an indirect suggestion) should not be used as synonyms. We normally *infer from*. "I *infer* from your letter that you are too busy to come to the meeting, though you do not actually say so." But "Your letter *implies* that you are too busy . . . say so."

Unique does not mean merely 'rare'; it is applied to something that is the *only one* of its kind. It is, therefore, absurd to say that a thing is 'quite unique' or 'most unique'. The words 'quite' and 'most' are pointless. If we mean that the object is 'very rare' or 'most unusual,' then we should say so. On the other hand, it would be sheer pedantry to object to 'almost unique,' which is a meaningful phrase. If there is only one copy of a book in existence, it is *unique*; if there are only two or three copies, then any one of them is *almost unique*.

Clichés

A cliché is a hackneyed, stereotyped phrase used by a writer who is too lazy to think about his own writing. The name comes from the French word for a stereotype block (*i.e.*, a block made for printing a phrase that is in constant use, to save the need for setting up each letter separately). "Suddenly, *like a bolt from the blue*, the headmaster appeared in the doorway." Such writing is bad because it indicates slovenly thinking. If you are going to use a simile to add vividness to what you are writing, let the comparison be one that you yourself have observed and appreciated. If you have actually seen a thunderbolt fall from the sky, and if the headmaster walking into a room really suggests this unlikely image, then it might be excusable to use it; but the condition is improbable. If a genuine simile does not naturally present itself to your mind while you are writing, then you do not need one. "The headmaster suddenly appeared in the doorway" could, in the right context, be good, effective English; its effect is ruined, not helped, by the addition of a cliché.

Here are some other stereotyped phrases which should never be mechanically used: *The cup that cheers* ('a cup of tea'); *filthy lucre* ('money'); *good in parts, like the curate's egg* (the joke has long been worn away); *the fair sex* (the writer does not really believe that all women are lovely—or blonde!); *more easily imagined than described* (the writer is trying to excuse himself, but actually draws attention to his failure).

It would be wrong to say that a writer must never use a proverbial expression or a familiar phrase. But when you find yourself tempted to use one, ask yourself if you are using it because it precisely expresses what you are trying to say, or because you have not bothered to think what you are trying to say.

Jargon

This term is applied to language that is considered hard to understand, especially if such language is full of technical terms relating to some branch of science, art, or trade.

There is a right use of jargon as well as a wrong. Technical terms are necessary to people who engage in a specialized technique, scientific or any other, and these terms are likely to mean very little to the outsider. They are jargon, but they are perfectly correct when used by technicians communicating with each other. Some of these terms may eventually find their way into the common language, and they are still correct when they express an idea that cannot be adequately expressed otherwise.

Jargon is wrongly used when it is a pretentious substitute for simple language, or when its effect is to befuddle the averagely intelligent reader instead of to enlighten him. It is wrong to use the psychologist's jargon, 'inferiority complex,' when we merely mean 'a feeling of inferiority,' or the educationist's jargon, 'fulfilling the urge for self-expression,' when we merely mean, 'doing what he wants to do'.

Slang

Slang expressions are reasonable currency in familiar conversation with friends. They save trouble; and it would be ridiculous to insist that people passing the time of day, or just taking pleasure in each other's company, should address themselves to these activities in the spirit of Milton writing *Paradise Lost*. But slang should not be used in any kind of formal writing, for here it is not the communicator's business to save himself trouble. His task is to convey his meaning with exactness in terms which are acceptable to a wide range of readers.

On certain special occasions a judicious use of slang may be permissible. Thus during the last war airmen giving talks on the radio or writing articles in magazines sometimes helped to suggest the appropriate atmosphere and to avoid an impression of unreality by the natural use of such terms as 'kite,' 'flat spin,' 'hadn't a clue,' 'the gen,' and so on. This was legitimate if not overdone; a specific purpose was served. Again, a serious writer may legitimately refer to the 'couldn't care less' attitude of mind, where he is quoting the slang term to illustrate and represent the mentality of those who use it. But apart from such deliberate use for some special purpose, slang should be avoided. There are more acceptable and precise synonyms available for such expressions, for instance, as 'fed up,' 'browned off,' 'bloke,' 'guy,' 'O.K.,' 'dough' (money).

Foreign Words and Phrases

A sound rule of good writing is to avoid using foreign expressions (that is, expressions which *remain* foreign, not words, such as 'garage', which have been absorbed into the language to serve a purpose). There is nearly always an English equivalent; if there is not it is usually best to think out afresh what you are trying to say. If you are writing in English you should stick to your chosen medium of expression.

Nothing is gained by writing, for instance, *de novo* for 'anew', *mirabile dictu* for 'wonderful to relate' (a cliché in any case), *hors de combat* for 'disabled' (not 'war-horse', as the schoolboy is reputed to have written), *modus operandi* for 'plan of working', *coup de soleil* for 'sunstroke', *entre nous* for 'between ourselves', or *en passant* for 'in passing'.

On the other hand, such words as *post mortem*, *dénouement* (the last stage, revealing the final situation, in the plot of a novel or play), *vice versa*, *rendezvous* (place or time of meeting, arranged beforehand) have been introduced to fill an obvious need, and are now virtually English words.

Tautology

Tautology is an unnecessary and usually unconscious repetition of words or ideas in the same sentence, and hence involves the use of superfluous words (sometimes called **Pleonasm**). For example: "Tautology is an unnecessary *repetition* of ideas *that have been indicated already* in the same sentence." Here 'repetition' and 'that have been indicated already' express the same thought (you cannot repeat an idea unless it has already been indicated), and the clause 'that . . . already' should be omitted.

The term *tautology* is usually confined to the *wrong* use of repetition, though some grammarians have applied the term to any kind of repetition. We must be careful not to confuse tautology (in its usual sense) with deliberate repetition for emphasis or rhetorical effect. "There must not be any rowdy behaviour in the corridor: every pupil must go quietly from one room to another." 'Not be any rowdy behaviour' and 'go quietly' repeat a single idea; but the repetition is intended to stress the importance of the rule. This is not tautology in our present sense of the term.

Misuse of the Hyphen

A failure to use common sense in applying the hyphen to closely connected words may result in absurdities. Here are a few examples to indicate the kind of errors to avoid, the chief of which is the connecting of the wrong two words:

a pickled herring-merchant (*for* pickled-herring merchant)
a small tooth-comb (*for* small-tooth comb)

In the following examples the error is the omission of a hyphen altogether, where the very close connexion between two words makes a hyphen necessary, and where the omission leaves two separate epithets qualifying one noun when a single (hyphenated) epithet is really intended:

a red hot face (*for* red-hot face)
a top heavy bookshelf (*for* top-heavy bookshelf)
three floored houses (*for* three-floored houses)
good hearted people (*for* good-hearted people)

Explain the effect of misplacing or omitting the hyphen in each of the examples above.

ERRORS IN STYLE

Breach of Proximity

There is no more important rule of good writing than the *Law of Proximity*, which lays it down that any qualifying word or group of words should be placed as near as possible to the word qualified. Failure to observe this rule is a common cause of vague, woolly, and feeble writing.

EXAMPLES

1. I was surprised to see the man who was due to play tennis to-day at Wimbledon in Paris last night.

COMMENT. This sentence plays havoc both with geography and with time. Parisians will be surprised to learn that the home of English tennis is in their city, and every one will be surprised to learn that to-day is included in last night. What really happened in Paris was not the tennis at Wimbledon, but the surprisal. The qualifying words "in Paris last night" should be placed as near as possible to the words "surprised to see." The neatest place to put them is at the beginning of the sentence, where they correctly qualify the whole of the main clause ("I . . . man").

CORRECT. Last night, in Paris, I was surprised to see the man who was due to play tennis to-day at Wimbledon.

2. The umpire ought to replace the bails, not the batsman.

COMMENT. The sentence indicates that the batsman is subjected to treatment which no spirited cricketer ought to tolerate. The real antithesis, of course, is not between "bails" and "batsman," but between "umpire" and "batsman."

CORRECT. The umpire, not the batsman, ought to replace the bails.

3. The books should only be replaced by the librarian.

COMMENT. The librarian's function seems to be confined to putting books back on the shelves; by implication he is forbidden to *find* books for library-users. But no doubt the writer of the notice really meant that no one but the librarian was allowed to replace the books.

The word 'only' has a way of slipping out of its proper place if it is not watched. Generally speaking, it should be put immediately in front of the word (or very closely connected group of words) which it is intended to qualify.

CORRECT. The books should be replaced *only* by the librarian.

Ambiguity

Ambiguity may arise:

1. From a breach of the Law of Proximity. (See above.)

2. From the omission of a necessary preposition or article, especially after *and*:

(i) We ought to use our fuel for cooking and warming ourselves.

COMMENT. "Cooking and warming" appears to be a phrase qualifying "ourselves." Unless the writer is actually advocating self-cannibalism, he should make it clear that the two gerunds are not intended to be connected, but are separately governed by the preposition "for."

CORRECT. We ought to use our fuel for cooking and *for* warming ourselves.

(ii) The Secretary and Treasurer agreed to address the meeting.

COMMENT. Is there (*a*) one official holding a double position or are there (*b*) two separate officials? The sentence implies the former, but probably means the latter. The ambiguity should not be tolerated.

CORRECT. (*a*) Mr Jones, the secretary and treasurer, agreed to address the meeting. OR (*b*) The secretary and *the* treasurer agreed . . . meeting.

3. From the attempt to crowd too much into a single sentence:

> I confess to having felt irritated, not to say disgusted, when, as I was fated to listen to some time ago, a well-fed and well-groomed individual—he was a cleric, too, by the way—contributed his share to a discussion on the social problem by the statement that it was a question of over-population.
>
> C. J. MELROSE, *The Data of Economics*[1]

COMMENT. The writer is trying to say too many things at once, and the result is a confused construction and a confused reader. The preposition "to," after "listen," appears at first to be governing "individual," but a little later we find that this word is the subject of "contributed"—by which time we give up in despair.

The only cure for this sort of ambiguous muddle is to start all over again, to think out afresh what we are trying to say, and to put the subsidiary points in one sentence and the main point in another. (While we are about it we will take care to avoid the misuse of the word "individual.")

CORRECT. Some time ago I was fated to listen to a well-fed and well-groomed gentleman—a cleric, by the way—contributing his share to a discussion on the social problem. I confess that I was irritated, not to say disgusted, when he made the statement that it was a question of over-population.

4. From vagueness in the use of pronouns, particularly in reported speech. (See pp. 128, 216.)

Non Sequitur

The parts of a sentence should be related in sense. When they are not, the author is guilty of a *non sequitur*. (*Latin:* "It does not follow.") Journalists and compilers of biographical dictionaries are apt to commit this fault through the attempt to put together a lot of miscellaneous information without using too many short sentences.

> Born at Brede in Sussex, she published her first novel in 1908.

COMMENT. The sentence implies that if she had been born not at Brede, but at some other place, she would not have published her

---

[1] Quoted in *Standard English*, by E. H. Grout.

first novel in 1908. This might conceivably be true, but the writer does not know it, and obviously is not really trying to say it. He is merely putting two unconnected ideas together.

CORRECT. She was born at Brede in Sussex. In 1908 she published . . .

Verbosity

Verbosity is the using of more words than are required for effective expression, with the result that expression becomes *less* effective. Often it takes the form of *circumlocution* (*i.e.*, saying in a roundabout way what could be better said more briefly).

In the majority of instances Brown's runs were scored from boundary hits.

COMMENT. The italicized phrase simply means 'most.

CORRECT. Most of Brown's runs were scored from boundaries.

GRAMMATICAL ERRORS

Error of Attraction

A list of all the players, with their Houses, were put up on the notice-board.

COMMENT. The verb "were" has been attracted into the plural by the proximity of two intervening nouns, "Houses" and "players." But the subject-word "list" is singular, so the verb should also be singular.

CORRECT. A list of all the players, with their Houses, *was* put up on the notice-board.

Non-agreement of the Relative

A. W. Carr made one of the hardest hits that has ever been seen at Lord's.

COMMENT. A relative pronoun must agree with its antecedent in number. "Hits" is plural, and therefore the relative "that" must be plural too. As it is the subject of its clause, it must take a plural verb "have."

CORRECT. A. W. Carr made one of the hardest *hits that have* ever been seen at Lord's.

(Compare "A.W.C. made the hardest *hit that has* ever been seen," where the antecedent "hit" is singular and the relative therefore requires a singular verb.)

Distributives with Plural Verbs

Neither of the boys were present at the prize-giving.
Each of the boys will be allowed to say exactly what they think.
Nobody present dared to say what they really thought.
Have either of you ever been up in an aeroplane?

COMMENT. The distributive adjectives and pronouns—e.g., *each, either, every, everybody, anybody, nobody, neither*—are singular, for they imply that each individual person or thing is separately considered. They must be given *singular* verbs and other parts of speech.

CORRECT. *Neither* of the boys *was* present at the prize-giving.
Each of the boys will be allowed to say exactly what *he thinks*.
Nobody present dared to say what *he* really thought.
Has either of you ever been up in an aeroplane?

Note. Strictly, *none* (= no one, not one) should also be followed by the singular, but usage, even among educated people, more often favours the use of the plural verb. ("There are none so deaf as those who won't hear.") The *Oxford English Dictionary* explicitly states that the plural construction is commoner.

Relative in the Wrong Case

1. He was surprised to see that there were several people present who he did not know.
2. That is the man whom I think is the finest footballer in England.
3. That is the man who I gave the best years of my life to.

COMMENT. Confusion between *who* and *whom* often arises from neglect of one basic rule: *the case of the relative pronoun depends on its function in its own clause.* If it is the subject of the clause it must be *who*: if it is the object it must be *whom*.

Let us take the relative clauses in the examples above, arranging the order of words so that they read: Subject / Verb / Object.

1. "he / did not know / *whom*" (not *who*)—Object of "know". (A useful way of checking is to substitute *he* for *who*, and *him* for *whom*

Thus we should obviously say "he did not know *him*," and not "he did not know *he*.")

2. "*who* (not *whom*) / is / the finest footballer. . ." "Who" is not the Object of "I think" (which may be regarded as a kind of parenthesis), but the Subject of 'is the finest . . .'' (Check: "*He* is the finest footballer . . ." not "*him* is the finest . . .")

3. "I / gave / the best years of my life / to *whom* (not *who*)." "Whom" is the Object of the preposition "to." (Check: "I gave the best years of my life to *him*," not ". . . to *he*.")

CORRECT. 1. He was surprised to see that there were several people present *whom* he did not know.

2. That is the man *who* I think is the finest footballer in England.

3. That is the man *to whom* I gave the best years of my life. (This is correct, but would be stiff in conversation; the relative would normally be omitted and the 'to' left at the end.)

Note. The following is correct:

There is some doubt *as to who* really is the senior prefect.

(Here "to" is not a preposition governing the relative pronoun, but part of a compound conjunction "as to." "Who" is the subject of its clause. The conjunction is really unnecessary.)

Wrong Use of Superlative

Both the boys were tall, but John was the tallest.

COMMENT. The superlative is used when more than two things are compared; the comparative when there are only two.

CORRECT. *Both* the boys were tall, but John was the *taller*.

Misrelated Participle

Arriving at the top of the hill, a wonderful view of the surrounding countryside made us gasp with delight.

COMMENT. The participial phrase "Arriving . . . hill" grammatically qualifies "view" (the nearest noun); but this, of course, is nonsense, as a view does not arrive at the top of a hill. The pronoun ("we") to which the phrase ought to be applied is, in fact, not expressed at all. We must correct the sentence either (*a*) by supplying the necessary pronoun immediately following the participial phrase, or (*b*) by changing the phrase to an adverbial clause.

CORRECT. (*a*) *Arriving* at the top of the hill, *we* gasped with delight when we saw the wonderful view.

(*b*) *When we arrived at the top of the hill*, a wonderful view of the surrounding countryside made us gasp with delight.

Confusion of Gerund with Present Participle

Our opponents do not like us *telling* the truth about the matter.

COMMENT. Here "telling" is not a participle (*i.e.*, adjective), but a gerund (*i.e.*, noun), for the sentence states that our opponents object to "the telling" of the truth by us: it does not indicate that their objection is to "us" in general. As the gerund is a *noun* it must be qualified not by the personal pronoun (in this case "us"), but by the possessive *adjective* (in this case "our").

CORRECT. Our opponents do not like *our telling* the truth about the matter.

Note. Strictly speaking, if there is a noun, not a pronoun, in front of the gerund, this noun should be put in the possessive. (*E.g.*, "I do not like the candidate's telling the truth about the matter.") Fowler, in *Modern English Usage*, has argued vigorously in favour of this, under the heading *Fused Participle*. But most good writers feel that the possessive noun with the gerund is often clumsy and pedantic; and the construction is best avoided altogether. (*E.g.*, "I do not like the candidate to tell the truth about the matter.")

Inconsistency in Use of Pronouns

It is right that one should do the best he can in helping lame dogs over stiles.

COMMENT. The indefinite pronoun *one* and the personal pronouns *he, they*, are not interchangeable. If you start off with *one* you must keep to it (and the possessive *one's*), and not switch over in the middle of a sentence or passage to a different kind of pronoun. And if the result turns out to be clumsy or ridiculous (*e.g.*, "One should have one's early-morning tea brought up to one, shouldn't one?") the cure is to avoid using this usually unnecessary pronoun. The indefinite use of *personal* pronouns is more satisfactory, because they change their form for different cases, and clumsy repetition is thus avoided. (*E.g.*, "*We* should have *our* early-morning tea brought up to *us*, shouldn't *we*?")

CORRECT. It is right that *one* should do the best *one* can in helping lame dogs over stiles. OR It is right that *we* should do the best *we* can in . . . .

Misuse of 'Due'

Due to the very bad weather this summer, the cricket club suffered a serious financial loss.

COMMENT. The word *due* is an adjective. It has not established its right to be used as part of a compound preposition with *to*; the correct form is *owing to*. A safe rule is to use *due* (+ *to*) only after the verbs *is, are, was, were* (or other forms of the verb *to be*), where it will normally be correctly used as a predicative adjective.

CORRECT. *Owing to* the very bad weather this summer, the cricket club suffered a serious financial loss. OR The cricket club's serious financial loss *is due* to the very bad weather this summer.

EXERCISES ON THE CORRECTION OF ERRORS

Comment on the following, and where necessary rewrite the sentence:

1. The pupil whom I thought would be at the bottom of the class was in fact near the top.

2. In learning to skate, the boots must not be too large.

3. You can rely on me doing my best to win the Long Jump.

4. This year there were less accidents outside the school than there were last year.

5. Every one thought of their own safety in this distressing accident.

6. The film was quite different to what I had expected.

7. Passengers should only alight from the bus when it is stationery.

8. Those sort of newspapers are full of sensational crime stories.

9. If you mean to infer that I am telling lies you had better say so straight out.

10. This is one of the most interesting films that has appeared for some time.

11. The great majority of motorists drive carefully in a greater or lesser degree.

12. Being a plain and straightforward person, the suggestion strikes me as hypocritical.

13. He told his father that he had lost his bicycle, and he couldn't tell him before because he didn't know where he was.

14. Walking along the road, there was a space of about fifty metres between each lamp-post.

15. I am returning the corrected exercises and examination papers.

16. Having climbed an iceberg to get their bearings, their canoes went adrift, and Nansen was forced to swim through the icy water to retrieve them.

17. If you will kindly reply by return I would be obliged.

18. The management regret that we cannot serve refreshments to people bringing their own food.

19. His children go for a ride in the wagon, and play in it when stationary in the shed.

20. These rubber boots are just the thing for fishing or walking in the snow.

21. I cannot work like I used to do.

22. In a number of cases companies start the completion of the form before the end of the year.

23. The hut was not very comfortable, but there was no alternate accommodation.

24. At the Shakespeare Memorial service at Southwark Cathedral Mr Leon Quartermain recited passages from the plays, while Mr Kenneth Barnes read the lessons.

25. I was surprised to meet my brother whom I thought was in London in Scotland.

26. The subject of our speaker's talk this evening is about "Good English".

27. Shakespeare is better than any author at portraying profound feeling.

28. When I got home, there was Jack and his friends waiting for me.

29. If there had been an opportunity of asking a question at the end of the lecture I should have liked to have done so.

30. We came to the same place as we had passed earlier in the day.

31. After the service the congregation was free to go their way.

32. The dull-eyed pupils listened wearily to the visitor's indeterminable lecture.

33. When conjuring with liquids the performer should exercise care or he will literally spill the beans.

34. Hearing strange noises above, the thought at once occurred to me that thieves had broken into the house.

35. If I was you I should stay at home, the reason being because there is an interesting talk by the wireless.

36. I shall be only too delighted to come to your delightful party.

37. The two men were born respectfully at Paris and The Hague, neither being British subjects at the time of his birth.

38. It has been well said that a man's religion is the chief fact with regard to him.

39. What one experiences in a barber's shop the first time he enters one is what he always experiences in barber's shops till the end of his days.

40. Such employment does not involve the necessity of obtaining a certificate of fitness.

41. The cessation of house-building operated over a period of six years.

42. He put his suitcase when he sat at the table under his feet.

43. I told my mother I would return on the next train and would she meet me.

44. She was very proud the first morning she rode a new horse with a new riding habit on.

45. She was surprised at the cordiality of her reception considering all she had heard of her host's masterly ways.

46. The only way of catching a train I have ever discovered is to miss the train before.

47. When he married the car lent by his brother took them to the station.

48. The old story that the Spaniard can live on a little bread and wine doesn't happen to be true. He needs food like you and I.

49. What Mr Thomas wants to see is a more comfortable taxi. . . . The driver will be entirely enclosed, and the passengers will have comfortable seats and better interior fittings.

50. He fired a pistol at the burglar's head, which he always kept under his pillow.

51. (a) Water was pumped into the flames to stop the fire from spreading at the rate of two-thousand litres per minute.

(b) Cycling through a busy thoroughfare, traffic jams made me late for work.

(c) The shopkeeper placed the beautiful vase on the shelf after admiring it.

(d) John Smith is cleverer than any boy in his class.

(e) I only go skating, like my brother, when the weather is cold.
(*Associated Examining Board*)

52. (a) It looks like he'll be more effected by this than he thought.

(b) I don't like him playing cricket on the lawn which I mown yesterday.

(c) Being unused to it, the chapel services disinterested him.

(d) Those whom we believe are natural leaders are seldom slack in the performance of his duties.

(e) The forest was remarkable for it's luxurious undergrowth.
(*Oxford and Cambridge*)

CHAPTER X

FIGURES OF SPEECH

THIS chapter has deliberately been left till last, lest the student should be tempted to regard figures of speech as ornaments with which to adorn his own writing. A good writer uses figures of speech unconsciously. He expresses himself in certain terms because those terms best convey what he is trying to say. If they happen to include certain figures of speech, as they often will, the inclusion is usually incidental and without premeditation.

It is often interesting, however, to examine figurative language when we are studying a piece of writing in detail; and questions on these matters sometimes occur in examinations. Various figures of speech and literary terms in common use are given here in alphabetical order, the more important figures being marked with an asterisk.

állegory. A fictitious narrative. in which the persons and events have a symbolic meaning. (*E.g.*, Bunyan's *The Pilgrim's Progress*, George Orwell's *Animal Farm*.)

alliteration. The repetition of the same consonant at the beginning of closely connected words. It was a characteristic of Old English poetry, and is still common in titles of articles and books, and in popular sayings and phrases. (*E.g.*, "In a *s*ummer *s*eason when *s*oft was the *s*un" [LANGLAND, *Piers Plowman*]; *The Pilgrim's Progress*; '*d*ead as a *d*oornail'; '*p*retty as a *p*icture.')

anticlimax. An arrangement of ideas in which an unimpressive item is put at the end, following some items which are more significant. It is often due to muddled thinking. When done deliberately it usually has a satirical or humorous effect. (*E.g.*, "Love your country; tell the truth; and don't dawdle."—THE FIRST LORD CROMER, at the Leys School.)

***antíthesis.** A balancing of contrasted ideas, usually in the same sentence. (*E.g.*, "Men who make money rarely saunter; men who save money rarely swagger."—BULWER LYTTON.)

apóstrophe. An exclamatory address made rhetorically to an absent person or to a personified object. (*E.g.*, "Milton! thou shouldst be living at this hour."—WORDSWORTH; "O eloquent, just, and mighty Death!"—RALEIGH.)

assonance. The rhyming of vowels, but not of the following consonants. (*E.g.*, load, moat; farther, harder.)

blank verse. Poetry not restricted by rhyme, but regular in metre.

> Our revels now are ended. These our actors,
> As I foretold you, were all spirits, and
> Are melted into air, into thin air:
> And, like the baseless fabric of this vision,
> The cloud-capp'd towers, the gorgeous palaces,
> The solemn temples, the great globe itself,
> Yea, all which it inherit, shall dissolve.
>
> SHAKESPEARE, *The Tempest*

climax. An arrangement of ideas in which the most impressive is put last, and gradually led up to. Its effect is usually dramatic and intense. The last three lines in the example of blank verse above are also an example of climax, expressing, in ascending order of intensity, the ideas: great buildings, royal palaces, religious temples, the whole earth, every living soul.

elegy. A song or poem of mourning, or one connected with the dead. (*E.g.*, Gray's *Elegy in a Country Churchyard*, Milton's *Lycidas*, Arnold's *Thyrsis*, Binyon's *For the Fallen*.)

epigram. A brief, witty saying, often satirical, with an unexpected sting in it. (*E.g.*, "Speech was given to us to conceal our thoughts." —OSCAR WILDE.)

epitaph. An inscription on a tomb, or a short tribute to a deceased person. (*E.g.*, "Nature and Nature's laws lay hid in night: God said, 'Let Newton be!' and all was light."—POPE.)

euphemism. A less offensive or less direct way of expressing something unpleasant or coarse. (*E.g.*, 'gentlemen of the road' for highwaymen; 'liquidation' for 'wholesale slaughter.')

euphony. A pleasing combination of sounds.

free verse. Poetry unrestricted as to rhyme or metre.

*****hypé·bolé.** Exaggeration for the sake of emphasis. (*E.g.*, 'a thousand thanks.')

innuendo. Indirect, unfavourable reference or insinuation, often ironical. (*E.g.*, "Conscience . . . had told us that we ought to visit Napoleon's house—now, very suitably, a natural history museum." —ALDOUS HUXLEY.)

*****irony.** A statement which means the opposite of what it says, usually with critical intention. (*E.g.*, "For Brutus is an honourable man, So are they all, all honourable men."—Antony, in *Julius Caesar* [SHAKESPEARE].)

sarcasm, which may or may not be ironical, is a cutting, sneering statement intended to wound.

dramatic irony relates to a situation (in a novel or play) which is very different from what one of the characters supposes it to be, the reader or audience being aware of the truth. (*E.g.*, as in Goldsmith's *She Stoops to Conquer*, when Marlow gives Kate Hardcastle, thinking her to be the barmaid, a falsified account of an earlier meeting he has had with her in her own person.)

litótés. Understatement; the opposite of hyperbole. (*E.g.*, "Falling down that flight of stairs hasn't done me any good.")

lyric. The words of a song. Also a type of poem which is usually fairly short, and often expresses the poet's feelings. It is a general term, and is not restricted to any specific form.

*métaphor. A compressed simile (see below) with the word of comparison omitted. An image is made more vivid by an implied resemblance to something more familiar or more concrete. (*E.g.*, "the grim jewellery of winter"—EDWARD THOMAS; "peep through the blanket of the dark"—SHAKESPEARE.) All speech and writing are full of metaphor, much of it unconscious. A metaphor may correctly be *sustained* (*e.g.*, "The germ-centres of hatred and revenge should be constantly and vigilantly purged and treated in good time."— CHURCHILL), but it must not be *mixed* (*e.g.*, "the germ-centres of hatred and revenge must be cut to pieces before they flood the world").

metónymy. The representation of one thing by something closely associated with it. (*E.g.*, "Since the First World War almost every beauty spot has been threatened by the builder"—*i.e.*, in danger of having buildings erected on it, "the builder" being used to represent the houses with which he is normally associated.)

ode. A rather vague term, usually applied to a poem addressed to some one or something, or to celebrate some special occasion. (*E.g.*, Keats's *Ode to Psyche* and *Ode to a Nightingale*; Marvell's *Ode upon Cromwell's Return from Ireland*.)

ónomatopoéia (pron. *-peea*). A word or group of words which suggests the sound it represents. (*E.g.*, "cuckoo," "thud," "the bare black cliff clang'd round him" [*i.e.*, Sir Bedivere in his armour descending a great rock].—TENNYSON.)

oxymóron. An apparent contradiction expressed in words placed close together, the surprise of the contradiction emphasizing a hidden truth in the thought behind it. (*E.g.*, "Kings too tame are *despicably good*."—DRYDEN.)

*paradox. A statement which appears contradictory, but which contains an element of truth which stands out by reason of the unexpected form of expression. It often takes the form of a contradiction of some well-known saying. (*E.g.*, "Any game that is worth playing is worth playing badly"—*i.e.*, the man who is not too good at a game gets the most fun out of it, for he is delighted at the most modest success, whereas the expert is depressed when he falls below perfection.)

parody. A deliberate burlesque of an author's style, often with critical intention.

*personification. A reference to inanimate or abstract things as if they were persons. (*E.g.*, "Warm Charity, the general friend, With Justice, to herself severe. And Pity dropping soft the sadly-pleasing tear."—GRAY.)

pun. A humorous play on words having a similar form or sound, but differing in meaning. (*E.g.*, "Most plays are content with a run. but *The Bat* has scored a boundary hit.")

saga. Originally stories dealing with ancient semi-legendary Scandinavian families; but now applied to any fictitious novel or series of novels dealing with family chronicles. (E.g.. *The Forsyte Saga*, by John Galsworthy.)

satire. Verse or prose which holds up to ridicule either individual people or human failings.

*simile. A vivid illustrative comparison of one thing with another. A simile is introduced with a word of comparison (usually *like* or *as*); and the two things compared must, if the simile is to be effective, be inherently *un*like except in the one respect. (*E.g.*, "Half wintry, half vernal, the mountain looked patchy, like a mangy dog."—ALDOUS HUXLEY.) Note that "the mountain looked patchy, like the hill we had seen earlier" would not be a simile, but merely a simple comparison, for the two things compared are inherently alike.

sonnet. A poem of fourteen lines, usually containing a slight change of thought or break in continuity between the octave (first eight lines) and the sestet (last six lines). There is more than one rhyme scheme. (*E.g.*, see sonnets by Shakespeare, Milton, Wordsworth, Keats, Rupert Brooke, etc.)

syllepsis. The use of one word in two different senses, usually literally and figuratively, in the same context. (*E.g.*, "That girl I met upon the beach so sunny, She stole away my heart—and then my money.")

synecdoche (pron. *sin-ék-do-kee*). The representation of a whole thing by a part of it, or of a part by the whole. (*E.g.*, "a fleet of fifty *sail*"—*i.e.*, ships; "Will *Surrey* win the county championship this year?"—*i.e.*, the Surrey County Cricket team.)

zeugma. A grammatical construction where, either by mistake or for the sake of brevity, a verb or adjective which is applicable only to one noun is applied to two. (*E.g.*, "There were more weeds than (there was) grass on the tennis court.") It is a construction which generally is best avoided.

EXERCISE

Point out any figures of speech in the following:

1. At the age of ten I had read the whole of Scott and most of Shakespeare.

2. In the foreground on the right a tall pink house went up, glowing like a geranium, into the sunlight.   ALDOUS HUXLEY

3. Their thoughts are often new, but seldom natural; they are not obvious, but neither are they just; and the reader, far from wondering that he missed them, wonders more frequently by what perverseness of industry they were ever found.   JOHNSON

4. Whence are thy beams, O sun! thy everlasting light?

5. God was palpably present in the country, and the devil had gone with the world to town.   HARDY

6. Chaucer is the most English of all poets, and the least read by Englishmen.

7. I have but one simile, and that's a blunder,
   For wordless woman, which is silent thunder.   BYRON

8. Necessity invented stools,
   Convenience next suggested elbow-chairs,
   And luxury the accomplish'd sofa last.   COWPER

9. The murmurous haunt of flies on summer eves.   KEATS

10. Justice is open to all—like the Ritz Hotel.

11. Thou hadst a voice whose sound was like the sea,
    Pure as the naked heavens.   WORDSWORTH

12. Wistfully watching, with wonderful liquid eyes.
    D. H. LAWRENCE

13. The sunlight on the garden
    Hardens and grows cold,
    We cannot cage the minute
    Within its nets of gold.

LOUIS MACNEICE

14. If you have the good fortune really to talk with a statesman, you will be constantly startled with his saying quite intelligent things.

G. K. CHESTERTON

15. On the coast of Coromandel
    Dance they to the tunes of Handel;
    Chorally, that coral coast
    Correlates the bone to ghost.

OSBERT SITWELL

16. The best way to learn a subject is to teach it.

17. Death lays his icy hand on kings:
        Sceptre and Crown
        Must tumble down,
        And in the dust be equal made
    With the poor crooked scythe and spade.

SHIRLEY

18. Fifty thousand horse and foot
    Going to Table Bay.

KIPLING

19. Pleasure was still the only business of Maxentius.

GIBBON

20. Sorting out one's ideas is not the least important part of essay writing.

INDEX

ABBREVIATIONS, 92–93, 114
Accusative case, 218
Active voice, 212
Adjective clauses, 225–227
Adjectives, 99, 216–217
Adverb clauses, 227–229
Adverbs, 217, 218
Affix, 188
Agreement, 246–247
Allegory, 253
Alliteration, 253
Ambiguity, 128–129, 244–246
Analysis of sentences, 223–234
Antecedent, 216, 246
Anticlimax, 253
Antithesis, 253
Antonyms, 197, 199
Apostrophe, 113–115, 253
Apposition, 99, 226, 227
Argument, 71–73
Assonance, 254

Between, 218
Blank verse, 254
Business letters, 74–81

CHOICE OF ESSAY SUBJECT, 15–23
Circumlocution, 246
Clause analysis, 229–234
Clauses, 99–100, 222
Clichés, 239–240
Climax, 254
Collecting ideas, 24–27
Collective nouns, 215
Colon, 107
Comma, 97–102
Commands, 126, 223
Complement, 212, 225, 226
Complex sentences 224–225, 229–234
Compound sentences, 222
Comprehension, 171–178
Compression of ideas, 236
Conjunctions, 219, 226, 229

DASH, 107–109
Defining clause, 99–100
Definitions, 182–183
Description, 56–65
Dialogue, 110–113

Direct speech, 107, 122, 135–138
Discussion, 71–73
Distributives, 215, 247
Double sentences, 222
Dramatic irony, 255
Due (to), 250

ELEGY, 254
Ending of essay, 46–48
Epigram, 254
Epitaph, 254
Essay, 15–49, 85–89
Euphemism, 254
Euphony, 254
Exclamation mark, 95–97
Explanation, 65–71
Exposition, 65

FIGURES OF SPEECH, 253–258
Finite verbs, 211, 229
Foreign words, 241–242
Free verse, 254
Full stops, 91–94

GERUND, 213–214, 249
Greek, derivation from, 188–192

HOMONYMS, 201, 203
Homophones, 201, 203
However, 101
Hyperbole, 254
Hyphens, 242–243

INCOMPLETE PREDICATION, 212
Indirect command, 126
Indirect question, 94, 126
Indirect speech—see Reported speech
Infinitive, 211, 213
Interpolations, 101
Intransitive verbs, 211
Inverted commas, 109–113
Irony, 254
It, 216, 226

JARGON, 240
Joining sentences, 235

LATIN, DERIVATION FROM, 188–192
Letter-writing, 74–83
Litotes, 255

MALAPROPISM, 201
Metaphor, 255
Metonymy, 255
Misinterpretation (reported speech), 129–130
Misrelated participle, 248
Multiple sentences, 222

NARRATIVE, 51–56
Nominative of address, 101, 130
Non sequitur, 245–246
Noun clauses, 225–227
Nouns, 215

OBJECT, 211–213, 225, 226
Ode, 255
Onomatopoeia, 255
Opening of essay, 39–46
Oxymoron, 255

PARADOX, 255–256
Paragraph, 29–39
Parenthesis, 108
Participles, 214, 248–249
Passive voice, 212
Personification, 256
Phrase, 218, 221
Pleonasm, 242
Plurals, 114, 246–247
Possessive case, 113
Possessive pronouns, 114, 216
Précis, 139–170
Predicate, 223
Prefixes, 188–189
Prepositions, 217–219
Pronouns, 128, 215–216, 217, 249–250
Proper names, words from, 193
Provisional subject, 226
Proximity, law of, 243–244
Punctuation, 90–121

QUESTION MARK, 94
Quotation, in essay, 41
Quotation, punctuation of, 107, 109–113

RELATIVE ADVERB, 225
Relative conjunction, 225

Relative pronoun, 215, 216, 225, 226, 246, 247, 248
Reported speech, 122–135
Roots, 188, 191

SEMI-COLON, 104–106
Sequence of tenses, 214
Short story, 84
Similar words, 200–203
Simile, 256
Simple analysis, 223–224
Simple sentence, 223
Slang, 240–241
Spelling, 203–210
Stem—see Roots
Stops, 90. See also Punctuation
Stress, 235
Style, 179, 243–246
Subject, 211–213, 223, 225, 226
Subjunctive mood, 212
Subordinate clauses, 222
Suffix, 188, 189–190
Summarizing—see Précis
Superlative, 248
Syllepsis, 256
Synecdoche, 256
Synonyms, 195–199
Synthesis, 234–237

TAUTOLOGY, 242
Tense, 214
That, 226, 227, 230
'Tin-opener,' 22
Topic sentence, 29
Transitive verbs, 211

UNITY OF THEME, 29

VERBOSITY, 246
Verbs, 211–215
Vocabulary, 182–210

What, 226
Which, 227
Who(m), 247–248
Words in contexts, 184–185
Words wrongly used, 238–239

ZEUGMA, 256